ALSO BY BEACH CONGER

It's Probably Nothing

It's Not My Fault

Bag Balm & Duct Tape

We Have Met the Enemy and He Is Us

WE HAVE MET THE ENEMY
AND
HE IS US

THE OPIATE EDUCATION
OF
A VERMONT DOCTOR

By

Beach Conger, MD

191 Bank Street
Burlington, VT 05401

Onion River Press
191 Bank Street
Burlington, VT 05401

Printed in the United States of America
ISBN: 978-1-949066-41-8
Library of Congress Control Number: 2020901045

Names: Conger, Beach, 1941-, author.
Title: We have met the enemy and he is us : the opiate education of a Vermont doctor / by Beach Conger, MD.
Description: Burlington, VT: Onion River Press, 2020.
Identifiers: LCCN: 2020901045 | ISBN: 978-1-949066-41-8
Subjects: LCSH Conger, Beach, 1941- | Opioid abuse--Vermont. | Opioid abuse--United States. | Drug abuse--Treatment--Vermont. | Physicians (General practice)--Vermont--Biography. | Medicine, Rural--Vermont--Anecdotes. | Physicians (General practice)--Vermont--Anecdotes. | Public health--Vermont. | BISAC BIOGRAPHY & AUTOBIOGRAPHY / Personal Memoirs | BIOGRAPHY & AUTOBIOGRAPHY / Medical | PSYCHOLOGY / Psychopathology / Addiction
Classification: LCC HV5822.H4 C55 2020 | DDC 362.29/33092--dc23

Book and Cover Design: willmottstudios.com

To Trine

for sharing the journey
and
for showing me the way

INTRODUCTION

In January of 1964, less than three months after unexpectedly taking office, President Lyndon Johnson declared war on poverty. Within two years, Congress had created Medicaid, Medicare, food stamps, Head Start, legal aid, and community health centers. Much of the responsibility for conducting the war fell to a department called the Office of Economic Opportunity (OEO).

I was a first-year medical student when the War on Poverty was declared. The following summer, I went to Holmes County, Mississippi, with a group of other medical students to conduct health assessments preparatory to the creation of the country's second OEO-funded community health center. It turned out, however, that the folks of Holmes County were more concerned about voter registration, so that's what I did.

In the years that followed, fewer Americans lived in poverty. A lot fewer.

Richard Nixon came into office five years later. He did not like the War on Poverty. He did not like it at all. Like any good Republican, he knew that the problem was not poverty, but those who suffered from it. Determined to right the wrong, he strove to end it by shutting down the OEO. The courts rebuffed his efforts. (It remains to be seen if the current administration's efforts will be more successful, but given its relentless determination it may well be.) But Richard Milhous Nixon, if he was anything, was a resourceful chap. He knew very well he could not fight the war he wanted to fight, the War on Poor People, so instead he declared a war that would accomplish the same end.

The War on Drugs.

The weapon with which Nixon chose to fight this war was incarceration. It has been a potent weapon. Over the next forty years the number of drug arrests tripled, and the number of those incarcerated for drug law violations increased tenfold; the vast majority were incarcerated for possession of drugs— in other words, for being addicted to drugs. This war has made the United States number one in the world in the rate of incarceration. (Russia is a distant second.)

The results have been dramatic. Since 1970, the number of deaths from opiate overdose has tripled. Until recently, most of these deaths had been caused by prescription opiates. But now that we are cracking down on prescription opiates, people addicted to opiates have had to find alternatives. The cheapest and most potent alternative is fentanyl, although in all fairness, it should be noted that fentanyl also started as a prescription drug. And now even more people die from opiates.

Now those thought to be responsible for these deaths are being taught a lesson. Major pharmaceutical companies especially are being roundly chastised for their role. We like to blame big companies for things that go wrong because— well, because they are big companies. And since the companies don't seem particularly to mind, because they can always pass on the blame, nobody gets too upset. So, we have fined them large amounts of money, being careful not to make it so much that it put too big a dent in their profit margin. They are, after all, big companies.

When you think about it, placing the blame solely on pharmaceutical companies is a bit odd. Not that they are innocent in the matter. They are indeed complicit, and we should extract every penny we can from the profits they made on this epidemic. But the pharmaceutical companies are not the primary culprits, because they only manufacture the drugs. They send them to the pharmacies only because the pharmacies ask for them. And the pharmacies ask for them only because their clients come in with prescriptions for those drugs.

And the only way that someone can go to a pharmacy with a prescription for these drugs, either to use themselves or to sell to others to use, is if someone has written a prescription for them. Which means we should hold accountable, especially, those who write those prescriptions.

That would be doctors.

Medicine has changed greatly since 1964, and overwhelmingly for the better. It is an honor and a privilege to be able to use the tools and the treatments we have today. But the advances have come at a price. Our devotion to technology has led us to neglect people. And in the rush to make sure we have done everything we possibly can, we fail to see what we should not do.

We have become unable to recognize when we have got it all wrong.

Nowhere is this more important than in accepting responsibility for our current addiction epidemic. We have remained silent as blame upon blame has been heaped upon greedy pharmaceutical companies, as if we were innocent dupes, unaware of the risks of a category of medications whose potential for harm we have known well for almost a thousand years. And we have been all too eager to shift blame to the actual innocent victims, treating them as if their disease was a result of their moral failing rather than ours.

This book is about trying to do the right thing.

CHAPTER 1

It has been said that medicine is like a religion. Although the analogy is imperfect, it is an instructive one. We have rituals and robes. We have priests and congregations. We have a bible. Several, in fact. And, as with any religion, one of the duties we take most seriously is the initiation of those who wish to join the ministry.

Knowing how vulnerable its novitiates are, medicine carefully protects them. For the first two years, they are not allowed to venture beyond the cloistered walls of the medical school. By the third year, however, they are considered sufficiently initiated that they are allowed, for brief periods, to leave the cathedral and venture into the world. There they are exposed to those who, like myself, were once high priests in good standing, but who, for any of a variety of reasons, have fallen from grace and now must satisfy themselves with preaching in a humbler church. It is considered an invaluable experience, an opportunity to see the fallen in their natural habitat, so that they may witness for themselves what happens to a doctor when she strays too far from the fold.

One such experience is the primary care clerkship, of which, for many years, I have been a preceptor. It is one of my favorite activities. I like medical students. They are eager and curious and caring and respectful of their elders. Their enthusiasm for doctoring is, even for a cynical old soul like me, contagious. And they actually listen when someone talks to them. As children are to adults, so are medical students to doctors—role models studiously ignored.

*****

"Davida Macleod Edwards, DMS III," read the name tag pinned to her too short white coat as she presented herself for the first day of her clerkship with me. Davida is striking. She has bright red hair that falls to her shoulders, she stands six feet two inches tall, and she has an erect posture that emphasizes what is even more apparent in her movement: that she is not the least uncomfortable with herself. So gracefully does she move that when she walks, it almost seems as if she is dancing.

Davida has a warm and open look that makes one immediately want to like her. Despite her youth, she displays not a trace of naivete. It isn't so much that she looks older—just somehow more complete. And when she looks directly at you, as she always does when speaking with you, she tells you as clearly as if she is speaking the words aloud: You can trust me, but you cannot fool me.

If I have given the reader the impression that I am fond of Davida Macleod Edwards, it is because I am. If there is a heroine in this work, it is Davida.

What is most striking about Davida, however, is not her height or her grace or her demeanor. It is her eyes. They are deep set and of a color that is not quite gray and not quite green, but sometimes gray and sometimes green and sometimes something else altogether. Most of the time there is a twinkle in them that is warm and friendly, but at times they will flash with a fire that shows she is not simply a nice person.

Her size has never intimidated me. Her eyes have. It may seem odd that a seventy-five-year-old could be intimidated by a twenty-one-year-old, and I agree that ordinarily such would be the case. But the eyes that cowed me more than once, though they looked identical to those that Davida wore, did not belong to her.

"Hi, Doctor Conger," said Davida, smiling.

"Hello, Vida. Are you ready to learn how to save lives and stamp out disease?"

She pointed to her name tag. "It's Davida," she answered, still smiling. "And I am."

*****

Rob Roy Macleod was born in 1847 on the island of Skye, in the town of Broadford, off the west coast of the Scottish Highlands. His father was a crofter, as had been his father and his father's father before him. They all had lived on the same twenty-acre plot of land. And their modest livelihood, like those of everyone else in the land, was entirely dependent upon one crop—potatoes.

In 1846 the potato blight that had devastated Ireland came to Scotland, and although it did not produce the same degree of starvation and pestilence as in Scotland's neighbor, it was an economic disaster. The Macleods survived the famine, but because Rob Roy was the youngest of three sons, it was inevitable that there would be no place for him on the family farm. Which was just fine with young Rob. He had no desire to be a farmer. The Industrial Revolution was just beginning, and Rob Roy wanted in.

At the age of sixteen, with no more than the clothes on his back, he set off from home to see what the rest of the world had to offer. His first stop was the coal mines in Ayr. He did well there, but after nearly being buried when a mine shaft collapsed, he decided it was time to move on. From there he went to the steel mills in Glengarnock, and from Glengarnock to the St. Rollox Locomotive Works in Glasgow. The pay was good, and so was the job, but Rob Roy was a restless lad, and when he had saved enough to book passage on a boat to America, he left his native country without a glance back.

New York City was not the place for a factory man, and so he headed north, first to Middleton, Connecticut, where he learned the pistol-making trade, and from there to Samuel Colt's factory in Hartford. One day Rob Roy saw a flyer advertising a new plant in Dumster, Vermont. The Jones & Lamson machine company was offering the unheard-of wage of thirty cents an hour with guarantees of a sixty-hour week. Rob had been in Hartford almost a year, and the itch was returning. It was all he needed.

It is impossible to say where he might have gone next, had not a French-Canadian named Francois Gagnon, in answer to the same flyer, come down to Dumster from Sherbrooke, Quebec. With him came his wife and his pretty young daughter, Emilie. Within six months Rob and Emilie were married, and within another year they had twin boys. Rob's wandering days were over. Rob and Emilie had four more children before Emilie died giving birth to her last child in 1876. The child, a girl, was a sickly little thing. "Bare enough to spit on," Rob said when he first laid eyes on her. "Won't live three months," said the doctor.

He named her Vida, after his mother. In Scottish it means "beloved," and beloved she surely was. Rob quit his job at Jones & Lamson and nursed her himself until it finally looked as if she might make it.

*****

Like Rob Roy, we came to Vermont in search of a better life. The year was 1977. I was working at a clinic in San Francisco, and Trine, my wife, was in her first year of law school. Life in the city had become too hectic for our young family. We decided to move. There were three things we would need in our new home: a hospital, a law school, and snow. The snow was for Trine, who is Norwegian. "For my soul," she says.

We had visited Burlington, home of the University of Vermont. We liked it. Burlington was a nice, small town. We were confident it would suit us well. Unfortunately, Vermont Law School is situated not on the university campus, but in the town of South Royalton, sixty miles to the south. South Royalton had a population of 500.

We had just about decided to wait in San Francisco until

Trine finished law school when an ad appeared in the *New England Journal of Medicine*: 'Excellent opportunity for a well-qualified internist to assume practice of retiring general practitioner in a small but fully equipped modern hospital in central Vermont. Superb outdoor recreational and cultural facilities nearby. Send curriculum vitae to Box 26, NEJM."

The ad had been placed by Emmeline Talbot Memorial Hospital, in Dumster, Vermont. Dumster was just a few miles down the road from South Royalton.

Emmeline Talbot was the last in a string of Northeast hospitals that were founded in the late nineteenth century. It was preceded by Mary Fletcher in Burlington, Mary Hitchcock in Hanover, Fanny Allen in Colchester, Mary Imogene Basset in Cooperstown, and Alice Peck Day in Lebanon. They were all founded with money donated by wealthy men who had made their fortunes off the not wealthy, except in the case of Fanny Allen, which was built with money from a collection of men—the Catholic Church. The hospitals' names were considered a tribute to the vital role that women played in medicine.

Missing from this distinguished set of in-name-only women's hospitals is a small hospital in Boston. Built in 1862, a full seventeen years before the first of the Marys, the hospital's original building is still standing, its historic importance overshadowed only by its historic neglect. You will not find any mention of the hospital in Frommer's. It is not on any of the historical tours of Boston. It did not make Trip Advisor's top forty-seven places to see in Boston, an elite list that includes such landmarks as Storrow Drive and the statue of Red Auerbach.

The New England Hospital for Women and Children was the creation of Doctor Marie Zakrzewska, a Polish immigrant who knew that to name a hospital after herself would be presumptuous. She arrived in the United States in 1853 at the age of twenty-four and as an experienced midwife. She was determined to become a physician but quickly discovered that such desires were frowned upon by the boys of Boston medicine. Her choices at that point were limited: move back to Europe or disguise herself as a man. Neither was an attractive option. So, she made do working with her sisters as a seamstress. Then she met Eleanor Blackwell, the first woman to graduate from an American medical school, Geneva Medical College in Upstate New York. Blackwell had been accepted to Geneva after a unanimous vote of the male student body, a prerequisite to her admission. Doctor Blackwell managed to get Marie admitted to Case Western Reserve School of Medicine in Cleveland. Case Western was far ahead of its time, allowing, as it did, a total of six women through its doors from 1850 to 1860. Graduating in 1856, Marie Zakrzewska quickly discovered that obtaining work was as difficult as obtaining her degree. In 1859, she finally found a place in Boston, as a professor of obstetrics and gynecology at New England Female Medical College, which had just opened as a medical school solely for women. The source of its funding was one Samuel Gregory, an enlightened chap who believed that women should be allowed to attend to their own sex, although his motivation was primarily on moral rather than egalitarian grounds. That women should ever be in charge of anything was not a concept he entertained. He and Marie soon parted ways.

Doctor Zakrzewska was not a quitter, so she set out on her own. Without any assistance from the other gender, and with a capital reserve totaling one hundred and fifty dollars, she opened a ten-bed hospital in Boston's Roxbury neighborhood, the New England Hospital for Women and Children. It was the first hospital in the city to offer obstetrics, gynecology, and pediatrics in one facility. So successful was the model that it was eventually appropriated—a little more than a century later—by its more well-endowed Ivy League neighbor on Longwood Avenue. The original charter of the New England Hospital for Women and Children stated that "the medical officers of the hospital shall consist of one or more resident physicians, all of whom will be women."

Born out of the sexism and segregation of the nineteenth century, the hospital gradually fell victim to its own success. As women became integrated into medicine, the all-women's hospital, like the women's medical college, became obsolete. Although the New England Hospital for Women and Children opened its doors and medical staff to men in 1962, it was too late. In 1969, the hospital closed. Some thirty years later it was resurrected as a community health center, and where it once served the needs of poor immigrants in Roxbury, it now does the same for the community's poor minorities. In a tip of the cap to its origins, it is called the Dimock Community Health Center. Doctor Susan Dimock was a colleague of Doctor Zakrzewska. Her name was chosen for the honor instead of Marie's presumably on the grounds of being easier on the tongue.

I was a resident at Boston City Hospital in 1967. I lived in Roxbury. It was a little less than two miles to work, and as the MBTA was not convenient for the trip, I usually walked—down Humboldt Avenue to Warren Street, and then down Massachusetts Avenue to the hospital. In scenic beauty, the journey was rather lacking, consisting, as it did, mostly of vacant lots and squat tenements, many of which were abandoned, the rest of which ought to have been. The only businesses were liquor stores and the occasional corner market. Usually I was either too eager to get to work or too tired at the end of my shift to notice my surroundings. Sometimes, however, the neighborhood's dispiriting nature got to me. When that happened, I took a slightly longer route—across Washington Street and up Columbus Avenue, until I came upon the New England Hospital for Women and Children. Situated on a slight hill, it rose like a castle over the surrounding land. It was a magnificent four-story Victorian building. A grand portico graced the entrance, and a set of porches ran along the entire north side of the building on each floor. The structure was topped by four great steeples, one at each corner. That it was elegant and extravagant is undeniable, but it never gave the feeling of being greater than its more humble surroundings. Just the opposite. It radiated a sense of comfort, offering sanctuary to any who wished to enter. And it spoke a promise that things would be better within its walls.

Robert Frost wrote a poem called "The Death of the Hired Man." Silas, the hired hand for farmers Warren and Mary, had been let go some time past because he could no longer do the work. One day he returns. He goes into the barn where he used to sleep and lies down on his usual bed of straw. Mary and Warren talk about his return:

'Warren,' she said, 'he has come home to die:
You needn't be afraid he'll leave you this time.'
'Home,' he mocked gently.
'Yes, what else but home?
It all depends on what you mean by home....'
'Home is the place where, when you have to go there,
They have to take you in.'

They have to take you in. This was the New England Hospital for Women and Children.

*****

In 1972, the people of Dumster had an ancient hospital that was no longer safe. They were faced with two stark choices: close the hospital or raise the money to build a new one. They chose the latter, although by naming the new hospital in honor of the wife of Elmer Talbot, founder of Dumster's most successful factory, Acme Tool and Die, they hoped his descendants would be disposed to make a substantial contribution to its construction. They were sorely mistaken. They had forgotten that the mother of Elmer's children was not Emmeline, but Margaret. Margaret had died in childbirth. Emmeline was her replacement. Emmeline was a severe woman who felt that the children had been spoiled by their mother and devoted all her energy to correcting that mistake. Although she was determined, she did not succeed in her mission. Elmer's four children had, in truth, already been spoiled rotten and were entirely inedible. They were an unpleasant, selfish, avaricious bunch who had no intention of ever giving a penny of their unearned money to anyone.

The entire town pitched in, the money was raised, and in 1973, the hospital opened. It had an emergency room, a modern operating room, and even a two-bed intensive care unit that looked out on a cow field.

*****

I was thirty-six years old. I had practiced for ten years at major medical centers in Boston and Atlanta and San Francisco. Dumster was a town of 3,000 people. Emmeline Talbot had twenty-two beds. Although it would not be the kind of practice to which I was accustomed, I was not concerned. With my training and experience, I knew I would be able to handle anything that came up.

CHAPTER 2

Until I met Vida Edwards.

Vida Edwards, born MacLeod, was 102 years old. She had survived not only her first three months, but three husbands and six children after that. She had witnessed four wars and twenty-one presidents. She had seen the invention of the telephone, the light bulb, toilet paper, the steam engine, the automobile, the camera, the dishwasher, radio, the vacuum cleaner, the zipper, insulin, the toaster, Scotch Tape, plastic, the airplane, the ballpoint pen, penicillin, the polio vaccine, the computer, the bikini, the credit card, the birth control pill, Tupperware, the disposable diaper, and television. Vida's was quite a life. I asked her once, what, in all those years, was most memorable.

"July 26, 1927," she said without hesitation.

"Just that one day?"

"Less 'n that, actually."

"What happened on that day?"

"Lindbergh."

"Charles Lindbergh?"

"Yep."

"That was when he landed in Paris?"

"Claremont."

"He landed in Claremont, New Hampshire?"

"Was on his tour. Flying from Concord to Springfield. He landed at the Claremont airport on his way. We all went down to see him."

"How long was he there?"

"Five minutes."

"Not very long."

"He waved at me."

At the time of our first meeting, her living descendants consisted of one child, one grandchild, and one great-grandchild, all male. The last of these was a lad of nine who had inherited, along with the name of his great-grandfather, the gray-green eyes and bright red hair of Great Grandmama. In 1994, he would become the father of Davida MacLeod Edwards.

It was my routine each evening to review the records of Doctor Franklin, whose practice I had inherited, for those patients due in the following day. Doctor Franklin had come to Dumster as a young physician in 1937, having done his medical education and residency at the University of Vermont.

I liked Doctor Franklin. He was intelligent, generous, and dedicated. And he had a good sense of humor. Like most physicians of his era, he had little time for reading, and none at all for conferences, so he relied primarily on his experience. I asked him why he was retiring.

"I'm tired," he said.

"I can understand that," I said.

"Besides, I've been at this a long time. Don't want to make it *too* long."

Doctor Franklin's workday pace, when it wasn't fast, was hectic. He didn't have much time for the niceties of medical record keeping. He didn't need to. He knew his patients, and he knew what he had done. So, all he really needed was a bit of a reminder. To call his charts concise would be charitable.

"Wants checkup—feels okay. Looks okay."

"Feeling puny—looks it. Wait and see."

"Belly ache—McBurney. OR."

"Bad cough—right side rales. Amox."

His last entry for Vida read. "Still fibrillating—dig on Tuesday."

From which I gathered that she was in atrial fibrillation, and that he was treating her with digoxin. With the arrival of newer and safer drugs, digoxin has fallen into some disrepute, but in 1977, it was still one of the mainstays for treatment of heart disease.

The reference to Tuesday puzzled me. Although an elderly woman would need less digoxin than most, one pill a week was hardly therapeutic. I made a note to ask her about it when she came in. Regardless of how much she was taking, I knew that guessing the right dose was no longer necessary. I was confident that by measuring her blood levels and adjusting the dose accordingly, I would be able to improve her cardiac status.

At first glance, there wasn't much to Vida. She was barely five feet tall and weighed a scant ninety pounds. There was not an ounce of fat on her and not much muscle either. One would be tempted to call her a frail elderly woman, and one would be two-thirds right. Her gender was not in doubt, and at one hundred and two, no one would argue for her youth. But frail she was not. It was her eyes that gave frailty the lie. Gray-green and deep set, they burned with a fire that could scorch one if one were not careful in one's dealing with her.

Vida Edwards was not someone to condescend to.

I started to introduce myself. "Good morning, Mrs. Edwards. I'm..."

She held up a bony finger. "Hold it right there, sonny. I know who you are. Leastways I know your name. What I want to know is this: Are you a whippersnapper?"

"Am I a what?" I stammered.

"Whippersnapper. Sure look like a whippersnapper to me. An' I don't have no use for whippersnappin'. Just so you know, Doc Franklin had one here once to help him out. Useless he was. Fussed and fussed and fussed and never amounted to nothing. Lasted two months. Two months too long, I'd say."

"I intend to last longer than that," I said, trying to lighten the conversation.

"Intend, outtend. Don't make no never mind. What matters is doin'. We'll see 'bout your intend. An' we'll see about your whippersnappin'."

Having completed this judicial pronouncement, she paused, not so much to allow me to respond as because she had run out of wind.

I chose to consider the comments rhetorical.

"Maybe you could tell me how you are feeling," I said, hoping to get the conversation on ground that was firmer for me.

"Just dandy."

"Really? Well, that's certainly good to hear, especially from someone your age."

"I bet it is. Lot less work for you. Now look at me, you damn fool. Do I look like a dandy-feeling person?"

She did not. Her face was pinched and drawn into a contorted grimace, all on account of a spine that was so bent and a neck so stiff that she had to strain to look up at me. She wheezed as she spoke, and her chest was so thin that I could see her palpitating heart heaving rapidly underneath. But her hands were the worst. Her joints were three times their normal size, contracting her fingers into knobby fists that resembled more a cluster of grapes than a hand. To open them she had to laboriously unbend each finger, one at a time, a process obviously painful and only transiently effective. How she could dress herself, let alone bathe and toilet, was hard for me to comprehend.

"So," she snorted. "Don't look so dandy then, do I? Well, I'm not—not a bit of it. I don't have a bone in my body that doesn't ache. All I can eat is mush, and even that most times makes me sick to my stomach. I can't go when I want to, and I can't stop when I don't. Talking wears me out. Walking is worse. Can't get up my stairs. Gotta sleep in my chair. Fact is, I'm miserable."

Which I could see. Just watching her strain her neck to look at me was painful. I felt bad for her. "I can see how difficult it must be for you," I said sympathetically.

Vida glared at me.

"Hah!" she exclaimed. "Sonny, you don't have a clue how I feel! Not one bit of it. You know what would be dandy for me? If I could feel the way I felt when I was *ninety*. Then I was dandy."

She was right. I didn't have a clue how she felt.

"And these things," she waved her hands at me. "Useless. I can't hardly smoke anymore. And don't you say nothing about smoking," she added, sensing correctly that I was about to make some comment. "It's all I got to look forward to now."

"But how can you..."

"I can't. Onliest time I can is when my grankid comes over and lights one for me. If I could just..." She stopped abruptly and put her hand over her heart, which was now pounding away at a rate of about 140. "Be still my beating heart." Looking at me grimly, she added, "Don't worry. It's not the excitement of you that does it."

"More likely your atrial fibrillation," I offered.

"Fibrillations, tribulations," she snorted. "Damn nuisance is what it is."

"I read in Doctor Franklin's notes that you take your digoxin on Tuesday. Is that only on Tuesdays?"

"Course not. Ain't a complete fool."

"What other days do you take it?"

"Wednesday."

"Tuesday *and* Wednesday? That's a rather unusual schedule."

"Would be, 'cept it's not what I do. Take it Tuesday mostly. Wednesday only iffen I forget Tuesday."

"Is that what Doctor Franklin recommended for you. Just one day a week?"

"Never asked him."

"I see. You know, digoxin is usually a medicine one would take more than once a week. And it might well help your fibrillation if you did. I'm sure Doctor Franklin would agree with me on that."

"Don't know 'bout that. One thing, though, Doc Franklin did agree with me on."

"What was that?"

"He wouldn't give me advice lessen I asked for it."

It seemed like a good time to change the subject. "Let's talk about your blood pressure," I said.

"Talk away."

"It's rather high."

"Yup."

"One hundred and eighty over one hundred and ten."

"Been higher."

"So I see. Over two hundred most of the time."

"Was two-thirty once."

"That's a dangerously high blood pressure. When was that?"

"A while back."

"Could you be a little more specific perhaps?"

"April 12, 1945. That spific enough?"

"Er, it certainly is. Was there something about that day in particular?"

"Day Roosevelt died. Only president ever amounted to anything. Got me all to dithers. Went to see Doc Franklin. He said it was okay. He had high blood too, ya know."

"Doctor Franklin?"

"Don't know about him. But Roosevelt sure did. Worse 'n mine. By a lot. 'Specially on the day he died."

"Three fifty over one ninety-five, I believe." I knew the story of FDR's blood pressure. My cardiology professor always brought it up in discussing the evolution of the treatment of hypertension as evidence of how much medicine can change in a short period of time.

"Somepin' like that. Anyway, Doc Franklin said if I wasn't going to quit smoking, I better at least take something for my blood pressure."

"That sounds like good advice. Did you?"

"Yup. Snake oil it was."

In the 1940s the most commonly used medicine to treat hypertension was reserpine. It is a natural substance found in rauwolfia serpentina, a small flowering plant native to India. The common name was Indian snakeroot. It was also used to treat anxiety. Gandhi took it. It is a good antihypertensive. The problem is, it can be *too* good. Especially when someone stands up.

"How did it work?"

"Worked fine."

"But you stopped taking it."

"Did."

"Why?"

"Passed out."

"There are plenty of other medicines available for treating hypertension. Certainly, Doctor Franklin recommended you try something else rather than just ignore it."

"Did. But Doc White said not to worry about it. You do know Doc White, don't ya?"

"I don't believe I do. I haven't been around here very long."

"Not from around here. From Boston. Thought that was where you were growed."

"Doctor White was from Boston?"

"Yep."

"Doctor Paul Dudley White?"

"That's him."

I certainly did know Paul Dudley White, my cardiology professor. In those days he was considered one the fathers of modern medicine. (It was before gender had entered the profession.)

"You saw Paul Dudley White about your blood pressure?"

"Didn't have to. Was a piece in *Eagle Times* he had writ some years ago 'bout blood pressure. Made sense to me, so I followed it.

I quoted from memory: "The greatest danger to man with high blood pressure is the discovery, because then some fool is certain to try and reduce it."

Despite herself, she almost smiled. "Hmm. Mebbe you're not so bad—for a whippersnapper."

I didn't think it would be well received to tell her that he always used that quote to remind us that the most important thing in medicine is to be always aware of the possibility that what you now know for sure may someday turn out to be completely wrong.

A new subject seemed in order.

"You mentioned you were tired."

"Course I am. Whaddya expect *at my age?*"

"True. But it's possible that there may be something to do about it."

"No ther-a-pee. Grankid keeps fussin' 'bout that. Not gonna happen."

I agreed with her about physical therapy. Both for her sake and for that of the physical therapist.

"I was thinking about doing some tests."

Vida was skeptical. "What kind?"

"Blood tests."

"An' that's it?"

"Well, yes—most likely. It would depend on what the tests showed, of course."

She offered up her arm. "Well, okay then. S'pose you gotta do some pissin' on the tree. Blood seems harmless enough."

I expected it to be my only opportunity to find out just what was going on inside Vida, so I ordered the full blue-plate special. Liver, kidneys, sugar, vitamins, chemistry, blood count, metabolism. While today such an approach would be taken for granted, at the time, it was quite novel.

*****

The doctors of Doctor Franklin's day were too busy taking care of the sick to pay attention to those who were not. Doctor Franklin never went searching for problems. He had enough on his hands with the ones that were given to him.

But in the 1960s all that changed. It was a time when young people wanted to do good things for the world. Doctoring was a natural outlet for such passions. And it did not go unnoticed that one could also do very nicely for oneself in the process. The number of physicians increased rapidly. The number of patients did not. Thus it was that in just a few short years, the profession passed from scarcity to surplus. The combination of a plethora of energetic young doctors and a paucity of new patients left us with a lot of time on our hands. There was much discussion within the profession about what could be done to remedy the imbalance. It wasn't long before we hit upon the solution.

In medicine, as in any business, whenever we see a need to expand our services, we look for a new product line. And as luck would have it, technology came to our rescue. Machines had just been developed that could run up to thirty tests on a single sample of blood. Using these machines, we could cast a wide net for as yet undiscovered diseases and see what could be hauled in. This process of diagnostic trolling is called health screening, a clever play on words, for screening usually involves selecting something *out* from a larger group, whereas in this case it is designed to selected something *in*. On the off chance that a first cast yields an empty net, it is of no consequence. Fortunate as a person might feel to have passed a screening one year, it is but a temporary reprieve—until the next and the next and however many it takes to haul something in. And just to be sure, every few years we change the standards for the tests, so that a result that was normal one year could become borderline the next and ultimately abnormal. Cholesterol guidelines alone have ensured that before long, everyone will become a patient.

*****

Not surprisingly, in Vida's case, a normal result was the exception. But eager as I might have been to fuss with her sodium and her anemia and her liver and her kidney, I was certain that the efforts would be futile, not so much because of age, but because of Vida. There was one test, however, that I knew might actually lead to a treatment that could make her feel better.

Her thyroid was low.

"Your thyroid is too low," I told her when she came back the next week to go over the results.

"Only the thyroid?" she asked skeptically. "Bet most of 'em was, 'cept those that were too high."

"There were others," I conceded. "But I think the thyroid is the most important."

"'Cause you got a pill for it? No thanks. Me an' pills just don't get along. You're so smart, shoulda figured that out by now."

"This pill might make you feel better."

"Hah!"

"Would you do me a favor, Mrs. Edwards?"

"Just Vida. Had too many Misters. I'm done with Missus."

"Would you do me a favor, *Vida?*"

"One week."

"It will take at least three,"

"Okay."

I knew she wouldn't get the full effect in two weeks, especially as I doubted she would take it as prescribed and I would have to start slowly because of her atrial fibrillation. But two weeks was better than one, so I wrote her a prescription, and off she went.

Two weeks later she came back.

"Alright, sonny," she said before I had a chance to ask, "I'll take your pill."

I was surprised. But then her thyroid had been awfully low, so even a partial effect must have been something. "So you feel a little better?"

"Don't feel no worse. An' I figure you'll pester me to death iffen you can't do somepin', so I figure I'll stay on this pill, which at least don't do no harm. But only, iffen..."

"I promise not to try to do anything else."

She gave me a real smile. "You're learning, sonny. Mebbe there's hope for you yet."

As Vida would say, for two years I *fussed* at her. Although strictly speaking I was her doctor, what I was, in fact, was a negotiator on behalf of the medical establishment. I proposed a course of action. She rejected it. Then we tried to find a compromise. Which always wound up with me doing much less than I thought ought to be done, and her doing hardly anything at all. She did continue to take her thyroid medicine, but every time I proposed something additional, she held it out as her shield. "Doin' just fine with these pills, sonny. No need to change."

It was the middle of May 1979, on a Saturday afternoon. I was at home tending to our garden when I got a call from Loree Ellis in the emergency room. "It's Vida," she said.

I was surprised. Vida never went to the emergency room. And other than a ruptured appendix, she had never been in the hospital. I assumed she must have been hit by a car or collapsed outside her house. "How is she?"

"Didn't say."

"How does she look?"

"Don't know."

"Who brought her in?"

"No one."

"But, how did she get there?"

"Didn't."

The shock of the call had discombobulated me, and I had forgotten how literally an old Vermonter answers questions. I corrected my line of inquiry.

"Could you tell me please, Loree, what's going on?"

"She's on the phone. Wants to talk to you."

"Tell her I'll call."

She answered on the first ring. "Morning, Doc," she said.

Something was up. Vida had called me many things in our two-year acquaintance. Doc was not one of them.

"What can I do for you, Vida?"

"Remember that p-nemonia was so bad you wanted to put me in the hospital?"

"I certainly do. It had just about worn you out. If you had come in the hospital to get antibiotics, with oxygen and some bed rest, as I recommended, you would have been better off."

"'Spect you're right. I'm willing to come in now."

"Really?"

"Yup."

"For the pneumonia?"

"Yup."

"That was six months ago."

"You gonna take me in or not?"

Now this was at a time when if someone was sick and I wanted to put that person in the hospital, I didn't need a reason. I just admitted the patient and cared for her until she got well enough to go home. And sometimes a bit longer—just to make sure.

It was a long time ago.

"Certainly, Vida. If you want to come into the hospital, I will bring you in. I just have one question."

"Why?"

"Yes, why?"

"Don't wanna make a mess."

"Are you having diarrhea?"

"Nope."

"Vomiting?"

"Nope."

"I'm afraid I don't understand."

"I die at home, no one finds out until my Billy comes by, which is not 'til Sunday. Could be pretty messy by then."

Further questioning, I knew, would be fruitless. "I'll meet you there."

She looked no worse than usual. She had no new symptoms that made me think anything was different. Grudgingly, she allowed me to listen to her heart and her lungs and poke on her belly. She refused all tests. And the only medicine she would accept was her thyroid pill. So I put her to bed, and I said I'd see how she was in the morning, and she said she doubted that.

And she was right.

CHAPTER 3

D avida looked at my name tag.

S. Beach Conger MD
Attending Physician
Upper Connecticut River Medical Center

It had my picture on it, just to make sure I was I.

"It's okay," she said. "You can call me Vida, if I can call you Doc. After all, you've known me forever—even since before I knew myself. And at least you didn't call me Clutch."

"Not a name to be ashamed of."

"No, but I can't take any credit for it. I just turned out that way."

"And your fadeaway jump shot just turned out that way too?"

"Well…"

I *had* known her forever. The first time I met her she was only a few months old. She was with her mother, who had come in for an office visit. I didn't wear a name tag then.

"Okay," I said, "here's the deal. I'll call you Davida if you call me Beach."

"Deal."

*****

Davida's father played basketball for Dumster High School. Her older brother, Rob, had as well. Father and son

often went down the street to the town courts to shoot hoops.
Young Davida always went with them. They let her carry the
ball. She liked the ball. She liked the way it felt when she held
it in her lap. She liked the way the grain on the ball tickled her
skin when she turned it. She liked how it felt when it came
back into her hands after she bounced it. Once, she fell down
on the court. She skinned her knee. She didn't cry. She grabbed
her ball and held it against the wound. Her father said to her,
"Now it's in your blood, sweetie." She wiped her palms on her
knee and then clutched her ball. She looked at him and said,
"Now it's in my hands." She was seven.

When she got older and could actually play, she discovered that there was a fluidity to the movement of the game
that was not unlike dance. And Davida loved to dance. When
asked as a child what she wanted to be when she grew up,
she would reply without hesitation, a ballerina. While her playmates idolized movie stars and actresses and singers, on the
wall of Davida's room were pictures of Anna Pavlova. Her
childhood dream was someday to dance Odette in *Swan Lake*.
She was a good young ballerina. Very good, many said. But she
was unable to pursue her love beyond childhood. Because as
she grew, she grew a lot, and by the age of ten, she towered
above her classmates. Too tall for ballet, she was told. So, she
turned instead to perform on a different stage, one where her
height served her well. But although she excelled on that stage,
and although she enjoyed playing the part for which she was
so well suited, that was all it meant to her. Ballet remained her
unrequited passion.

But she never looked back at what might have been. She
took up basketball as if it were all she ever cared for. And
when Davida took up a thing, she stayed with it. She had a
dogged determination to succeed that kept her at it. But her
goal wasn't to become the best, for Davida knew that to be
not only pointless, but vain. Nor did she seek approval from
others. Not from her coaches, not from her friends, not even

from her parents. Only when her older brother, Rob, gave her the occasional "Not bad, Vids" did she feel a bit proud. Davida was outgoing, but she was also completely within herself. And she knew that only one person could be the judge of how good she was. She was willing to accept failure when it came because of things beyond her control. But if she thought that the failure would not have occurred had she worked a little harder or been a little smarter, she did not let up until she had succeeded.

At being the best she could be.

Her size and coordination made her a good basketball player. Her determination made her very good. But what made her the best was her focus. When she was intent on a task, nothing could distract her. Opposing crowds quickly gave up when she was at the foul line. It was pointless. And whenever she made a play that changed the tide or sealed the win, and the crowd erupted in cheers, she got a startled look on her face. She hadn't noticed that anyone else was watching.

When Davida was in high school, Dumster won the girls state championship in basketball three years running. It would have been four, but she got appendicitis the day before the finals her freshman year and didn't play. What earned her the name Clutch, however, was that in each of the three championship games, Dumster won because Davida had taken charge in the final minutes. Her senior year, with Dumster down by two, and fifteen seconds left, Davida got the ball. Everyone in the building knew what she was going to do, and everyone, including the opposing team, knew it would be useless to try to stop her. And at the top of the key she let fly with the game winner, her trademark fadeaway jump shot. The crowd went wild. This time, at least, Davida did manage a smile.

Davida was recruited heavily by several Division One schools, including UConn and Tennessee, but in the end, she went to Middlebury on a full academic scholarship. Her freshman year she went out for the team and was quickly put in the starting lineup. But she never played a game for the Panthers. She left the team after a couple of weeks. Her official explanation was that she wanted to devote her energies to her studies.

"I've always played basketball because it was fun," she told me once. "At Middlebury, they seemed to have forgotten that it's only a game. Besides, they weren't nearly good enough to take it as seriously as they did."

She graduated summa cum laude. She chose Dartmouth for medical school because it was close to home. And here she was.

"Can I ask you a question, Beach?"

"Certainly."

"What was she like?

"Your namesake?"

"Yes."

I shook my head. "She was something else—like nobody I had ever met. Even at one hundred and two she was a force that couldn't be reckoned with. Stubborn, crotchety, always on the edge of mean, but never really. She had a good sense of humor. And she was a great teacher."

"I didn't know she was a teacher."

"Well, tutor would probably be more accurate. She had only one student."

"Whom I might know," she said smiling.

"Whom you just might."

"What did she teach you?"

"Nothing—and everything."

"Can you teach it to me?"

"No."

"Oh," she said, disappointed. It wasn't so much because she expected that I would give her some pearls of wisdom passed down from her great-grandmother. It was that she just wanted to know more about her.

"You see, what she taught me mainly was that I had to teach myself." I paused. "Well, there was one thing she said to me once. Sums her up better than anything, I would say. I had just unsuccessfully tried to convince her to engage upon some unnecessary course of action. Best I can remember, it was an x-ray of her aching hip. 'Sonny,' she said. She always addressed me as sonny when she was about to give me a lesson. 'Took the Hippocratic oath, din't ya?'"

I allowed as how I had.

"Four words," Davida said.

"I know," I said.

"Not two."

Davida smiled. "First do no harm—not, first do."

"Correct." I said. "And that's the lesson for today. Let's go save lives."

Students in their third year are just beginning their genuine clinical experience. In their first two years, they learn the trade on an assortment of less than real-life activities: lectures, mannequins, Stepford patients. Invariably they are excited to step into the clinical world. Davida was no exception.

"And stamp out disease," she said grinning.

CHAPTER 4

"So, what's on the list for today?" I asked.

"Blood pressure."

"That's all?"

"They said they wanted us to start slowly. Until we got used to things. It needs to be both arms. And then lying, sitting, and standing."

"Four blood pressures! Well, that's another matter altogether. We better hop to it if we want to finish by end of day."

"You know it's not *my* list," she said defensively.

"Not mine either."

The students always come with a list. This is to make sure what they do is exactly what they are supposed to. Nothing is left to chance. At this early stage of their education, students are prone to acquiring the bad habits of community preceptors. It is a kind of educational imprinting. The list is quite specific. Take a blood pressure. Look in an ear. Ask about chest pain. But Davida didn't have to come all the way to Dumster to learn how to examine a body or take a history. There are plenty of bodies with plenty of problems at the medical school that more than suffice for the purpose.

Rather, the real purpose of this clerkship is to teach the students how to construct a building that, as its architecture does not quite fit in with its campus, the medical school prefers to have constructed at some more distant site.

They come to us to learn how to build a medical home.

Now, most likely you have never heard of a medical home. And it is also quite possible that the pairing of the words *medical* and *home* sounds, on the face of it, like an absurd coupling. And you would be right.

The medical home is the creation of the National Committee for Quality Assurance. The NCQA, as the name implies, is in charge of insuring quality in the practice of medicine. In order to do that, of course, the NCQA had to figure out what it is that doctors actually do. For specialists, this was pretty easy. They put things in, and they take things out, and you could check to see if the things went in and came out as they should. But for primary care, they got stuck. As far as they could tell, what we did mainly was send people to specialists so the specialists could put things in and take things out. And we talked a lot. But the committee members were undeterred. They set about to make standards for talking. (Setting standards is the NCQA's second-favorite thing to do, the first being to have meetings to discuss the standards.)

I'm not sure how they came up with the idea of the medical home, as their deliberations are highly classified, but maybe it was because they figured that people talk a lot at home. Regardless, they took to the idea of a medical home like a dog to a bone. And as a result of continued meetings and continued settings of standards, those standards have now grown to include no fewer than 121 elements. It has been an impressive undertaking, and it is a tribute to the remarkable ability of a bureaucracy to take credit for common sense.

If you are not a primary care doctor, you are probably not as familiar with the 121 elements that are required in constructing a medical home as we are. Let me say just that it is quite different from any kind of home you know.

Imagine your own home. The living areas contain the kind of furnishings that suit your taste. Your bedroom has a comfortable bed and cozy down. The bathroom might have a nice tub for taking long, warm baths. Your kitchen pantry and refrigerator are well stocked with your favorite foods. It is, in short, a place just suited to the comfort of you and your family. A castle it has even been called.

Then your doctor comes in to make it into a medical home. Here is what she would do. Tear down the walls. Throw out the allergy-laden furniture and the rugs. Pack up the family photos and pictures on the wall and the knickknacks you are so fond of. You need to be looking forward to your new life, not backwards at your old one. Empty the refrigerator. Clean out the pantry. Now, you are ready for the *blueprint*—that is the actual word—that will be used to build your medical home. There are no living rooms or dining rooms in a medical home. Shared space means shared germs. Tubs are an accident waiting to happen. But you will have a shower chair. The kitchen will not be changed. Only the larder. Gone are the unhealthy foods that you were unable to resist—foods laden with salt and sugar and saturated oils. Foods like bacon and cheese and Chunky Monkey. There will be eggs. But not very many. There will be no chocolate in your medical home.

Now, this is just an analogy, of course, and I know the image of an architectural redesign of your current home is not very appealing, so I will try to frame it in a more positive light. Imagine instead that you are at your favorite trattoria, and you are sitting down to a full five-course meal. What you have just sampled above is the antipasto. Here is what follows:

Primo. The patient health questionnaire. Designed by the mental health folks, who wanted in on the boon that screening has been to their colleagues over on the physical side of the aisle, the purpose of this course is to make you a mental health patient. It asks a series of questions, and it particularly emphasizes that you should think carefully about each one before answering. This last step is most important, for when we are asked to think carefully about our mood, we invariably become depressed. It's designed, like our current blood pressure and cholesterol standards, to ensure that no one will pass.

Have you ever been tired?

Do you ever sleep too much?

Do you ever sleep too little?

Do you sometimes wish people would just leave you alone?

Do people sometimes just want to leave you alone?

Do you ever feel you are not as good a person as you could be?

Why don't you do anything about it?

Secondo. Shaping up. This course is loaded with filling dishes. Smoking, alcohol, marijuana, weight, exercise, diet, safe sex, seatbelts, and gun safety are just a sample of what is on the menu.

We call this counseling. I have to admit that it has been hard for me to talk about these things. Except for smoking. Smoking is something that I can prescribe medicine for. Take weight, for example. When I first started, the idea of talking to someone about his weight was considered beneath the dignity of a doctor. Now, we recognize that nobody weighs what he should, and we are exhorted to address it forcefully. I tried diligently for a while. But it was discouraging. Back when I never tried to encourage weight loss, most of my patients were thin. But now that I am playing a more active role in their lifestyle, most of my patients are not thin. I don't mean to imply that doctors addressing obesity is the cause of its increase. That, of course, would be absurd. Still, it does tend to take a bit of the wind out of one's sails. Not to mention that, although I have had patients who, with the combined exhortations of me and our dietician, have temporarily misplaced their weight, all of them eventually have managed to find it again, and often a bit they didn't previously possess. I barely remember anyone who has managed to lose it altogether. At least not on purpose.

To talk about exercise is what I call a reflective conversation. I can hear the reflection of the words I utter coming back to me, entirely unabsorbed by the person to whom I am addressing them.

My brain is a fairly tolerant organ. It puts up with no end of disrespect, insults, and even downright abuse without so much as a peep of complaint. Counseling patients about things that are none of my business, however, is an activity that really gets on its last nerve. "Enough is enough," it says. "Cut it out." So, whenever I try counseling, my brain breaks into one of those infernal jingles, like how small the world is after all, that drive every other thought from my head.

Dolce. Be a better person. This is stuff that usually falls under parental or spousal jurisdiction. Don't interrupt. Put down the toilet seat. Look at me when I talk to you. We call them behavioral modification strategies. It sounds better than, "Shape up, you." They are important. Mostly they apply to men, so we diligently collect the information, and then we forget about it.

Digestivo. Guidelines, algorithms and protocols. Diabetes, hypertension, heart disease, emphysema, depression are complex diseases that, actual patients being a rather unruly lot, often present in a multitude of confusing ways. Finding a plan that fits the needs and desires of each patient can be a frustrating, time-consuming, and often unsuccessful process. But when the student has a guideline and an algorithm and a protocol, the patient no longer muddies the waters. With these essential tools, the student can quickly arrive at the desired treatment plan, *completely independent* of the actual patient. We know we can rely on these tools because they are based on evidence from double-blind studies.

Double-blind studies are those in which neither the doctor nor the patient knows whether they are getting the actual treatment or just fake medicine. This prevents bias, which is when the doctors try harder to help the patients who they know are getting the real treatment, and the patients try harder to get better because they know they are supposed to. Double-blind is considered the latest advance in quality of medicine. There was a time, probably before any reader's memory, that double-blind was standard care. Back then, not having the faintest idea whether the treatment you were prescribing was doing any good at all was nothing to be particularly proud of. But times change.

We understand that for a patient to digest the entire meal in one sitting is a bit much. And we don't want to place any unrealistic demands on patients. All we ask is that the patient sets goals. Goals are really what the medical home is all about. So, the patient can come back on a regular basis to review them and revise them and then make another appointment to do the same thing all over again.

*****

Building a medical home is quite time-consuming. For the serious student, an hour and a half per visit is not unusual. Which is a long time to sit with one person. Were I ever able to spend ninety minutes with a patient, I might rely on the list to pass the time also, although, truth be told, I am more likely to ask about their grandchildren. Medical schools know that doctors in the community can't do this. It's not that they think we don't know how. And it's not that they don't trust us. Both of those would require that they actually consider our role in the education of the medical students. Which they don't—because we are clinicians, those who spend all our time taking care of people. Clinicians tend to see medicine in the light of our own clinical experience. Furthermore, we are overly fond, when it suits us, of prescribing treatments that are not strictly evidence based.

The schools understand that this is not our fault—that one of the prices community doctors pay is that we deal a lot with uncertainty, and that, as a consequence, we have to try to figure out what to do without the help of guidelines. They understand how easy it is to fall into this type of behavior. But they know how dangerous it is to the education of young, impressionable minds to be exposed to us without any protection. If the medical schools had their way, practicing doctors and real patients would be completely removed from the curriculum. Like society at large, they know that there are certain things that the young are too young to handle and should be shielded from until they can make mature decisions about what to do. Things like sex and alcohol and driving. And voting.

Left to their own devices, medical schools would just as soon not have anything to do with us. But there is money in medical homes. A lot of it. And so, they send their charges out. But it makes them nervous, and even with the lists and the instructions and the admonitions, they are not really at ease until the students return safely back in the fold.

The reason I know all this is true is that once I was on the other side myself, and my view then of me now was just like theirs. But that was a long time ago and in another land.

CHAPTER 5

The year was 1965. I was a third-year medical student on the Harvard wards at Boston City Hospital. The kind of doctor I now am was called an LMD, local medical doctor. LMDs didn't have names. They were the doctors who actually took care of our patients, and they belonged to a professional caste far below ours. They had nothing to do with us, and we had nothing to do with them. We knew that our patients came from them and went back to them, but as to what they actually did, we had not the slightest notion, and we cared not a fig.

When it was founded in 1864, Boston City Hospital was intended "for the use and comfort of poor patients." One hundred years later it was still for the use of the poor, but as regards comfort, that has been transferred to others more deserving—to the medical schools, their professors and their students. Not one, but three medical schools staked their claim to mine the wealth of disease that Boston City Hospital possessed. Boston University, Harvard, and Tufts each had its sphere of influence. It was a division of spoils not dissimilar to the means by which the Europeans partitioned China in the nineteenth century.

The Harvard medical service had its home in the Peabody Building. It was there that I passed my professional infancy and childhood, first as a student and then as a resident.

It was a dismal place, the Peabody. Two large wards, one for men and one for women. Along each side of the wards was a set of stalls, separated one from the other by a thin partition, giving the wards more the appearance of stables than places of healing. The lower half of each stall was metal, so that a person lying down might be encouraged in the illusion that he had some semblance of privacy. The upper half was transparent glass. This allowed anyone who entered the ward to look down the rows and detect at a glance any signs of undesirable activity on the part of an occupant. Large windows ran the entire length of each wall. Some were cracked, a few were broken, and all were covered in a perpetual layer of grime, upon the contents of which I would not care to speculate. Pale yellow lights overhead cast an unhealthy glow on everything and everyone. When we wanted to know if the yellowed appearance we beheld in our patient was actually due to a failing liver rather than bad optics, we would take her outside in order to inspect her in the natural light. Often this simple act would effect the instant cure of her jaundice.

At the far end of the ward, looking quite out of place, was a large marble fireplace. Above the fireplace was a portrait of our founding father, George Francis Peabody. Doctor Peabody looked down at us from his place of honor with a stern and all-seeing eye. No matter which corner of the ward I was in, should I happen to look up, he would have me fixed in his admonishing gaze, reminding me not to forget where I was and who had preceded me. "I've got my eye on you," he warned. "Don't disappoint."

How could I help but? I was bright enough, but just in an ordinary good-student way. I knew I would never rise to the ranks of his descendants, our professors, whose careers were as distinguished as his. Brilliant doctors all, they were among the great minds of medicine.

Edward Kass was a renowned infectious disease physician. His work on urinary tract infections in pregnancy would lead to preventing thousands of premature births, and his discovery that a deadly strain of staphylococcus could lurk within a woman's tampon, only to erupt in toxic shock syndrome when deployed, saved many lives.

Max Finland, our chief emeritus, had discovered that penicillin could cure pneumonia, thereby reducing a once deadly disease to a minor illness.

And William Castle, because he vomited, almost won the Nobel prize.

In 1920 George Whipple was conducting research at John Hopkins on iron deficiency anemia. He discovered that raw liver cured patients' anemia. At the same time, in Boston, George Minot William Murphy and William Castle were studying a different type of anemia in humans. Because the anemia was associated with other symptoms, such as confusion and inability to walk straight, it was called pernicious anemia. Iron therapy had been of no benefit, so they decided to try Doctor Whipple's cure. They fed a pound of raw liver a day to their patients. It worked.

The question was why. What about the rest of us, wondered Doctor Castle. We don't eat raw liver every day, but we don't have pernicious anemia. He reasoned that although there must be something in the liver that is necessary to the cure, there must also be something in the body that allows the consumption of a more palatable diet without producing pernicious anemia. To prove it, Doctor Castle ate not raw liver, for he thought that was disgusting, but instead a nice beef tenderloin, medium rare. After fully digesting the meal, he made himself vomit it back up. He then fed just a small portion of what he had vomited to his patients. I realize it may seem surprising that patients would agree to this experiment, but you must remember this was before informed consent was invented, and at the time it was universally known that the worse something tasted, the better it was for you. Sure enough, Doctor Castle's gastric juices alone cured the anemia. Doctor Castle called that which was in the liver extrinsic factor, and that in the stomach intrinsic factor. Eventually, Doctors Whipple and Minot isolated the extrinsic factor. They called it vitamin B12. (At the time eleven other B vitamins had been discovered, although since then, we have discarded vitamins B4, B8, B9, B10, and B11. They turned out to be fake vitamins.)

The Nobel Prize committee is a notoriously squeamish lot. Doctors Minot and Whipple won the Nobel Prize for their discovery. Doctor Castle did not.

Every Monday, Wednesday, and Friday from 10:30 a.m. to noon, our professors descended from their ivory towers to give us their words of wisdom. I don't mean to imply that they would spend their entire ninety minutes seeing all our patients. That simply wasn't done. Each day the resident would select a few choice patients for consultation, and we would troop to those bedsides. There, the student caring for the patient recited the patient's story at the head of the bed. After the presentation was finished, the professor would perform an examination on some particularly choice part of the body. Then we retired to a conference room, where the professor enlightened us upon a subject that might, or might not, be related to the patients in questions, but which, in the professor's experience, was worthy of enlightenment.

Which was only as it should be. It was understood that our professors should not waste their valuable time on the actual treatment of our patients. Their days were spent in the laboratories, not at the bedside. Patient care was not what they did. So, for the sick and poor of Boston, medical care was rendered by those of us who had been doctors for either one day, one year, or, in the case of experienced senior physicians, almost two. And assisting them in the task of caring for the sickest of the sick was a cadre of dedicated young almost doctors. We were the Boys of Boston City.

There were no women doctors in our ranks at Boston City. This was due to a long-standing Harvard tradition of institutional misogyny. In 1847, Harriett Kezia Hunt, who had been a practicing physician in Boston for twelve years, applied to attend lectures at Harvard. The corporation duly considered her request and then denied it. They considered her request "inexpedient." Twenty years later, Doctor Zakrzewska's colleague, Susan Dimock, then a student at the New England Female Medical College, applied for admission to attend lectures. The faculty turned her down by a vote of seven to one. Heartened by the vote, she decided to try her luck. The faculty was outraged. It informed the president that "this faculty do not approve the admission of any female to the lectures of any professor." It was not until 100 years later, in 1945, that Harvard finally admitted its first class of women, a move prompted less by recognition of its pompous stupidity than financial necessity. The World War II draft had substantially depleted the pool of qualified applicants, and the school realized it was faced with two choices, starkly presented in a report analyzing the predicament: "Harvard will have to seriously lower her standards in the immediate future or content herself with smaller classes." The admission of women was approved by a vote of fifty-four to three. The irony of the choice of personal pronouns for the institution was presumably not noticed.

Although the medical school was willing to set foot in the feminine forest, it did so with trepidation and not very far. Twelve women were admitted that year. Eighteen years later, when I entered, there were eleven women in our class of 162.

But the Peabody had held firm.

We worked hard. Too hard. But we were guys. And being guys, we knew we needed no adult supervision. Whatever it was, we could figure it out. We made a lot of mistakes. But that was to be expected. Mistakes were good. Because we learned best from our mistakes. And the ideal time for mistakes was when we had been up for thirty-six consecutive hours.

In 1997 an overworked resident in Illinois was driving home after a thirty-six-hour shift. She fell asleep at the wheel and struck a car operated by Heather Brewster, a promising young gymnast. The accident left Heather permanently brain

damaged. The family sued the hospital for requiring the doctor
to work excessive hours. They lost. The court, in its wisdom,
ruled that the hospital was not responsible for the doctor's
condition. But the Accreditation Council on Graduate Medical
Education decided the question of work hours needed urgent
attention. A study committee was formed, and after spending
six years thoroughly evaluating the subject, it issued a ruling
that a doctor's work week should not exceed, on the average,
eighty hours. Proving yet again that in medicine, nothing is too
obvious to preclude a study.

When we had no more to do to our patients, we returned
them to the care of those from whom we never heard and
to whom we never spoke. Had you asked me at the time if I
would ever become an LMD, I would have been shocked at
the question. We knew that LMDs came from somewhere, but
it was not a subject upon which we were encouraged to dwell.

Nor were we encouraged to dwell upon the fate of those
to whom we ministered. Not that we were uncaring. We honestly wanted the best for our patients. We were happy when
they got better, and we were disappointed when they did not.
How much of this reflected our desire to show we had done
a good job I could not say. What I can say was that as people,
our patients hardly existed. We were oblivious to their hopes
and fears. We were not involved in their wants and needs. We
knew them by the diseases that allowed us to learn our trade.
We did not call them by name, but by condition. Cardiac, GI
Bleeder, Chronic Lunger.

I had been assigned the case of Billy O'Connor, a dock
worker from South Boston who was admitted with vomiting.
On rounds, it would be my duty to present Billy to the chief.
Present not so much in the style of "Chief, may I present Billy
O'Connor. Billy is visiting with us from South Boston, where
he lives with his wife, Mary, and their three children. Chief,
Billy. Billy, Chief." Followed by the customary "Pleased to meet
you" by both parties. Rather in this instance, the presentation

was more like what a chef would do when bringing in the pièce de résistance of a meal, a well-dressed rack of lamb or a flaming chocolate soufflé.

This was not Mr. O'Connor's first admission to the hospital. Nor was it his second or his third. On sixteen previous occasions Billy had occupied a bed on Peabody One.

It was not unusual, in those days, for patients afflicted by chronic illness to have an extensive hospital record. With respect to heart disease and emphysema, to name but two of the most common reasons for admission, we had little more to offer than a few days of rest in a relatively more stable environment. Billy was just such a patient. Billy was not, however, a Cardiac or a Chronic Lunger. But we had a special name for Billy too: Alcoholic.

Billy O'Connor was twenty-nine years old.

My first task, upon being assigned to Billy's case, was to review his entire record in detail, so that I would be able to delineate accurately the catalog of his complaints. It began when he was thirteen and passed out on the street. His subsequent admissions included the full range of alcohol-related complications: stomach bleeding, pancreatic inflammation, broken bones, pneumonia, delirium, and more recently, cirrhosis of the liver. It took me an hour and a half, but by the time I had finished, I was confident I knew everything there was to know about Billy, including the fact that for the past six months, as a result of the combined complaints of his wife and pancreas, Billy had been abstinent.

I knew furthermore that Billy was no ordinary alcoholic. There was ample evidence on physical examination of the ravages of his disease. His liver could be felt almost in his pelvis. His fluid-filled abdomen, covered with numerous spidery blood vessels, protruded like a barrel. The whites of his eyes were canary yellow. And when poked with a needle anywhere from the soles of his feet to his knees, he felt no pain.

Billy was an interesting case.

One day, not too long ago, I was visiting one of my patients at the medical center. She complained bitterly that she never saw any doctors. I explained that was because she was not interesting. She was upset to hear this. We generally like to think of ourselves as interesting. I had to explain to her that interesting to a doctor is something you do not want to be. To see doctors and our minions gathering regularly at your bedside is a very bad sign indeed. It brings to mind a bird of similar intent.

*****

Back in the fifth century, a young English novitiate from Giannoventa was sailing his boat on the Irish Sea, when he was captured by a band of Irish pirates. They took him back to their native land. There he was kept captive for six years, until he managed to escape and return home. He completed his studies for the priesthood, but he was never quite the same. By day and by night, he was haunted by voices urging him to return to the land of his capture. "And they cried out, as with one voice. We appeal to you, holy servant boy, to come and walk among us." And so he did. Things were a bit dicey in the early going, for the local authorities were none too eager to have their deities challenged. The druids had been in charge of things since time immemorial and were not pleased as slowly but surely, he won converts to Christianity. He was beaten and jailed and almost executed, but in the end, he prevailed. It has been said that a large measure of his success was attributable to his identification of the three-leafed shamrock as a sign that the Holy Trinity were among them. It has also been said that he banished all snakes from Ireland. Whether this is apocryphal or not, I cannot say. I do know this much. The shamrock does have three leaves. And there are no snakes in Ireland.

His name was Patrick. Patrick became the patron saint of Ireland, and March 17, his feast day, has ever since been a day for great celebration, both in Ireland and among the Irish emigrants abroad.

When the Irish potato famine triggered mass emigration, South Boston was one of the places where the Irish settled. Accordingly, Saint Patrick's Day is a much-celebrated day in Southie. In honor of the day, the shipyards are closed, and the bars serve free beer. And the beer, in honor of St. Patrick's adopted land, is green.

*****

Beer is hard enough to resist for any hardworking man. Free beer on Saint Patrick's Day is impossible to resist. Billy O'Connor got terribly drunk on March 17. He came to the hospital early the next morning with protracted vomiting of a bilious color. As it could signify serious intestinal obstruction, bilious vomiting was considered a grave sign. We called the color Kelly green, in honor of the land of origin of so many of our patients.

By the time I saw him, Billy's green vomit had turned to dry heaves. He was shaky and sweating profusely—and penitent.

"I was doing good, Doc," he said. (In those days, students were allowed to pretend that we were doctors. It was thought to be beneficial to our education.) "But I couldn't help it. I see that green beer, and it calls to me. And I gotta answer. Missus says she was thinking of locking me in the house but held off on account o' I'd surely just jump out the window and bust my neck. Must be somepin' in my jeans, doncha think?"

I allowed as how the genetics of alcohol cravings are a bit obscure, but the power of what we now call triggers is not. Further discussion on the subject was cut short by another round of vomiting.

We gave him intravenous fluids for his dehydration and Compazine for the vomiting. The medicine stopped his vomiting but made him groggy and confused. Sleep deprived and sedated, he soon fell sound asleep. All things considered, this did not seem such a bad outcome. By the time rounds occurred, he was awake but not quite himself. When we arrived at his bedside, I stood at attention and faced the chief.

"William O'Connor is a twenty-nine-year-old white male who was in his usual state of health until the night prior to admission, when he consumed large amounts of alcohol. He came to the hospital with a six-hour history of protracted bilious vomiting. On examination, he was sweating and agitated with a moderate tremor. Vital signs showed a pulse of one hundred and twenty-six and a blood pressure of ninety-eight over sixty-two. He was oriented and alert. His skin turgor was diminished, and his mucous membranes were dry. There was marked scleral icterus. Cardiac examination revealed…"

"His usual state of health?" interrupted the chief. "Tell me, *Doctor* Conger, exactly what was his *usual* state of health?"

"Usual state of health" is one of those things doctors often say to each other. It is like "Have a great day" or "May it please the court." No one expects it to be taken at face value.

I had no idea what it meant.

"W-w-well," I stammered. "Pretty much as usual."

"As u-su-al," the chief repeated slowly. "Of course. Which would not be unusual for one's *usual* state of health. I gather then that this usual state of health did not include a night of binge drinking to the point of protracted vomiting."

"Uh, no sir. Yesterday was an unusual day for him."

"Ah, an *unusual* day. So, in this *usual state of health,* he does not partake of alcohol to excess?"

"No sir."

"All right, perhaps you could enlighten me as to how much he drinks in his *usual* state of health."

At the time of my education, intimidation was considered an educational technique par excellence. It was thought to sharpen the mind and enhance one's concentration. Unfortunately, at this stage of my education, it served completely to muddle it. Although I had obtained a complete medical history from Billy, including his daily alcohol consumption, which, when I eventually looked back at my notes, I confirmed as "used to be three to four beers after work, a few extra on Saturday, and Sunday, but not a drop for the past six months, until yesterday." At the time, however, this information had completely fled my memory.

"Er, I'm not exactly sure, sir."

"No? Pity that. Well, perhaps we can find out for ourselves." The chief turned to Billy.

"Tell me, Billy," he said, addressing him with an ingratiating smile and a confidential tone. "How much do you drink on an *ordinary* day."

For a minute Billy stared blankly at the chief. At first, he didn't seem to recognize that the question was addressed to him. After some hesitation, he answered slowly. "Well, used to be no mor 'n any fella, I s'pose. But now…"

"Then," interrupted the chief, "all we have to know is the average alcohol consumption of the ordinary fella, as you so nicely put it, and we'd have our answer, wouldn't we?"

Billy shrugged. "Dunno 'bout averages, Doc. 'Cepn' Yaz. Over three hundred last year, he was."

"Well then, let me ask you something about *this* year. Do you know what day it is today?"

Billy was still disoriented from the medicine. Close questioning was not something he was quite up to. "Not exactly," he answered uncertainly. "Not a very good one, I'd say."

"No, it doesn't seem to be," said the chief. "And do you know, perchance, where you are—now?"

Billy looked at the unfamiliar surroundings. He looked at the bare walls of his cubicle. He looked at his flimsy hospital johnnie. And he looked at the unfamiliar faces in front of him. For all he knew, these people were dressed in butcher's frocks. He stared blankly at the chief and for some time said nothing. "I'm in trouble," he said finally.

The chief turned his attention back to me.

"Okay, Beach. What we have here is a man who is tremulous, sweating, and confused. He is oriented neither to place or time. He has been drinking heavily. So, the important question would be…"

"Is he in DTs?" I ventured cautiously.

"Precisely."

His question caught me completely unprepared. I hadn't even considered the diagnosis. During my entire interview, Billy, although shaky and weak, was coherent. But that was then. And now, I had to admit, he was not. It was a distinct possibility. "I hadn't appreciated it, sir," I confessed.

"Well then, let's see if we can improve your appreciation. Tell me, what would you consider some of the signs of delirium tremens?"

"Well, tachycardia for one."

"Yes, tachycardia most definitely for one." The chief picked up the bedside chart displaying the vital signs. "Pulse of one twenty-six. Would that meet your standards for tachycardia?"

"Yes, Chief."

"Mine also. What else?"

"Tremors."

"Which?"

"Are present."

"Indeed they are. And what would you consider the most important single sign. The one that would separate DTs from mere alcohol withdrawal?"

"I believe that would be visual hallucinations."

"Very good," said the chief, his tone like that of a parent praising a young child for just having completed some simple task.

"And did Mr. O'Connor have any such?"

I had thought Billy was quite lucid when I talked to him, but at this point, I was not certain of anything. " Er, I don't think so."

"You don't *think* so?" he said facetiously. "What have I told you about thinking, Doctor Conger. You do remember, I hope."

I certainly did. It was a refrain he drummed into us every chance he got.

'What you *think* it is doesn't matter. What matters, is what it *is*."

"Correct. So. let's see if we can make the transition from thinking to knowing. Did he have a positive string sign?"

There was no mention of the string sign in my textbook or in our lectures on alcohol. I had no idea what it was. "I don't know the string sign, Chief," I confessed.

Although admission of ignorance by doctors, as it led to bad habits later on, was strictly to be avoided, an exception was made in the instance of a neophyte third-year student. This was not so much out of indulgence for our sensitivities as for the opportunity it provided our elders to expound. "Well then," the chief said, "allow me to demonstrate."

He turned his attention to Billy. "If you don't mind, Billy, I would like to check your eyesight."

Receiving no objection, the chief put his right hand in his coat pocket and, after fumbling about for a few seconds, brought out a closed fist. Extending his right arm before him, he took his left hand and brought it into approximation with the right. Then, pinching his left thumb and index finger, he slowly drew them apart, rubbing the two fingers back and forth. Finally, he extended the two outstretched arms in front of Billy's face,

"Do you see anything, Billy?" he asked, jiggling his hands slightly.

Billy looked at the chief. Without hesitation, he answered flatly, "a string."

"Yes," said the chief, "a string. That's just what it is. Now tell me if you can, what color is the string?"

"Brown."

The chief smiled. "Exactly right, Billy. It is on the brown-ish side. But what about over on this end?" he nodded toward his left hand. "Wouldn't you say it looks a little green here?"

"Sure," Billy agreed quickly. "Green it is. Green as the beer on Saint Paddy's Day."

"Yes, Billy, it is." The chief turned away from Billy and addressed me. "That, Doctor Conger, is a positive string test. Whatever he may have been on admission, this patient now has visual hallucinations and is in impending delirium tremens. What he needs is Thorazine one hundred milligrams IM, mag-nesium sulfate two grams, and thiamine two hundred milli-grams IV stat."

And with that, the chief left Billy's bedside, and we moved on to the next bed.

It was an impressive demonstration, and I could hardly wait to try it out myself after rounds were over.

In the next bed was another interesting case. We knew about it already, because the student to whom it had been as-signed was so excited about his examination that he couldn't wait to tell us.

"He's got the murmur, of course," he had told us with a pride of ownership. "But get this, he has splinter hemor-rhages and Janeway lesions. He's even got a Roth spot on his left retina. I saw it myself."

We were all impressed—and rather envious. Such mani-festations of an infected heart valve were not an everyday oc-currence

"Thomas Johnson is a forty-five-year-old black male her-oin addict who has been admitted with endocarditis of the mitral valve. He has a three out of four holosystolic murmur at the apex, splinter hemorrhages on his right third and fourth digits, a Janeway lesion on his left thumb, and a Roth spot in the superior temporal quadrant of his left eye. Preliminary blood cultures show a gram-positive organism."

There followed the usual interruptions by the chief and the student's responses, after which we were all invited to partake of the delicacies that the patient offered for our inspection. During the presentation I had the unsettling feeling that the patient was staring at me.

When it was my turn to listen to his heart and look at his hands, he spoke to me.

"Don't I know you, Doc?"

"Uh, no, I just started my rotation this week. I don't believe I've seen you before."

"No," he said with a sad smile, "I don't believe you have. Snickers."

"Excuse me?"

"Joe's Market on Humboldt."

"Oh," I said uneasily. The chief was fixing me with a less than pleasant stare. It was not quite fraternizing with the enemy, but rounds were not considered a social event, at least not between doctors and patients. "I know the store, but…"

"Know you do," he said. "I'm Joe. You come in for a Snickers bar. Sometimes a Coke."

"I'll let you two catch up with each other later," said the chief briskly. "And now, if you don't mind, we will proceed to the business at hand." With that he marched us off to the next bed.

After rounds, I went back to Billy's bedside to administer the ordered medications.

"You seemed to be confused back then on rounds, Billy," I said.

"Truth be told, Doc, I felt kinda drugged from the stuff you gave me earlier. Di'n't help none, neither, him being so big. Intimidating, he was, if you know what I mean."

I did.

"That's okay," I said. "You did the best you could. I'm going to give you some medicine that should make you feel better. But before I do, I just want to check your eyes again." I

put my hand in my pocket. "Now, I want you to look at this."
I went through the string test that the chief had just demon-
strated

"Okay, Doc," Billy said. "Let's call it green—with a bit of
blue on the ends." He smiled at me indulgently. "Not too bad
for your first time on the string. But you were a little quick on
the unravel. More like this." He reached under his johnny and
in a perfect duplication of the chief's demonstration unrolled
the imaginary string. I was dumfounded, and more than a little
embarrassed.

"Yeah," he said, "I don't mind you poke at my liver, and
you can stick needles in my toes, and you can look at my eyeballs. I know you gotta learn, but I wouldn't bother with the
string. You don't need me. You can practice it at home."

"But—I don't understand."

"You know how many times I been in this hospital?"

"Seventeen."

"That many huh? And how many for drinking?"

"In one form or another, just about all of them."

"Right. So, let's say seventeen students on admission, then
another seventeen residents after, and another who knows how
many others they want to show off to. How many times you
figure I been given that string test?"

"Uh, quite a few."

"Yep. And how do you think it makes me feel?"

"Well, I don't…"

"At first, I was kinda angry, then I got over that. And now,
well, now I feel it's kinda a privilege."

"Privilege?"

"Yeah. Here I am, an uneducated drunk from Southie,
and I'm at one of the great teaching hospitals in the country,
and I'm part of it. I'm one of your teachers, actually."

He was, of course. "Yes, I guess you are, Billy. I never
thought of it that way."

"Don't 'spect anybody did. Anyway, makes for a better

feeling than humiliation. Only…" He stopped talking and looked away.

"That it does," I agreed readily. "Only, what?"

"Only sometimes I wish that one of you would show even a little interest in me disregardless of my findings, as you call 'em."

"Oh," I said quietly. "Well, better late than never. Tell me then, what have you done that you are most proud of?"

"That's easy, Doc," he smiled. "Everybody in Southie knows. Was a first-class pitcher in school. Senior year undefeated and an ERA of zero. Course high school competition not that great, but still. Was drafted by the Yankees and played a year of class D ball in Kansas. Guy named Mantle came down and worked out with us."

"Holy cow!" I blurted. (In my youth, this expression was considered the highest accolade of appreciation.) Mickey Mantle was my childhood hero. "You played with Mickey?"

"Just that once—in practice. Hit three out of the park on me."

"Still, it was Mickey Mantle."

"Yeah," he said wistfully. "Long time ago."

Billy recovered uneventfully from his Saint Patrick's Day setback and never drank again. Unfortunately, his liver disease was already too far advanced, and he died less than a year later. Too soon, unlike his playing buddy, with whom he shared more than baseball, to get a new liver. The first successful transplant was done the year of Billy's death.

I can't say exactly why, but for some time after that day I avoided Joe's Market on Humboldt. A couple of years later, during my residency, I did stop by. At the counter was a young man. I asked him about Joe.

"Joe passed," he said.

*****

Two manifestations, in black and white, of the same illness. It was 1966. The civil rights law was less than two years

old, and cultural integration had not yet come to Boston.
Heroin was confined to Roxbury. No one paid it much attention. Alcohol was just one of those things, like bad weather or
taxes. It would not be until decades later that equal opportunity spread heroin to Billy's people. At which time it became
belatedly recognized for its toll. So, opiates get our attention
now. Perhaps it is because the deaths are more dramatic, but
mainly it is because we think it is something new. An epidemic
we call it. Which, if you don't look at Roxbury or Harlem or
North Philadelphia or any of the communities where it has
taken young lives for over sixty years, it might well be. In 2018,
48,000 people died from opiate overdose. That's a lot.

The same year, 88,000 died from alcohol. The same year
almost half a million died from smoking. We don't keep figures
on how many die from sugar. Of course, the comparison isn't
really fair. Slightly fewer than 2 million people are addicted to
opiates. Alcohol claims 15 million, smoking over 30 million,
and as for obesity, it's responsible for about one in three deaths.

Addiction is the most deadly of preventable diseases. But
back in 1966, the addiction itself was not our concern. Content to fiddle with its outward and visible manifestations, we
ignored the fundamental precepts of medicine, that the first
step is prevention. And the most effective treatment is that
which is designed to attack the underlying cause. But to treat
addiction that way would have required us to see the people
behind our patients.

We recently had a medical school reunion. Our fiftieth. As
is common at such gatherings, fond reminiscences over past
glories tended to take precedence over present realities. There
was much waxing nostalgic about the good old days, and how
great our training was, and how it isn't any longer anything like
what it used to be. Which it certainly isn't.

For when I look back on my years at Boston City Hospital, I am not nostalgic.

I am ashamed.

CHAPTER 6

As I said before, 1966 was a long time ago. The practice of medicine has changed greatly since then. It is so much better. Medical schools—not so much. Tethered to the certainty of tradition, they remain almost as hidebound and dogmatic as ever, determinedly ignorant of the existence of a world beyond their noses.

Students have changed, though. They are smarter. They are more aware of the world around them. They can see how it functions. And they know how it should function. Overall, they are better equipped to minister to people than we ever were.

It helps that, collectively, they have a lot less testosterone.

Davida Edwards, for one, has heard much from her olders and wisers about how devoted we are to the well-being of her generation. She has seen how we act upon this devotion. From parents who are more concerned with their own needs than the needs of their children. From teachers who are more impressed with their ability to teach than their students' ability to learn. And especially from coaches who are more interested in their moves on the athletes than those the athletes perform on the ball. She has seen enough of the folly of those in charge to be skeptical that older does not necessarily mean wiser.

But it is the receivers of medical care who have changed the most. It was not that long before my time that a patient was satisfied to emerge from a medical encounter (that is the word we now use, the adversarial connotation of such a term apparently lost on those who have adopted it) none the worse than when she entered it. By the time I started, patients were, if not actually optimistic about the outcome of our ministrations, at least hopeful.

*****

There is a character in *David Copperfield* by the name of Wilkins Micawber. He is prone to the making of philosophical pronouncements that he follows not one bit. There is one in particular that is relevant here. It is as follows:

Annual income twenty pounds, annual expenditure nineteen pounds nineteen pence, result happiness. Annual income twenty pounds, annual expenditure twenty pounds one pence, result misery.

Although the principle refers to matters financial, it serves equally well in the matter of expectations.

We have a son and two daughters. All are accomplished in their professions. All have helped to raise healthy and well-adjusted children of their own. But there is one big difference. Our daughters see not what they have done, but what remains yet to be done. Our son sees that what he has done is more than he might have. Our daughters' expectations exceed their accomplishments. Their result, misery. My son's expectations are less than his accomplishments. His result, happiness.

*****

So it often is with patients. It used to be that when they received treatment, they considered how much worse it could have been. Then they were happy. Now, when they receive treatment, they think upon how much better it should be. Now, they are miserable.

But not in Dumster. Like our son, the people of Dumster have been blessed with low expectations. If crops were not so good this year, at least they weren't as bad as three years ago. If they have a particularly harsh winter, they remember when there were four such in succession. If the departure of Acme Tool and Die deprived the townspeople of high-paying union jobs so that they had to work long hours at two jobs to make ends meet, it was better than being out of work. And if my ministrations didn't quite achieve the desired effect, "You did the best you could, Doc," was their invariable response.

But even in Dumster, the winds of change are rustling the trees. Not long ago, after I had discussed a treatment with one of my most devoted and trusting patients, he said, "If you think maybe a second opinion, Doc, well, er, I guess it would be okay with me. Not that I'm thinking I need it. I mean, only if you thought. You know I trust you, Doc. Sure do. Just saying." He was hesitant and apologetic, but there it was, the bane of the primary care doctor's existence, the S.O. As if I couldn't give him any number of opinions myself. It was a sign of the times.

The patient was William Fusswood.

I have known William Fusswood—Fusswood, as he prefers to be called—for over forty years now. I met him shortly after my arrival in Dumster. When first he came to me, his philosophy of medical care was like that of his fellow townspeople. Laissez-faire existentialist would best describe it. That something might happen in the future that could be prevented by action in the present was a concept with which he was familiar, but with which he did not hold much truck. He was a disciple of the if-it-ain't-broke-don't-fix-it school of maintenance, for all objects, both inanimate and animate. And if it did happen to be broken, if it wasn't too badly broken, he would fuss at it with whatever he had handy, like Bag Balm or duct tape, and then he would temper it with a heavy dose of tincture of time. Fusswood would no more think of going to the doctor when he wasn't sick than he would think of replacing his shingles if the roof wasn't leaking.

A town full of people with such a philosophy was not favorable to the new approach to medical care that I brought with me. But as luck would have it, just about the time I came to town, an enterprising young man by the name of Jerry

Sclikowski Slick, as he was known—decided to leave his job as head salesman at Davidson Ford Lincoln Mercury New and Used Cars and go into business for himself. The business he chose was insurance. It was the perfect choice. Slick is one of those people who has that remarkable ability to convince a person that what he wants you to do is exactly what it is you had in mind to do, only you just hadn't happened to think about it. It is a powerful ability and when wielded by the likes of Abraham Lincoln or Mahatma Gandhi, it can be a great force for good. In a salesman, it is deadly.

Although there were vehicles in Dumster that had not been sold by Slick, there weren't many, and they invariably belonged to those who had not lived here long enough to need a new car. No matter what you were looking for, Slick would find a car to sell you. His motto was, "You don't see it, I'll get it." And he was as good as his word. New or used, foreign or domestic, pricey or cheap, if it wasn't on the lot at Davidson, Slick knew where it was, and he got it. He never took a commission on these sales— "just a small handling charge." "Public service" is what he called it. "Better they get it from me than someone else," he said. "Someday they'll need a truck." Which they did. Hardly a driveway in town did not sport in the place of honor a new or used F150 with a Davidson license plate holder on the rear bumper. Trucks were where the profit margin was. "Sedans," he told me, "are just a loss leader. They always want to save on their sedans. And I let 'em. Makes them feel they got a good deal. But a truck is another animal altogether. A man's truck tells you who he is. And no man wants his truck to say, 'Second class.' A man may have a dog, and he may even let the dog ride shotgun, but in Dumster, it's a truck that's man's best friend."

He was right. Trine had been a family court magistrate for many years. "Hardest thing I ever had to do," she always said, "was tell the man his child support had to come before his truck payments." They just couldn't understand. "But, yer honor," they'd plead, "it's for my *truck*."

Slick took the savings he had accumulated at Davidson and invested it in his new venture. He bought the old Woolworth building on Main Street and set up his office on the ground floor. Upper Valley Insurance Company, he called it. He started with auto insurance. Up until then, townspeople went to the State Farm office in White River Junction for their insurance. Switching to Slick was only natural. He was a local boy. Everyone knew him. Everyone trusted him. They had bought their cars and their trucks from him, and when Slick started calling them all in "just to gab," in they came. And they walked out with Upper Valley auto insurance.

But Slick had grander designs than just autos.

So, when one of the boys came in to get his car insured by Slick, and after all the papers had been signed and Slick had congratulated him on what a great deal he had made, Slick would lean back in his chair, smile, and say, "Got a sweet little truck there, Joe [or Armand or Hiram]."

And Joe or Armand or Hiram would answer, "Thanks to you, Slick."

"Just doin' my part," he'd answer deprecatingly. "Anything I can do to help my boys, you know I'm good for it."

And Joe or Armand or Hiram would concede that truer words were never spoken. At which point Slick would pause, look him straight in the eye, and ask, "Now tell me, buddy, what's more important than that ol' truck of yours?"

Which would pretty much stump his man. So, Slick would suggest helpfully, "Family, good buddy. The missus and the little ones. Nothing beats family."

To which assertion, the good buddy in question had no choice but to agree that certainly, nothing beats family.

"And you already done made sure that truck of yours will be taken care of should, God forbid, anything ever happen to it. So, let's see what we can do to make sure that family of yours is just as safe." Slick ended the analogy here. Unlike in his former job, he did not bring up the subject of replacement.

Slick's logic was impeccable, his manner irresistible. Dumsterians started sprouting life insurance policies like crabgrass. And for every new policy holder there had to be a medical examination.

Accustomed as he was to Doc Franklin's feel-okay-look-okay checkup, Fusswood, when I first met him, was fully expecting something along those lines. But as he discovered to his chagrin, I was not Doc Franklin. I examined him head to toe and, to his considerable discomfiture, a variety of places in between. I ordered a slew of blood tests. Just about all of them were normal.

Except for a little blood in the urine.

All of us, even those whose milk contains nothing but human kindness, are at times subject to feelings that we would definitely prefer to keep to ourselves. Feelings that do not make us prone to say, "You know what I was just thinking?" to our near and dear, or to anyone else who might be within earshot.

So it is with a doctor when she finds something in her examination that is not quite as it ought to be. Something that, if she were to have discovered it in herself, would cause her at least disquiet, possibly even frank alarm. Yet when it is found in a patient, she experiences instead a pleasurable flutter of excitement, as she anticipates what lies ahead.

"We exist in order to treat," we would argue if pressed. "And in order to treat, we must first discover." Which is true enough, but really begs the point. Because the simple truth is that things amiss are not simply our raison d'être. They are our joie de vivre.

The abnormal is what sustains us.

It is often argued—speciously, I must say—that the reason we order so many tests is because of fear of malpractice. This argument, on its face, is silly. The fact remains that no one ever sued a doctor for not ordering a test to diagnose a condition that the patient did not have. We order tests because we like to. And we like to because that's how we find things. Things that give us something to do. If nobody coming through our doors ever had anything wrong, doctoring would be a very dull business indeed. Call it what you will, health maintenance, preventive medicine, comprehensive care, in reality, it is a fishing expedition, trolling to be precise. Casting a wide net to see what we can bring in.

Blood in the urine opens a whole world of meddling.

"You have blood in your urine," I told Fusswood after we had finished.

"Nope," said Fusswood, misconstruing my statement as a question.

"I'm afraid I didn't make myself clear, Mr. Fusswood. I was explaining that we found some blood on the urine test."

"I never seen it."

"It's only a microscopic amount."

"Okay then."

"But it could represent a problem."

"Don't think so, Doc. I got no problems with my water works. Runs just right when I want it to. Stops when I don't—if you know what I mean. But I thank you for your concern. Now, if you'll just sign that paper for Slick, I'll be on my way. Already taken up too much of your time. You got sick people to tend to, I'm sure."

"Yes, I do, Mr. Fusswood, and I want to make sure you don't become one of them."

"Oh?" he said.

"It's probably nothing, of course."

"*Probably*, huh?"

"Yes, but it's because of the small chance that it could represent something more, well …"

I had his full attention.

"Serious?"

"I'm just saying that we should make sure. It's up to you, of course."

"Course," he agreed readily. "Whatever you think, Doc. You're the boss."

There is nothing quite so upsetting to a person's sense of well-being as a "probably nothing." It destroys in an instant that illusion of invulnerability to which we all cling for as long as we can. And which doctors labor tirelessly to destroy. Its loss is the first step on the long and arduous path a person travels in order to become a patient.

As Fusswood had worked for several years at Acme Tool and Die, including the years before exposure to chemicals was as strictly controlled as it is today, the possibility that some had gotten into his urine and caused mischief in his bladder had to be considered. Bladder cancer among the workers there was not uncommon, a fact of which Fusswood, like all former Acme employees, was well aware. Several among his colleagues already had their bladders removed. And there was a long piece in *The Valley News* about the carcinogenic risks at the factory.

I suggested that we should start by checking out his bladder. Fusswood readily agreed. I sent him to Elaine Flushing, our urologist. She looked inside with her scope and pronounced everything as clean as a whistle. Upstream from the bladder lay the ureters and the kidneys. They were next on the agenda. At that time, the standard diagnostic test was an intravenous pyelogram. It is an x-ray where the kidneys are highlighted by injection of a dye, which the kidneys concentrate and then excrete. On Fusswood's films, the ureters were wide open, but on the top of the left kidney there was a spot. The radiologist declared it to be "ill-defined." *Ill-defined* is a popular term with radiologists. They use it when they haven't the foggiest what something is. It conveys the idea that any uncertainty is not due to their lack of diagnostic acumen, but a failure on the part of whatever it is to own up to its identity. In 1977, a lot of ill-defineds cropped up at Emmeline Talbot. It may just have been one of those things, but it was also the year Emmeline Talbot acquired a new piece of diagnostic equipment, a computerized tomography machine, CT for short. CT scans provide much more detail than the old roentgen films. Like everyone else who had ill-defineds that year, Fusswood had a CT scan. The CT scan showed that the kidney itself was fine, but sitting on top of it was a lump. A lump that remained stubbornly ill-defined. The radiologist and Doctor Flushing had never seen anything quite like it before. They called a specialist in Boston. The specialist looked at the films. He opined that in the category of lumps, it was most interesting. *Interesting* is the word specialists use instead of ill-defined. It means the same thing. The specialist recommended an angiogram, an injection of dye into the bloodstream to highlight the circulation of the lump. This, he expected, would help to render the defined less ill.

The angiogram showed that the area in question was particularly rich in blood vessels. "Highly vascular" is the precise term. The radiologist spoke with Doctor Flushing, and Doctor Flushing spoke with the specialist, and they all agreed.

It was suspicious.

Unlike in the criminal justice system, in medicine, a suspicion is guilty until proven innocent. And so, sentence was passed.

"Out, out damned lump."

At surgery, Doctor Flushing found a large yellow lump. As advertised, it was highly vascular. Just to be safe, she removed the kidney as well. The pathologist examined the lump and sent slides to Dartmouth for review. The final diagnosis was an angiomyolipoma. In simple terms, a big blob of highly vascular fat.

I gave Fusswood the good news.

Fusswood was relieved. There is nothing quite so comforting as a near escape from disaster, to discover that a probably nothing is, in fact, nothing. So relieved in fact was he, that he never asked why we took out a perfectly normal kidney for a piece of fat. Which is only what one would expect from a patient.

After Fusswood had recovered from the surgery, I rechecked his urine.

It showed a small amount of blood.

Had Fusswood been able to see his experience for what it was, an excessive intrusion on the part of an overzealous medical profession, he could have emerged from it with a healthy skepticism of doctors and our claims. And there are those who can do just that. Those who, when I suggest a course of action, say, "What if I didn't?" But such clear-sighted folk are exceptional. Fusswood was no dummy. Nor was he naïve. But Fusswood was not an exceptional person. He had an ordinary confidence in his own judgment and an ordinary distrust of authority. And in an encounter with medicine, the ordinary is a woefully insufficient weapon with which to do battle. Thus it was that, rather than being reassured that his experience was much ado about nothing and feeling confident that he was as healthy as he felt, he became uncertain and anxious, fearful as to what the next such unexpected finding might portend. It may have been a nothing this time, but would he be so fortunate in the future? And so it was that for a person whose last thought in the world had been about his health, now the slightest ache or briefest twinge became grounds for concern.

From that time forth there was no complaint too trivial to pursue. A bit of indigestion became a possible heart attack. A minor disruption in the bowels was certain cancer. Fatigue at the end of a long day became Lyme disease. Misplacing his keys was the first sign of Alzheimer's. And a cough could only mean pneumonia. Unless it was something worse. Some might say that Fusswood had become a hypochondriac. For me, he was simply a good patient.

Chance had it that Mr. Fusswood was on my schedule for Davida's first morning. He came in with one of his regular complaints, a cough. As she would have only one patient for the morning, William Fusswood was the ideal subject. He was articulate and affable, and he had an extensive medical history. It could easily take her all the allotted time to find out everything there was to be known about Fusswood, and to develop her own plan for his management.

Having as much time as one needs provides an excellent learning opportunity. It allows for the kind of in-depth holistic approach that is all too often preached more than it is practiced. Being quite time-consuming, however, it does not necessarily equip the budding doctor to flower in an environment where the soil is less fertile and climate less favorable.

Except for a concierge doctor.

As the name implies, a concierge doctor surrenders her independence to her patients, promising, for a substantial fee, to be at their beck and call. The degree of beck in the call varies with the practice size. If your ideal practice size is one, then you might choose a Warren Buffet practice, or if a family medicine is more to your liking, a Bill and Melinda Gates. From there the size increases depending on your needs and the pocketbooks of your patients. I must admit, there are days when, faced with a waiting room full of patients, only a fraction of whose needs I can meet, it does have an appeal, even though it smacks of the kind of master-servant relationship the wealthy enjoyed with their doctors in centuries gone by. And it is less than ideal for meeting the needs of the entire community. Unless that community consists of the 1 percent.

It was not necessary for me to ask Fusswood's consent to see Davida. He quite enjoyed the opportunity of the undivided attention of a bright, young mind as a willing vessel into which he could pour his troubles.

"A student today, Doc?" said Fusswood when we walked into the room. "Great. Anything I can do to help. You know I'm there for you. After all you've done for me. Besides, sometimes, you know, talking with them, I can remember stuff I didn't have time to bring up with a busy guy like you. So, tell me, who is the unlucky one this time?"

His initial attention was so focused on me, he failed to realize that the student in question was not only someone he already knew, but a dignitary in her own right. Then he saw who it was.

"Clutch!" he exclaimed. "Is that really you?"

"It used to be, Mr. Fusswood," replied Davida smiling. "I'm Davida now."

"Right, Doc," Fusswood corrected himself. "Okay if I call you that? Davida's a kid's name. Besides, that's what I call *Doctor Conger* here." He jerked his thumb toward me, half in jest.

Davida looked at me a bit uncertainly.

"Well," I said, "the medical school has strict rules about how students are to be addressed, and it is no longer considered appropriate to employ the title until it has been earned. However, seeing as we are not in the medical school at present, and the appellation Doc has been applied honorifically to many who are not physicians, your patron saint, for one."

"You mean Doctor Seuss?"

"Correct. So, I think we may say, welcome Doc Edwards. Besides, who knows what the future holds." I turned to Davida with a mock salute.

"And Who isn't telling," said Fusswood.

"Well, I'll leave you two to it. Let me know when you need me."

"No worries, Doc," said Fusswood quickly, thinking about the prospect of spending a few hours alone with a bright, attractive, and personable young woman. "We'll be fine."

I closed the door and went out. As I walked back to my office, I thought how nice it was that the two of them had bonded so quickly.

And I felt old.

CHAPTER 7

I went back to my office and sat down at my desk. I checked my schedule. Start at 8:00. One patient every fifteen minutes. Stop at 11:30. Fifteen-minute break at 10:00.

For most of my years in Dumster, I was in private practice. I shared office expenses with Doctor Wetherby, and we covered for each other, but financially, we were independent. "You eat what you kill," he joked when I arrived, explaining how things worked in Dumster. He had gone to Dartmouth College and Dartmouth Medical School and he had done his residency at Mary Hitchcock. As he really had not had much contact with civilization, I forgave him his poor choice of metaphors. "How about: you keep whom you save?" I replied. He just looked at me.

We were the only show in town, and like our predecessors, we took care of our patients wherever and whenever they were—the office, the emergency room, the hospital, the nursing home, and, ultimately, King's Funeral Home. The multiplicity of venues made for a lot of interruptions, and a rigid schedule was impossible. To accommodate this, there were blocks of unassigned time scattered throughout the day. Rarely was a day perfectly planned, but equally rarely was it a complete mess. The people of Dumster didn't mind. A little inconvenience never bothered them. They had their Doc.

All that changed four years ago. After forty years of service, Herbert Shiftly, who had been the only administrator

Emmeline Talbot ever had, got up out of his swivel chair for the last time and moved to Cape Cod to farm cranberries on a two-acre plot in Chatham. "One bog to another," he said. "This one, I expect, will be more manageable."

In honor of his service, the trustees gave him a rocking chair with the hospital emblem on the back, and they put a picture of him in the hall at the entrance to the hospital. Then they hired a team of consultants to come in and make recommendations for the future direction of the good ship Emmeline, now that its only captain had left.

Which the consultants did. They didn't say it straight out. That's not the way consultants are. But they made it clear right from the start that not only had we been sailing in the wrong direction, but that if we didn't change course and crew pretty damn quick, we would run aground and founder.

First order of business, they explained, was rebranding. I remembered rebranding from when I was a kid. On Saturday afternoon I went to the matinee show at Rome Theater. Sometimes they showed a Western. Rebranders were the bad guys. In the dead of night, they stole cattle from the hardworking farmer, and they terrorized his devoted wife and good-looking daughter. Rebranders were guys who had to be chased down by John Wayne or the Lone Ranger or a federal marshal. Who always got them.

That was then. Now, rebranding is good. Essential, even. Without it, we wouldn't be able to get our message out. Getting the message out, the consultants explained, was very important. No message out, no people in. And we had to be quick about it. All the other hospitals up and down the river had already done their rebranding. Claremont General was now Valley Regional Hospital. Windsor Hospital had become Mt. Ascutney Hospital and Health Center. And our mother ship, Mary Hitchcock, was no more, imploded on a great funeral pyre. In her place was a spanking-new, magnificent building, the Dartmouth-Hitchcock Medical Center. It even had a shopping mall.

After much discussion, the trustees finally decided on their new name: Upper Connecticut River Medical Center. The consultants were paid, and they went home. Their job was done. A new batch came in right on their heels. They would be responsible for upgrading our services as best befit our new message. The new consultants came from California. California is a big state. It has 346 hospitals. A small hospital in California has 250 beds. But they were undaunted. They set about making UCRMC just like a California hospital, only smaller. First to go were the Docs. I don't mean they got rid of doctors. On the contrary; they doubled and then tripled the size of the medical staff. But the old-time Doc, they explained, was a thing of the past. A dinosaur. Too big and too clumsy to survive in the modern world.

There was now only one Doc.

Me.

Until recently, there had been four of us. The Gang of Four they called us. Doc Caplin, Doc Wetherby, Doc Sackett, and me. Everyone who began their life in Dumster started out with Doctor Caplin. When they reached adulthood, they would switch from her to either me or Doctor Sackett or Doctor Wetherby. When the transition occurred was variable. Davida transferred to me when she was twelve. And Jerry Williams, who never got over his teenage crush on his doctor, stuck with Doc Caplin until he had his first heart attack, at the age of forty. It didn't matter all that much anyway. Whoever was on call was the only doctor around, so we all did what had to be done. But by the time Shiftly left, Doc Wetherby had died, and Doctors Sackett and Caplin had retired. I was the last of the lot who had made Emmeline Talbot a place to call home.

For inpatient care, the hospital would need hospitalists. The nursing home would have geriatricians. And for the emergency room, emergency room doctors. Such people were trained in their particular arena to provide care that was the highest quality, the most efficient, the most comprehensive—and the most remunerative.

After the hospital staff had been thusly organized, in came the ologists, a whole battalion of them. Dermatologists, cardiologists, gastroenterologists, neurologists, rheumatologists, endocrinologists, pulmonologists. They even had a psychologist, but he didn't last long. When it comes to talking about one's troubles, Dumster folk belong to the "none of your beeswax" camp.

Now don't get me wrong. I like specialists. They perform a vital role in the care of patients. When I was in Boston and San Francisco and, more recently, in Philadelphia, I even considered them colleagues. Specialists are essential to the practice of modern medicine. No matter what the condition, there is always someone who knows more about that condition than I do. Except maybe the geriatrician. I know pretty well how not to mess too much with old people. Vida had taught me that.

Specialists are like good neighbors. They are really handy if you want to borrow a cup of sugar or get help fixing a mower. But you wouldn't want them moving in with you. They had no more business, as Vida would have said, pissing on my tree than I had rooting in their cabbage patch. Dartmouth had been just the right distance, close enough that we could get to them when we needed to, but far enough away that I was reasonably able to protect my patients from their clutches when it wasn't necessary.

You might well ask, what then was left for me?

Which I did ask.

The consultants from California said, "Good question," which is what the consultants always said when you asked them anything. It is the consultants' way of saying, "Shut up, please."

"You will be a primary care provider."

A primary care provider, PCP for short, is a doctor on a rather tight leash. My practice would be confined solely to the office, and the conditions upon which I could fuss would be solely those that specialists consider below their pay grade— conditions like chronic fatigue, ill-defined pain, and any other symptoms that did not qualify as specialist grade. I would also be expected, on a more frequent basis, to schedule visits for health maintenance, the primary purpose of which had less to do with maintaining a person's health than with finding something that would justify referral to the appropriate specialists. The acronym PCP was completely fitting. I would be a hallucinatory vision of a real doctor.

The consultants told me that as the senior physician I would have my choice. I could be a PCP. But if I preferred, I could be a hospitalist, an emergency room doctor, or a geriatrician.

"Okay," I said.

"Okay, which?" they asked.

"All of them," I said.

"You can't," they said.

"I will," I said.

"The bylaws don't allow it."

"Change the bylaws."

"We would lose our accreditation."

"Make an exception."

"Just for you?"

"Just for me."

"That wouldn't be fair."

"Ask."

"Ask whom?"

"Everyone. Ask the trustees. Ask the medical staff and the nurses. Ask the telephone operators and the receptionists and the billing people. Ask maintenance. And ask the other doctors. If any one person objects, I'll retire."

I had been there forty years. The medical staff consisted of a whole new cadre of smart, young doctors, none of whom had been there more than a few years. They liked having me around. I was a curiosity to them. The last of a dying species. They thought I was "cute." Whatever I did was fine with them. And most of the employees and the trustees were either my patients or had a relative who was. The others didn't care. They figured I wasn't likely to last all that long anyway.

Nobody objected.

But I did have to agree to become an employee of UCRMC and to abide by a contract, which specified, among many other things, the exact schedule for outpatient visits. It was a nuisance, but with the help of Crikett, my nurse and responsible adult, I managed to fudge my schedule enough to give me a modicum of flexibility in case someone happened to get sick or actually wanted to talk to me.

*****

Students vary considerably in the time they choose to spend with patients. A few are finished in ten minutes. They are the listening impaired. Which might seem to be a handicap in our line of work. But medicine has made a special effort to find places for such people. Accordingly, there are many areas of doctoring in which one doesn't have to listen much, and a few where listening does not occur at all. The same is true of the laying on of hands. For the touch-challenged, there is a whole set of specialties where you do nothing but take pictures or look through instruments. It suits them well. There are also students who take forever. They can listen endlessly to the most repetitive drivel. They have trouble coming to closure on the visit. They have a use, too. There is room for everyone in medicine.

To forestall floundering, I usually ask the students to check in after about thirty minutes just to see how things are going. After an hour had elapsed without word, I went to the exam room and knocked on the door. I heard voices inside, but no one answered. I opened the door and went in. Davida and Fusswood were huddled together over the computer, quite intent on whatever it was they were looking at. They didn't notice me.

"Everything okay?" I asked.

"Oh, Doctor Conger," said Davida, looking up. "I'm glad you came in. I was just going to ask you if it's all right that I go over some of Mr. Fusswood's records with him. He had some questions about one of his medicines, and I said I would do the best I could to answer them."

"Which medicine is that?"

"My cholesterol medicine," said Fusswood.

"Of course," I said, a bit snappish. "Fusswood and I *have* reviewed his statin quite extensively on several occasions in the past, but if he doesn't mind…"

"Not at all, Doc," answered Fusswood quickly. "Not that you haven't before. Not at all. I always appreciate how you explain things to me. But I figure if I can do anything to help with her education, I'm only too glad to—I mean, it's the least I can do after all you've done for me. And she's doing a really good job—for her experience that is. Doesn't talk down to me. Makes it simple and clear as can be."

"I see. Well, I'm glad to see things are going so well. And when you're done, we can get you treated for your cough."

"Oh that," said Fusswood. "That's all set. Turns out I don't need any antibiotics. Davida explained it all to me. How often a cough, even if there is a touch of pneumonia, doesn't require antibiotics, because mostly they are just viruses, and you will get better anyway. And that when you get antibiotics and then you get better, you think it is because of the antibiotics instead of your own body fighting the infection, which is where the credit really belongs. And she reminded me that antibiotics are not good for the environment. It just gives more of a chance for resistant bugs to crop up. And…"

"That's certainly true," I cut in. His soliloquy had gone on long enough. "I'm glad you appreciate the importance of taking antibiotics only when appropriate. However, antibiotics do have an important role in fighting infection, and their judicious use is important."

"Sure thing, Doc. And I only take what you prescribe for me. I'm just saying that Davida…"

"Of course. Well, I'll leave you two to your work. We'll go over it when you're ready."

"Okay, Doc. I'm in no hurry. She can take as long as it takes."

*****

I have been told there are people who can resist all temptation. Although I have never met such a person, there is something reassuring in knowing they exist. It gives the rest of us something to strive for. On the whole, I would consider myself a reasonably good temptation resister, although as Trine points out, doctors always have a higher opinion of themselves than is justified by their behavior. So, I'll just say that I am reasonably good at resisting temptation—for a doctor.

Doctors are beset by many temptations in the course of our work. And the inordinate trust placed in us by our patients makes it possible for us to succumb to temptations without suffering the consequences. There are financial temptations that make it easy to reward ourselves for activities that we may have performed but ought not to have. There is the temptation of easy access to any drug that strikes our fancy. And there is the worst temptation of all, the one that arises from the privilege that we are given of doing almost anything we choose with the bodies of those for whom we ought to be caring.

I can safely say that such temptations have never had any appeal for me, so resisting them has not been an issue. For not yielding to a temptation that doesn't tempt, I can take no credit, of course, but I just mention it in case any of my patients are reading this and beginning to wonder about me.

There is one temptation, however, against which I struggle constantly. And in which struggle I do not always prevail. It is the temptation to do what your patient wants, rather than what you know is the proper thing to do. And nowhere is this temptation stronger than in the prescription of antibiotics. The vast majority of illnesses of the respiratory tract—colds, sinus infections, bronchitis, even many pneumonias—do not need antibiotics, and for the very reasons that Fusswood pointed out, they should not be prescribed. It is not good for the individual, and it is not good for the environment. In the beginning of my career, we treated everything with penicillin. There were no such germs as MRSA, vancomycin-resistant enterococcus, or multi-drug-resistant Enterobacteriaceae. Now, penicillin is almost a relic, confined to two diseases, Group A streptococcus and syphilis. Some strains of syphilis have already acquired resistance. And although streptococcus is still generally susceptible to penicillin, it has learned a strategy that protects it equally well. Ordinarily, when strep invades the body, it lodges on the outside of cells, from which vantage point it can more easily wreak havoc on neighboring tissues. But some strains, when faced with a penicillin assault, now take refuge *inside* the cell, a place penicillin is unable to penetrate. And it won't be long before those strains teach this trick to the rest of their relatives

Today's antibiotics are both more potent and more toxic than penicillin. The best one can say about them is that they are sure to be safer than their descendants.

Many patients expect to have antibiotics when they are sick. This is not their fault. We have trained them to have that expectation. It allows us to do something for a condition that would get better anyway. And once they have had antibiotics and gotten better, it is only natural that they would credit the treatment, and the doctor who did it. It is good for business. People wouldn't bother to come to the doctor if they knew they weren't going to get anything other than the common-sense advice that their mothers gave them.

There was a time when I stood firm against Fusswood's pleas. Unfortunately, some years ago he came down with a

rather severe case of pneumonia, and antibiotics were indicated. He recovered uneventfully and was very appreciative of
his treatment. I did not emphasize that this particular illness
was not typical of the assorted coughs and congestions that he
suffered on a regular basis.

*****

A father and his young daughter go shopping. Usually, the
mother does the shopping. She never takes her daughter. She
knows better. This morning, however, the father offers to tend
to both, shopping and daughter. He may be doing it because he
is trying to be helpful. But it is just as likely that, under cover
of helpfulness, he is managing to get out of a more onerous
task that he has been avoiding for some time, like cleaning the
gutters or fixing the sump pump.

In the checkout line, the little girl sees a small, brightly
colored package. On the front there is a picture of her favorite
cartoon character. She knows better than to point or to ask.
She grabs it and looks up at her father with an innocent smile.
The father knows that she should not have it. He and her
mother have had long discussions about how bad sugar is for
little mouths and brains. They have no sweets in their home.
They have also discussed how important it is to establish good
behavior early in life, so that it becomes just the natural way
of doing things. So, the father knows full well that his little girl
should not have this package. But she is his daughter, and she
is the cutest, most precious thing he knows. Why not? he asks
himself, and before himself can answer with an explanation as
to exactly why not, he puts the package on the counter with
the rest of the purchases. "I love you, Daddy," the little girl
says sweetly. And she means it. It's only this once, he says to
himself. And he means it, too. Fat chance, says himself to the
father. But the father doesn't hear it.

*****

That's the way it is with Fusswood and me. Sometime
after that bad pneumonia, Fusswood came into the office for

the second time with what was no more than a bad cold that just wouldn't go away. He told me he needed antibiotics. Someone at work had the same cold, he said, and her doctor had given her antibiotics, and she got better. But, as he pointedly remarked, I hadn't, and he hadn't. Against my better judgement, I gave them to him. And each time after that it got a little harder not to do the same thing, until eventually, if Fusswood said, "This is a bad one, Doc. Think I need that Z-pak," I would write the prescription without objection. I knew I shouldn't.

I was not proud of prescribing antibiotics in this fashion. It bothered me. But I did it anyway. And the next time it bothered me less. That's the way it is with yielding to temptations. It is a vicious cycle.

A cycle which Davida, in one visit, had broken.

I wondered if Davida, as she progressed in her career, would be able to resist the temptation. Somehow, I thought, she would. And that her patients would be glad of it.

She came into the office after she had finished with her visit. We went back to see Fusswood. I asked him if he had any questions. He told me he was all set. Davida had done a great job.

"Let's see when we should make your next appointment," I said. "How about…"

"We're all set for next week," said Fusswood.

"Well, that seems a little soon. You just had your annual checkup two weeks ago, and everything seemed in order. I think we could go a little longer. Three months should be about right—unless you get sick, of course."

"Well, Doc," said Fusswood sheepishly, "I was sorta thinking—I mean if it's okay with you—that I could come in again sooner. I'd like to go over some more stuff about my cholesterol."

"Your cholesterol?" I said, not concealing my irritation. "We discussed it at your last visit. It's fine. At least it's as good as we can get it without side effects." Fusswood had an elevated cholesterol, but each attempt to increase his medication dose had produced a variety of symptoms that precluded a full therapeutic dose, and we had settled for the fact that some was better than none. Which was in line with this month's cardiologists' recommendation, reasoning, presumably, that as long as a person took *something*, that person was still a patient.

"I know, Doc, but I was wondering if I might have Chip."

"Chip?"

"Yeah. C-H-I-P. Don't know exactly what it stands for. Heard about it yesterday on *All Things Considered*, but the words were too fancy, and I couldn't figure out what it was."

"Well, that is certainty a consideration, and we should definitely discuss it at some point, but I see no hurry about that."

I had no idea what he was talking about. I had never heard of CHIP, but I did not consider it necessary to mention that fact to Fusswood.

Davida spoke up. "I told him I didn't know what CHIP was, but that I would do some research on it, and then he could come back and we could discuss it—if that's okay with you."

"As you wish."

"Great," said Fusswood. "You know, Doc, Davida here has a really good way of explaining things. Doesn't make me feel I am being talked down to. Not that you don't too," he added hastily. "But, of course, she has more time, you know, and…"

"Of course. We'll see you next week."

*****

I am pretty conscious about keeping up to date as to what is new in medicine. I subscribe to three medical journals. I attend our grand rounds regularly. And I take CME courses every year, usually in the Caribbean in winter—it's easier to concentrate there, being free from the distractions of home. But I do have to work for a living, and I don't have the time to spend all day listening to the radio.

I don't know if you ever listen to public radio. I used to, back when we first arrived in Vermont. They played the kind of music you couldn't get on regular radio stations. But somewhere along the way they got into news in a big way. BBC envy, most likely. First one hour, then two. Now it's up to seven hours a day. Which creates a problem. Day in and day out, there isn't much news that is actually new. Real radio stations usually cover it in about five minutes. Seven hours is a long time to talk about not very much. The problem is compounded by the fact that they don't have commercials. This means they have a lot of extra time they have to fill with something else. Mostly, they solve this by interviewing ignorant people to get their opinions on important subjects. Since such people are plentiful, this takes up a lot of the slack. But not quite all. So they have taken to reporting on articles in the medical journals. And the medical journals, eager for the publicity, have gotten into the annoying habit of sending their studies to public radio before they appear in print. Which means that if one of my patients is sitting at home with nothing better to do, he may tune in and hear about some new finding that says whatever we have been doing up to now needs to change. This is not beneficial to our doctor-patient relationship, because when someone asks me about what they heard, and I don't know about it, it can make that person wonder what else I might not know about, and maybe they should find a doctor who does know about it. So, when it comes to questions about reports that patients have heard on public radio, I keep my ignorance under wraps. And as soon as I get home, I listen to the podcast.

By the time Davida had finished with Fusswood, it was almost the end of the morning, so she accompanied me on my last two appointments. When we were finished, I asked her how she thought things went.

"It was *so* much fun!" she exclaimed. "To be actually working with you—I mean, all these years I have known you as our family doctor, and I am, well, maybe not exactly, but sort of…"

"A colleague."

"Oh no!" she said quickly. "I would never think that. I was thinking more like an apprentice."

"A protégé, shall we say?"

"Protégé. I like that. And, oh dear."

"What is it?"

"I spent so much time talking to Fusswood, I never got around to taking his blood pressure. And it was the only thing I was supposed to do."

"Well, we certainly don't want you to get in trouble for not doing your list on the very first day. Perhaps we can find a volunteer." I rolled up my sleeve.

"You don't mind?"

"Not at all."

Davida took my blood pressure in my right arm. Then she took it in my left arm. Then with me lying down and then standing up.

"Oh," she said.

She handed me the results.

I looked at them. "Well," I said, "that's it for today."

She looked at me for several seconds without saying anything. "Yes, I guess it is. Until tomorrow then."

"Until tomorrow."

CHAPTER 8

There are people who are afraid of spiders. There are people who are afraid of snakes. There are people who are afraid of heights and small places and thunder and rats. Such fears are so common that we have names for them: arachnophobia, ophidiophobia, acrophobia, claustrophobia, tonitrophobia, murophobia. Fear of flying is another. It is so common, it doesn't need a special name.

"Everyone is afraid of something," George Orwell said. He said that whatever it was, for each person it was "the worst thing in the world." The thing that they would do anything to avoid, even if it should run counter to every value and belief they had. I always pay attention to what George Orwell said, because he certainly knew what the world was going to come to. Even if he was off a bit in his timing.

I knew a guy in college who told he me wasn't afraid of anything. He was lying of course, but he was a big, strong guy, and when he said it, you could almost believe him, even though you knew that it couldn't possibly be true. One day we were walking across campus, and I took a shortcut on the lawn. He stayed on the path. Turns out he was afraid of something after all: dandelions. Terrified by them, he later told me. Said he didn't mind them so much when they had blossomed into pods and were blowing their seeds to the wind, although it did worry him to think about what that meant for the dandelion future. But when they were bright yellow and sitting in the grass, just

waiting for him to get near so they could reach out and... I
never knew exactly what it was he was afraid they would do, or
how it came about that he was afraid of them, because, being
a guy, he didn't want to talk about it. Anyway, the point is that
strange as it was, it was *his* fear. At least he had the advantage
of being able to stay off the grass and avoiding his fear. Not
like having, say, a fear of cockroaches, which are impossible to
avoid. I would not recommend cockroaches for a phobia.

So when I now say I have a phobia, you will understand
that it is a perfectly normal thing to have, even if it does seem
rather odd.

I am afraid of patients.

I realize this seems a little strange, given my line of work,
so I should explain. I am not afraid of the patients I see. Not
the least. If anything, a patient I treat is reassuring. Because
that patient reminds me that I am a doctor, and not a patient.
The worst thing in the world for me is *being* a patient.

Those of you who have been a patient are probably thinking that although it isn't necessarily your absolute favorite thing
to be, it's not exactly a big whup. And that such a phobia is
pretty silly, sillier than a fear of dandelions even. With which
I would agree. But it is what it is. Fortunately, I've managed to
avoid my fear so far.

You might also think that for someone to reach seventy-
five years old without ever having been a patient would require
that person to be some rare specimen of perfection, which
I am not at all. I have, in fact, been tended to from time to
time for an assortment of ailments, but in all of those inci-
dents I was a PINU, a patient in name only. The doctor was
always a colleague, and the nurses and staff were all people
with whom I had worked, and whenever they did something to
me—I know this may be hard to believe, but I am not making
it up—if it was the slightest bit inconvenient or uncomfortable, they would apologize profusely. Things like asking me
to give a urine sample or starting an IV. They even apologized

for the quality of the mattress I slept on, and the meals I was served. As I said, I was a patient in name only.

The reason, as you may have guessed, that I am bringing up this subject now is because of my blood pressure. It was high. Quite high, in fact. I can't give you the actual numbers, because that would be a violation of HIPAA, but suffice it to say that if you came into my office with the blood pressure that Davida got on me, I would not put you in the hospital on the spot, but I would start you that day on not one, but two medicines, and I would have you come back in a week to see how it was doing. I used to give blood when the Red Cross came to town, but the last time I went, after they took my blood pressure, they apologized (of course) and said I wouldn't be able to give that day. That was five years ago.

I know that I need to have my blood pressure taken care of. I don't want to have a stroke. And I also know that he who doctors himself has a fool for a doctor.

I knew what I ought to do. And I was not happy about it.

When I got home, Trine noticed my mood right away.

"Difficult day?" she asked sympathetically.

"Yeah," I answered

"Which you don't want to talk about," she replied, less sympathetically.

"Not just yet."

"Okay then."

"Any news?

"A letter came for you today from CMS."

"Oh?"

"Yes. It was a Welcome to Medicare letter."

"You opened *my* letter?"

"No, dear, I opened mine. Yours is on the table."

"Ah," I said. I made no move to get it.

"Aren't you going to read it?"

"Probably just another promotion. They're always trying to get you to do something."

"Mine mentioned that, as a new Medicare recipient, I was entitled to a free checkup, one that provides a complete evaluation of my health status. It says now that I have reached the Medicare age, it is a good time to take care of my health needs in a comprehensive manner. It lists what it recommends, and it says that all of it is covered by Medicare. Seems like a pretty good idea." She looked directly at me. "Don't you agree?"

"It can be excessive."

"Such as?"

"Testing how many seconds it takes you to get up from a chair, and how many objects you can remember after three minutes."

"Of course, dear, but surely you wouldn't claim that *all* of it is useless."

"No, not all."

"Checking your cholesterol and your sugar and your blood pressure, for example."

"Those are good."

"So…"

"So?"

"Have you done it?"

"Done what?"

"The Welcome to Medicare examination. That has been the subject of our conversation in the last three minutes. *If* you remember.

"Welcome to Medicare examination? Sure. I do them all the time."

"I didn't mean as a doctor, dear. I meant as a patient."

"A patient."

"Yes. You are a Medicare patient are you not?"

"Well, technically speaking…"

"So, you should be eligible for one also. I'll bet that's what's in your letter." She went over to the table and picked up the envelope. "Let's see."

"I don't think that's necessary. I know what I need."

"Well, that's certainly reassuring, *Doctor Conger*. But I am curious what Medicare has to say to Beach."

She went over to the table, picked up my CMS letter, opened it, and started to read aloud:

Dear Beach Conger,

It has now been ten years since you received your first Welcome to Medicare notice, and you have not yet taken advantage of the comprehensive health assessment it offers. We do recommend this highly. Early detection and treatment of health problems is especially important at your age. We urge you to take advantage of this free examination as soon as possible.

"Not yet taken advantage of," said Trine dryly. "I guess what is good for the goose is not so good for the gander."

"I keep an eye on things."

"I bet you do. Is it possible that two eyes are better than one? *At your age?*"

Judging this to be a rhetorical question, I felt it needed no answer.

"A sensitive subject, I gather. Well, I'm going to make my appointment. How about you?"

"We'll see."

"Yes, *we* will."

I was in my office the next morning when the phone rang. It was Sandy Brown, one of our receptionists. She was calling for Doctor Steinway. Heather Steinway is one of my new colleagues. She is an excellent physician. She is also a good person. I like her. When she arrived, I had recommended that Trine pick her for her own doctor.

"Doctor Steinway wanted me to let you know that she got a call from your wife today."

I knew Trine was planning to make an appointment, so I was not alarmed. But it was a little odd that Sandy was calling to tell me about it.

"Nothing wrong, I hope." I said

"Not at all. It's about the appointment she made."

"Yes, I know. We talked about it last night. The Welcome to Medicare examination. It is a good idea. I'm glad she did it,"

"Doctor Steinway could make it next Tuesday at ten. If that's convenient."

"I don't see why not. I'll let her know."

"That's just it, Doctor Conger."

"That's just what?"

"The appointment is not for her."

"I'm afraid I don't understand. If it's not for her, then why are you calling?"

"It's for you."

"What's for me?"

"The appointment, Doctor Conger. Your wife called to make an appointment for you to see Doctor Steinway next Tuesday, and I just wanted to make sure that fit in with your schedule.

"For me. Ah, well, let's see. I believe I have a conflict. I'll check my calendar."

I didn't need to check my calendar. Tuesday morning was always a free morning for me, as Trine knew perfectly well. "Yes, as I thought. I'm sorry, but I'm afraid I can't do it then. I have another obligation. I'll get back to you on that."

"That's what your wife said you'd say. She asked Doctor Steinway if she could keep every Tuesday at ten open until you came in. Doctor Steinway said that was fine with her. Would the following Tuesday suit you better?"

It was clear I wasn't going to get out of this. "Tuesday after next would be fine, Sandy."

"Thank you, Doctor Conger. I'll put you in. You should be fasting, nothing after midnight—but I don't have to tell you that. Sorry."

"Not at all, Sandy. Reminders never hurt."

*****

Heather Steinway joined the group just three years ago. Her father is a doctor, a general practitioner in Evansville,

Indiana. He is seventy-nine years old, and he is still practicing, although he no longer does hospital work or delivers babies. Like many small-town doctors, he is a solo practitioner with one employee, a nurse receptionist. Betty is her name. When Heather was growing up, he had his office in their home, and Heather used to visit him there. She saw her father and his nurse as they worked together. She loved her father, and she admired him. But she worshipped Betty. She decided that she wanted to be a nurse when she grew up. Her father was pleased that she was interested in medicine, but, of course, he would rather she became a doctor. When he thought she was old enough to understand the ways of the world, this is what he told her: "Betty is smarter than I am, and she is much better with my patients. But she barely makes enough money to support her family. And she will never get as much credit as she is due. Is that what you want?"

And so, like her father, Heather became a doctor. But she thought, and she acted, like Betty.

She went to college at Indiana University, and to Dartmouth for medical school. Her primary care clerkship was here in Dumster. She was a very good student. The patients liked her, and so did the staff. She went on to be a resident in family medicine at Dartmouth. After she finished her residency, she was appointed chief resident. Chief resident is an honored position awarded to a doctor who has particularly distinguished herself in residency, both by her knowledge and her leadership. The chief resident has substantial teaching and supervisory responsibilities over her peers. It is, therefore, a position that demands more maturity. It is also a position used for residents whom the faculty would like to add to its staff, but for whom a position is not immediately available, a kind of academic redshirting. After her year as chief, Heather worked in the primary care practice for two years. It took her less time than that to realize that for a large medical center to attempt primary care was in no way different than if Emmeline Talbot were to try to do open heart surgery. The shoe just does not fit. When she called me about a job, it was at the time when, fortunately for us, we were in our expansive mood.

I enjoy working with Heather. She is intelligent and thoughtful, and she has good clinical judgment. She is also courteous and respectful to everyone. She never raises her voice. If she is less than fully pleased with a situation, the most she ever says is, "I'm a bit disappointed." And whatever the situation was, it never happens again. No one wants to disappoint Heather.

One could do a lot worse than to be a patient of Heather Steinway. One would be hard pressed to do better.

Which should have been more consolation than it was when I came in for my appointment.

CHAPTER 9

Under ordinary circumstances, meeting with Heather would be a pleasure. She is a cheerful soul with a good sense of humor. She also has that special ability to make you feel good about yourself, just by being around you. She is a smart and thoughtful clinician as well, and despite the difference in our ages, and even though the cases we discussed were always hers and never mine, I was always more careful in my actions after talking with her.

This Tuesday, however, was anything but an ordinary circumstance.

Patricia, Heather's nurse, called me in as soon as I arrived. "Good morning, Doctor Conger," she said. "I hope you're well today."

"Just dandy," I replied. "And let's hope I remain so after the visit."

"It says here you are in for a Welcome to Medicare visit. Is that correct?"

"Well, yes, but I don't know that we need to go through all the…"

"I'll let you and Doctor Steinway figure out what to do," she said quickly, eager to avoid the preliminary paces of the visit. "I'll just take your vital signs."

She took my pulse and my temperature. She took my blood pressure. Then she took it again. "Oh," she said to herself in a small voice. "Doctor Steinway will be right in." And she hurried out of the room.

Heather was her usual self, as if our seeing each other was nothing out of the ordinary. "Good to see you, Beach," she said cheerfully.

"You too."

"It says here that this is a Welcome to Medicare visit."

"It is."

"Welcome to Medicare."

"Thank you."

"Now that we've got that out of the way, what's up?"

"It seems I'm due for a checkup."

"Any particular reason for a checkup now?"

It was a fair question. Except in the case of patients who believe in annual checkups, which she knew I did not, a checkup request out of the blue is invariably cover for something else.

"Well, it's been a while since I had one." I paused.

She waited.

"And my blood pressure is a little high."

"Okay." Heather looked at my recorded vital signs. "One sixty-eight over one-oh-two. Give me a sec, if you don't mind, so I can see what it's been in the past."

Heather scrolled through my medical record. It didn't take long. "Hmm," she said. "I can't seem to find any blood pressures in here."

"No," I said. "Probably have to look in the old paper chart." Our electronic medical record was only five years old.

"Right." She opened the file that contained a copy of all the records back to the opening of Emmeline Talbot in 1971. I knew from experience that these records often ran to many hundreds of pages. Reviewing the whole thing could take a considerable period. Heather was finished with mine in about thirty seconds. She looked at me.

"When did you come here?" she asked.

"Nineteen seventy-seven."

"A long time ago."

"It's all relative."

"As you always like to remind me. Still, as we are not talking about the melting of a glacier, I would say that forty years in the same job with the same medical record qualifies as long."

"I suppose it does."

"I see that when you fell off your bike in nineteen eighty-eight, and they brought you to the ER to get some stitches. Your blood pressure was high, but we can certainly write that off as due to the circumstances of the visit."

"Certainly."

"And then, in nineteen ninety-six, you had your Dupuytren's contracture repaired in same-day surgery. It was up in recovery, but by the time you were discharged, it had come down to one forty-two over eighty-four."

"Which would have been normal at that time."

"Yes. I guess it would. You would know more about it than I. That was before my time. And since then…" She made a show of studying the records again, although we both knew it was unnecessary. "Hmmm," she said finally, "I can't find any blood pressures recorded since then."

"I get it checked when I give blood."

"Of course. Might be something to address, wouldn't you say?"

"Uh, yes."

"Okay then. Anything else of concern?"

"Not really."

"Good. Well then, seeing as I don't really have any data in your current record, why don't we start from scratch. You know the drill. Why don't we start with your past history?"

"My past history. Okay. I was born in New York City, but we left when I was only two, so I really don't remember any of that, although my mother did tell me that I said my first complete sentence just before we moved. It was in Central Park. A bus came along, and I said, 'Here coming de buh.'

"Until I was ten, we lived in Hastings-on-Hudson. We lived in a big apartment complex that bordered on the river. I had two friends there, Tim and Pam. The first thing I remember was sitting in Pam's living room and peeling the aluminum foil off gum wrappers we collected from trash cans in the neighborhood. We rolled them into a big ball, size of an orange. Then we gave them to our parents, and they gave us a nickel for each one. They said it was for the war effort. We did it for the nickel. That was how much a candy bar cost in those days. Chunky was my favorite. I liked the crunchy feel. Pam liked Good & Plenty because they lasted longer. Tim was for Hershey's Bars, because that was what everybody ate.

"One of our favorite things to do was to go down to the river to swim. The Hudson was dirty and smelly, and the things we saw floating in it were pretty disgusting. But because we were absolutely forbidden to go down there, it was great fun. Part of the excitement was crossing the railroad tracks that went along the river's edge. That close to the city, the trains were all electric. They switched in North White Plains, and there was a third rail that we knew would kill us on the spot if we touched it. It wasn't true, but we didn't know it then. So, when we jumped over it, we never knew if we might slip and fall and be fried to a crisp.

"Then we moved up to Pleasantville, home of the *Reader's Digest*. But it wasn't. The *Reader's Digest* was in Chappaqua, the next town over, but Chappaqua, home of the *Reader's Digest*, didn't sound as good, so they used Pleasantville as their mailing address.

"Both my parents worked there, my mother ever since we moved, and my father for the last year of his life. He died there—in the elevator. The autopsy said it was a heart attack, but we all knew it was the *Reader's Digest*. He had been a newspaperman all his professional life. He had gotten a job at the

New York Herald Tribune right out of college. Until the news-paper folded in 1970, it was the only job he ever had. He went to the *Reader's Digest* to work, but he never liked it. 'It's not real news,' he said. It broke his heart to work for them. Literally, you could say.

"After Pleasantville High School, I went to Amherst for college, then Harvard for medical school. That was fifty-four years ago. The rest you pretty much know."

There was a study once that looked at how well doctors listened to their patients. One of the things they discovered was that when patients were giving their history, women doctors waited longer before interrupting them than men did. Almost twice as long. It's not really all that surprising, I suppose. Women in general are better listeners. Twenty seconds for men, thirty-eight seconds for women.

I had been talking for over three minutes. Heather hadn't said a word. She was a doctor like her father. But she listened like Betty.

"That's a very interesting history, Beach," she said. "And quite thorough."

"I tried to be thorough, but concise. I always believe concise is important in a history."

"Yes, you were thorough and concise. It's just that, well, often, as you know, the history *we* obtain tends to have a bit more focus on the *medical* parts."

"You mean—from patients."

"Yes, from patients."

There was an awkward pause. Neither of us spoke.

"Oh!" I said finally. "I see. And I..."

"Well..." Heather interrupted mercifully. "If you could imagine, just for the sake of our discussion, that you were a patient, and you, the patient, were telling a doctor, me, for example, about your medical history. What would that include?"

"Ah, yes. Okay, I think I can do that."

I told her about my father's diabetes and heart trouble and high blood pressure, my mother's lung cancer, and my sister's high cholesterol. I told her about my own history of Lyme disease, hand surgeries, a couple of concussions from bike accidents, and a tonsillectomy at age five. In those days, all kids had tonsillectomies, whether they needed it or not. Then she asked me about any symptoms, and I told her I didn't have any, and when I finished, she said, "How about *your* cholesterol?"

"Mine?"

"Yes."

"Oh, of course. Well, it should be fine. I'm not overweight. I exercise regularly. And I would say my diet is pretty good."

"That's good. I was asking not just because of your family history and your high blood pressure, but also because checking cholesterol is one of those things that we do these days, and it might be something we could think about."

"Oh, yeah. By all means. Good idea, Doc."

"Well then. That brings us to the examination. I'll let you get ready. Be right back." Heather left the room and closed the door.

She came back two minutes later. I was sitting in the same position.

"Uh, Beach," said Heather.

"Yes? "

"Your clothes."

I looked down at them. They seemed okay. "Is something wrong with them?"

"Not at all. It is customary, however, to take them off for an examination—unless, of course, it's embarrassing for you to be examined by a woman. In that case, it might be better to see Doctor Warnock. I'm sure he would do a fine job."

"Oh no! That's not it at all. I mean, seeing as how I am going to need to have a doctor, I want you to be it. I'm not embarrassed at all. Just kinda slipped my mind, I guess."

"I understand. You are just a lot more accustomed to being on the other end of the stethoscope, as it were."

I almost managed a laugh. "As it were."

I took off my clothes, and Heather examined me. It was a very thorough examination.

"Well, Beach," she said when she had finished. "I would agree that you are in good shape. There are just two things worth mentioning. First, your heart is not entirely regular. I did hear occasional skipped beats."

"That doesn't surprise me," I confessed. "A couple of times when I have been exercising hard, I've had palpitations. I counted it once. It was over two hundred. But," I added quickly, "no chest pain."

"That's good," she said. "I suppose, however, we could consider it a positive in your review of symptoms."

"Uh, sure. Must have slipped my mind. I mean, it doesn't really bother me."

"What's that your so fond of saying—about the longest river?"

"Oh, that. Yes, I suppose you could say that."

"Maybe not quite denial," she replied. "As you know, it's not unusual for people not to remember certain symptoms the first time they are asked."

I nodded. "Patients can be like that."

"Then there is your prostate. Here I will say *for your age*. It's large, but smooth. No nodules at all. Do you have any trouble urinating?"

"Well, my stream is pretty slow these days. And I do get up a couple of times a night. But I don't have urge incontinence. At least not very often—for my age, you could say."

"I believe I did. So, that brings up the issue of what we should do next. With your exercise-induced tachycardia, I would recommend a stress test. As regards the prostate, I'd be inclined to say leave bad enough alone. And I do think it would be good to know what your actual cholesterol is. As you know, you are well into the age of coronary disease.

Finally, the most important thing. Your blood pressure. It needs treatment, Beach. I hate to say it, but you've put it off too long already."

"I'll start today."

"Good. You pick your meds. I'll write the prescription, and you can get started."

"And I'll make an appointment for a follow-up in two weeks."

"I'm glad you said it."

"Me too," I agreed. I almost believed it.

"Okay, I think that about covers it."

I shook her hand. "Thanks, Heather. It was—Joy."

"Makes the examination almost nice."

"Wasn't that before your time too?"

"It was, but it's what my mom always said on the rare occasions when my father did the dishes."

I selected my antihypertensive meds, I got my blood drawn, and at the end of the day, I picked up my prescriptions at the pharmacy. I got some aspirin also. Then I went home. I can't say I was happy about the whole thing, but I was a bit relieved. Maybe, if I played my cards right, I could be a doctor *and* a patient.

"How'd it go?" asked Trine when I arrived.

I showed her my prescriptions and my appointment.

"Heh, heh," she said. "Join the club."

CHAPTER 10

Belief in immortality is an essential faith. When all others— love, religion, money, power—fall short as we travel along the road of life, it is the one that is always there. In the early going, it is sustained without any effort on our part. But as we get further, we will, from time to time, catch glimpses of the inevitability of the journey's end, and even though we avert our glance quickly, it makes us aware of the need for vigilance, lest it become a dispiriting vision that makes us stop in our tracks and refuse to proceed further.

It is not at all unusual, when I tell one of my patients that he has some potentially serious condition, for that patient to ask, "Am I going to die?" And though the Rational Self knows not only the answer, but that even to pose it as a question is absurd, Rational Self is rarely involved in such a conversation. And so it is that when I am asked this question, the only answer I can give is, "Of course not." At which point I may go on to explain that although it is technically true that everyone dies, all *my* patients are still alive. To answer any other way would only ensure that I never see that patient again.

In my own case, preservation of this illusion has been greatly facilitated by the fact that I am a doctor and not a patient. My visit with Heather had struck a serious, though fortunately not fatal, blow to my powers of self-deception. I returned for my follow-up visit to Heather after the tests had been completed. I knew my medicine was working. I had been checking my blood pressure several times a day, an act that gave me some concern, as I knew this was behavior attributable solely to a patient, and an anxious one at that. But it was an act that I could not avoid.

I showed Heather my blood pressure results. She agreed that the medication I had chosen had achieved the desired results.

"So," she said, "shall we go over your test results, or do you feel that isn't necessary?"

I hesitated. Doctor Conger had looked at the stress test. And Doctor Conger had seen his cholesterol. And Doctor Conger had reviewed the lipid studies. And Doctor Conger knew full well what the current guidelines would recommend. But it did seem unfair to not let Heather discuss them with Beach.

"Let's talk."

"Good. I think we'll agree. And it means I don't have to bring up a delicate subject."

I had no ideas what she had in mind. There was nothing at all untoward about my results—or the options for what to do about them.

"What subject is that?" I asked uncertainly.

"Permission to release information."

"To…"

"To Trine. She asked me to tell her if you decided not to discuss the results with me and come up with a mutually agreeable plan."

"I see."

"I'm sure you do. Anyway, the echo speaks for itself. Your exercise tolerance at twelve METS was excellent."

"For my age."

"Your age has nothing to do with it. You are in very good shape."

"I work at it."

"I know. And the occasional ectopy you had at peak exercise is of no clinical significance, especially considering the absence of any evidence of ischemia. So, as long as your blood pressure remains under control..."

"Which *we* will make sure it does."

Heather smiled. "Then all we have to do is to decide about your cholesterol. A total cholesterol of 154 with an HDL of 47 is exceptionally good, and normally I would say there is no need to talk about using a statin."

"However..."

"Yes. *However.*"

*****

When I started, back in 1967, high cholesterol was a rare disease. It was diagnosed, not by a blood test, but by the appearance of large globules of fat hanging from the eyelids. That an ordinary cholesterol could represent a disease just wasn't considered. Eggs, milk, and cheese were considered part of a healthy diet. (It is true that after forty years of exile in the nutritional wilderness some have returned to the table once again. But that is another story altogether, and it would only detract from the point I am trying to make). People rarely took cholesterol-lowering medication, primarily because the one drug that worked gave you stomach ulcers, gout, diabetes, and hot flashes. And it was a time when people failed to accept the value of taking something that made you feel worse solely on the grounds that it might forestall something that you never thought about anyway.

In 1970, Akira Endo, a pharmaceutical biochemist at Sankyo pharmaceuticals, was searching for a better cholesterol-lowering drug. He started, as most researchers do, by looking in the dirt. He looked at molds. And in 1971, he found one. Mevastatin, he called it. Produced, by one of the famous Penicillium family of fungi, it did a great job of lowering cholesterol in dogs. The only fly in the ointment was that most of the dogs taking it developed muscle damage and tumors and died.

Other researchers took up the search. After many years of turning over stones and digging in the dirt, they found what they wanted in Aspergillus terreus. It contained a substance that was just as effective as mevastatin, but the substance had the big advantage of not being lethal. They purified it, and they called it lovastatin. In 1987, it became the first statin on the market. Suddenly the treatment of cholesterol became acceptable. At first the standards were liberal. Anything lower than 240 was okay. But this was back when there were fewer cardiologists, and, accordingly, less need for cardiology patients.

Like all professionals, cardiologists have meetings. These are events designed to allow the full exchange of ideas and the introduction of new treatments that are expected to be of great benefit to their patients. One of the important things the cardiologists do at their meetings is review their guidelines, since guidelines are what cardiologists use to convert people into patients. As the number of cardiologists has increased, the guidelines have been adjusted. They have been adjusted in such a manner that no one who had previously been a patient would be excluded, but many who had been kept out have been welcomed into the fold. I do not mean to imply that they count the number of cardiologists and then count the number of cardiology patients, and that when the supply of the former becomes excessive relative to the latter, they adjust the guidelines to restore a proper balance. That would be preposterous. I'm sure that the increase in the number of cardiologists and the increase in the number of patients attendant upon their new guidelines is purely coincidental. I mention the fact only as a curious one. And I would not presume to predict exactly what the future holds, for I am never privy to their deliberations, but if they continue in the same direction, it won't be too long before *nobody will be exempt*. Everyone will be a patient.

As a doctor, I could hardly object to this. But as a patient, I had a rather different point of view.

*****

"The problem," began Heather, "as you well know, is that the guidelines *this year* are based not on cholesterol, but on a person's risk of having a heart attack within ten years."

"And you know my fondness for guidelines."

"There is that to consider. The pa…, the *person's* preference is always paramount."

"For someone *at my age,* it doesn't matter what my cholesterol is. My risk based solely on age is over twenty percent, and there is no way I can escape recommendations for treatment."

"Unless, at age seventy-five that person was not already on medicine."

"Which I was not."

"Which you were not. However, if you had been getting checkups on a regular basis…"

"And my lipids checked at age seventy or seventy-four, I would not have been exempt. I would have been put on medications. And now, I would be expected to stay on them."

"Yes, that would be according to the guidelines."

"Hallowed be thy name."

"It is your choice."

"Maybe."

"Good point. If I have your permission to tell Trine about our visit, I will let her know that we have agreed on a plan, and we'll leave it at that."

"For now."

"Yes, always *for now.*"

We shook hands and I left. I was strangely relieved, but not quite combobulated. I couldn't have asked for a better treatment than that which I received from Heather. I even felt that we had handled it as one colleague to another.

Almost.

CHAPTER 11

Once upon a time, doctors were selected primarily on the basis of being unsuitable for any more respectable line of work. Medicine was not an esteemed or remunerative profession back then, so those who were not fit to be businessmen or lawyers or ministers were sent off to study medicine. In the past hundred years, however, it has become not only an acceptable, but an honored career. This change is due in large part to a report issued by Abraham Flexner in 1905. Doctor Flexner, then president of Johns Hopkins University, was commissioned by the American Medical Association to evaluate the state of medical education in the United States. The report is detailed and comprehensive, but its conclusions can easily be summed up in one word.

Humbug.

The report states that if the edifice of medicine were to assume its rightful place in society it needed to replace a foundation that had been erected upon the sands of superstition, ignorance, and pretense with one built instead on the bedrock of science.

By and large we have succeeded, although two sections are not yet modernized. They are the museum and the art gallery. While the former is infrequently visited, the latter is still quite popular, especially among the older practitioners, for whom the belief in medicine as an art remains strong.

Among the arts, that which has always had the most appeal to doctors is performance art. To its patrons, the ability to act the part of doctor is as important as the skill with which one does the doctoring. When I entered medical school, my first class was an art lesson. We gathered in one of the great temples of medicine, the amphitheater of the Peter Bent Brigham Hospital. There the 151 men and eleven women were addressed by the chief of surgery at the hospital, Franklin Hall. Doctor Hall was a great surgeon, one of the leaders in the field. And he looked every bit the part as he faced us, standing tall and erect in his starched long white coat.

"Good morning, doctors," he began. "Look around you. Most you do not recognize. Some have been friends. A few, perhaps, more. Whatever they may have been, they are no more. They are now your colleagues. Together you will be the men—and women—who, in the years to come, will preserve and advance the practice of medicine. It is with great pleasure that I admit you to the noblest of professions. Welcome."

He then called out our names, each in turn, Doctor Bruce Burgess, Doctor Joan Cheesman, Doctor Beach Conger, Doctor Douglas Dorman. And we each came up on the stage, where we were handed a short white coat and a name tag. "Doctor Beach Conger," mine read. Before leaving, we also received a small black bag embossed with our name and designation, courtesy of the pharmaceutical manufacturers in anticipation of value they would receive in the future.

Then we went off to our class, Introduction to Doctoring. The sole purpose of the course was to teach us how to act the part we were to play in the years to come. It involved traipsing around the hospital in the wake of one of the senior faculty to see how a consummate performer played his role.

I heard an expression once about what it would take to master a certain sport. I think it was golf, but maybe it wasn't. "Be the ball" was the expression. I have no idea what it means with respect to sport, but the idea that in order to master whatever it is you are attempting, you must be so fully immersed in it that you lose yourself completely was, as I now realize, the primary function of the initial stages of my medical education. True, I had to learn a new language, and I had a new set of facts to acquire, but this was no different from what I had done in high school, only now, rather than being Latin or chemistry or solid geometry, it was pharmacology and physiology and anatomy. It was the kind of learning that we all excelled at, or else, as we were often reminded, we would not be there.

*****

Harvard had four teaching hospitals then. Three of them—Peter Bent Brigham, Beth Israel, and Massachusetts General Hospital—were among the elite hospitals, not only of the country, but of the world. Patients came from everywhere to be treated by their physicians. They expected the best, and they got it.

The fourth hospital was Boston City Hospital.

I spent most of my time at Boston City Hospital. Whether this was by chance, or whether the school knew that I would be better off performing before a more forgiving audience, I know not. Like those upon whom I now ply my wares, the patients at Boston City knew the importance of low expectations. They had no illusions about in whose hands they were. They knew that at best, their "doctor" would be someone who had two years under his belt, and that this privilege occurred but once a year, in June, just before a new crop came in. To be sick in July was their greatest fear. Student, intern, resident, we all looked the same to them. They knew we would do our best—and they knew it wouldn't be quite good enough.

Boston City Hospital suited me well. I would have been content to pass my entire four years there, but in my third year, I had a rotation at Mass General. It was in gastroenterology. My preceptor was Doctor Edgar Mansard III.

On the first day of the rotation I reported to his office. After we had a brief getting-to-know-you chat, he gave me my first assignment. I was to interview a patient who had been referred to him in consultation. As was customary, I was given no information about the patient other than her name and location, Katherine Bradley Choate, Room 2007, Phillips House.

Phillips House opened in 1917 as a purely private section of the hospital, a haven where the wealthy could be treated in the style to which they wished to remain accustomed. The original building no longer exists, but the name and function persist. It is located on the top three floors of one of the main buildings of the MGH campus. The rooms are spacious and well appointed, and they offer spectacular views of the Charles River and Boston Harbor. This is how the hospital describes it: "For more than 90 years, Massachusetts General Hospital has offered elegant, private, patient rooms and personalized service through Philips House."

It is often said in jest of Phillips House that the best thing about it is that it is close to a good hospital.

Outfitted in my white coat, badge, and black bag, I arrived at Phillips House at 1:30 in the afternoon, looking, if not feeling, every bit the doctor I was not. A man in uniform was sitting at the entrance. Adjacent to him was a bank of elevators. "May I help you?" he inquired as I approached the elevators.

"I'm here to see Mrs. Choate," I said, my tone sounding less confident than I had hoped.

"And you are?"

"Doctor Conger," I said, displaying my name tag. "I am collaborating with Doctor Mansard."

"Ah," he said, "Doctor Mansard." And he consulted a sheet of paper on his desk. "We have Doctor Williams listed as Mrs. Choate's doctor. Is Doctor Williams aware that you will be seeing Mrs. Choate *in collaboration with* Doctor Mansard?"

"I believe he is," I fibbed.

"I see," he said, unconvinced. "And is Mrs. Choate expecting you?"

"I believe she is."

"Very well. Let me see if she is receiving. It is not customary for Phillips House to receive visitors between the hours of twelve and two."

There followed a brief phone conversation, the result of which was that I was allowed, much to the displeasure of the concierge, to proceed to Mrs. Choate's room.

Her room was unlike any I had ever seen before—and since. The solid-wood door was trimmed in mahogany, and upon opening it, I found myself in the sitting room of a spacious three-room suite. The furnishings had the appearance of a nineteenth-century drawing room. There were two plush armchairs, a divan, a sideboard, and a polished table of dark wood. On the table was a fresh vase of flowers, a silver tea service, and a place setting for two consisting of white linen napkins, crystal goblets, fine china cups, plates, and saucers. On the sideboard were tasty looking pastries.

Reclining upon the divan was a woman who might have been in her early fifties or late seventies; the amount of her makeup made it impossible for me to tell. She was dressed in a lace gown with a cashmere shawl around her shoulders and a string of pearls around her neck. Her hair was faultlessly made up.

"Beach!" she exclaimed, extending a heavily jeweled hand to me in a gesture that seemed to suggest I ought to kiss it rather than shake it. "What an interesting name you have. You must tell me all about it. Please sit down." She motioned to the armchair closest to her.

I was completely flummoxed. I had no idea how I was going to proceed. I took the seat. "Well…," I said tentatively.

"Oh, silly me," she exclaimed, interrupting me quickly. "Here you have come all the way over from the office to see me. You must be parched. Would you like a drink?"

"Er, not right now," I stammered.

"Of course not!" she laughed. "You are a working man. But you don't mind if I do, do you? It's time for my afternoon constitutional." She rang a small silver bell at her side. Shortly a nurse appeared. "I'll have my usual now, nurse. You sure you won't have anything, Beach, even a small glass of wine? I have a very nice sauvignon blanc."

"No thank you."

The nurse left. She reappeared shortly with a tray bearing an amber colored beverage in a short, round glass. Mrs. Choate accepted it and took a long sip before settling back comfortably on her divan.

"Now, where were we?" she said. "Ah yes, you were going to tell me how you got that absolutely delicious name. It just reeks of a story waiting to be told."

So I told her the story of the three itinerant Ohio Presbyterian ministers who rode a parish circuit together back in the 1850s, and whose last names were Seymour, Beach, and Conger, and how Conger, when he had a son, named him after the other two. He was Seymour Beach Conger, my great-grandfather. I was the fourth in line.

"What happened to Seymour?" she asked. "Shouldn't you be Seymour Beach Conger the Fourth, then?"

There is a story behind that also, but I did not think it necessary to explain to her that I had dropped Seymour at the beginning of high school because of junior and senior boys who, when they saw me in the halls, would nudge each other, and one would ask, "Do you?" And another would respond, "Do I what?" And the first would say, "See more Beach?" Upon which one would grab my shirt, pull it up, and squeeze my breast until I said, "titty." That was the end of Seymour.

"Beach was simpler," I said.

"I'm going to call you Seymour," she said playfully. "It has a nice sound to it. Straight out of J.D. Salinger. You know, I knew Jerry from our days in the city. Quite the gay blade he was back then. But you didn't come here to ask about him. You want to know about me. So, let's play doctor and patient. It's one of my favorite games. You go first. Fire away Seymo..., *Doctor* Conger. I'm all yours." She lay back and spread out her arms over the divan, striking a pose that would have been, were she thirty years younger, provocative.

"Well, Mrs. Choate..."

"Kitty, please. I'm Kitty to all my friends. Besides, Choatie is a *such* a thing of the past." She smiled. "Long past."

"Perhaps you could start by telling me why you are in the hospital."

"You mean why I'm here at the Phillips? Oh, that's easy. That's Dickie's doing. Does it every year about this time. November is such a dreadful month. I just loathe it. I don't even like to travel then, so we agreed November was the best time."

"I'm sorry," I confessed. "I'm afraid I don't know who Dickie is."

"No? Oh, of course not! You would know him as Richard Williams. He's my doctor. Such a dear, he is. And he's just done wonders for me. Without him, I'd just be a complete mess."

Dickie provided me with an opportunity I did not want to waste. "Maybe you could tell me just what the medical problems are that Dickie is treating you for?"

"Me? Heavens, no! I don't have the faintest idea, darling. That's what I have Dickie for. He knows what I have. And what to do and, of course, when to call in outside help—like you and Doctor Mansard." She leaned forward and smiled intimately. "But let's not talk about me. I know all about me. I don't know anything about you, though. Except that you must be awfully clever to be at Harvard. Tell me all about yourself."

"That isn't exactly..."

"Exactly fiddlesticks. Let's start with what made you decide to become a doctor. Tell me about that." And with that declaration, she settled back again on her divan, folded her arms, and gave me a look that said she would brook no contradiction.

Even at this stage of my career I had already been asked this question on multiple occasions, and it has been countless more times since then. In my experience it is not a question that is asked because of any genuine interest in the answer. In that respect, it is in the same category as "How are you feeling today?" a category in which the asking of the question is an end in itself, and the answer is expected by both parties to be one that requires no further inquiry. "Fine" generally fits the bill quite nicely.

In my youth, like all children, I knew exactly what I wanted to do when I grew up. I wanted to be an airplane pilot. On Saturday afternoons, for twenty-five cents, the Rome Theater had a matinee for kids. There was no feature film. There were cartoons: Bugs Bunny, Donald Duck, Road Runner. There were short features, comedies such Our Gang and Laurel and Hardy. And then there were more serious works, like Flash Gordon. I liked them all, but what I liked best was the newsreel that appeared at the start of the show, *The Eyes and Ears of the World*. At the time, one story above all else dominated the news: The Korean War. *Eyes and Ears* made no bones about the fact that this was a battle, just like that of Flash Gordon and Ming, waged between the forces of good and the forces of evil. Those who fought were my heroes, especially our brave airmen and their magnificent flying machines. There were Grumman F9F Panthers taking off from aircraft carriers, Lockheed F-80 Shooting Stars dive-bombing enemy placements, and Boeing B-47 Stratojets flying in formation. All were on display, their heroic missions documented in detail and presented to the accompaniment of inspirational martial music.

The allure was irresistible, and I was smitten. I wore a pilot's cap. I hummed "Off we go into the wild blue yonder." And I built model airplanes, which I hung by strings from the ceiling of my room. They were the last thing I saw at night and the first thing I saw in the morning.

When I was fourteen, my mother explained to me that an airplane pilot was not quite, well, just not quite. If I wanted to pursue a career in aerospace, I should become instead an aeronautical engineer. Engineering would be more *suitable*. Pointing to my ceiling, she said, "And you do so like to build them."

I was at an impressionable stage. It didn't take long for me to make the transition from flier to designer. I subscribed to *Popular Mechanics*. I bought graph paper and made meticulous copies of the blueprints that accompanied my model airplane kits. I got a book on introductory aerodynamics. And I continued to build model airplanes.

This lasted until my junior year in high school, when I took an aptitude test that we all got so that Mr. Winter, our guidance counselor, could counsel and guide us in the proper career choice. After I took the test, I sat down with him. "Beach," he said, "you're a smart kid. You can do pretty much anything you wish." I told him how much I liked model airplanes, and that I was interested in a career in aerospace. "Model airplanes are okay," he said slowly, looking at my scores, "but leave your aerospace career at that."

He could see how disappointed I was, and, as he was a kindly fellow, he added quickly, "I'm sure you could be anything else you set your mind to."

"Like what?" I asked.

"Well, like a doctor," he said.

"Okay," I said.

The first time I was asked why I wanted to be a doctor, I told the person this whole story. "Really?" she said, in a disappointed tone. I didn't tell the story again.

"My favorite uncle is a doctor," I say. Which, although true, was unrelated to my choice. But it serves the purpose. There is something appealing in the idea of an inspirational role model.

As there was to Mrs. Choate. "Oh, that's marvelous, Seymour. He must be very proud of you."

"He is," I said. "Now, perhaps I could get some of your..."

Almost as if on cue, the nurse entered the room. "It's two o'clock, Mrs. Choate."

"Is it already?" she exclaimed. "Oh dear! And we were having such a lovely chat. But I'm afraid we will have to end it now. It's time for my appointment, and I just can't keep her waiting. You just must excuse me, I'm afraid."

"Certainly," I said, disappointed. And confused. Doctor Mansard had assured me that Mrs. Choate's schedule for the afternoon was free of tests and consultations. "I thought your Tuesday afternoon was free."

"Oh, yes," she answered brightly. "I keep that open for Mademoiselle Pourvoir. She does my nails. Every Tuesday at two. Has for the past twenty years. She is such a gem. I just couldn't risk doing anything that might upset her. Which reminds me. Nurse, she will have her usual, if you could."

"Yes, ma'am, a dry martini."

"Fine," Mrs. Choate declared, and turning to me she said, "I certainly hope I get to see you again, Seymour. And," she added with a sly smile, "I think I just might."

I mumbled a goodbye and left the room. I was disconsolate. I had failed my assignment utterly, and I was not looking forward to my review with Doctor Mansard.

We say that honesty is the best policy. It is a good policy. And like all good policies, it suffers from practice-and-preach dissociation. Whenever someone says to you, "To be perfectly honest," you can be pretty sure of one thing—that person is lying. Because the policy that everyone actually uses is that honesty is the best policy, if you can't get away with a lie.

Therefore, the first thing I thought of once I was outside was how I could avoid admitting I had flubbed my assignment. I considered telling Doctor Mansard that I was unable to interview Mrs. Choate because she had been away at some other appointment. And I thought about the stratagem employed, despite strict admonitions to the contrary, by some of my bolder classmates, which was to sneak a look at the patient's medical record. This not only made them look very skilled at interviewing, it also obviated the need to obtain any history at all from the patient. But my fear of discovery was too great. In the end, I went back to the office without any plan, though not at all ready to fess up.

Doctor Mansard greeted me with a genial smile. "Couldn't get any history?" he asked.

"Er, not really."

"Don't feel bad. It's not you. It's on account of her condition."

"She has some type of cognitive impairment?"

"I suppose you could call it that."

"Oh, what is her diagnosis?"

"There are two. I will tell you one. But you have to find out the other for yourself."

"The one?"

"Filthy rich."

"She is in the hospital just because she is rich?

"Yes. That's not her medical diagnosis, of course, but it should help you understand the difficulty in getting information from her. You've never met somebody filthy rich, have you?"

"Well, my parents had some friends who were quite well off. They had a big house in Pleasantville and a second home in Connecticut, and their kids went to private school."

"Mrs. Choate is worth over a hundred million dollars."

"No, I haven't."

"I thought not. You see, when people are as rich as Mrs. Choate, they have a different view of the world. They know they are important because of their wealth, but it tends to affect them in a way that makes them believe that everyone else exists only to serve them, excepting only someone wealthier.

In their eyes, doctors are no different from the mailman who delivers their mail or the gardener who maintains their lawns. More educated and skilled than other tradesmen, but in the end, we are, like the others, a servant. Which means that trying to play the role of master will inevitably result in failure. You must achieve your ends through subservience. So tomorrow you will go back and interview her again. This time, do a better job. She is looking forward to another visit. She thinks you're cute."

"Cute?"

"It's an asset. Use it to your advantage."

The next day I went back to Phillips House. This time the security man barely looked up. Mrs. Choate was again sitting on her divan, and again she had a glass of amber liquid in front of her.

"I couldn't stay away," I said. She waved her hand at me in greeting.

"Seymour!" she exclaimed, pleased. "It's so good to see you again." She smiled coyly. "I was expecting you, you know."

"So I gather. I'm glad. You're so much more fun than any of the others."

"Flatterer," she said with mock displeasure. "That's going to get you nowhere with an old woman like me."

"No, I wouldn't expect it to. But maybe with someone who has been young for as long as you have…"

"And now that you have buttered me up, I suppose you are going to ask me all those tedious doctor questions. Well, if you must, you must. Fire away. I'm at your mercy." She folded her arms across her chest and lay back on the divan with a smug look on her face that seemed to say, "Good luck."

"I'm afraid I have to. Otherwise I'll never get to be a doctor, you know. And then, who will be your doctor when Dickie retires?"

For the first time she looked at me without pretense. "Okay, Seymour. That's enough malarkey. Although, I must say it is rather good. What do you want to know?"

"I looked you up in the newspaper archives. I know just how old you are. And I know how good looking you were when you were young, which is not flattery, but only the truth."

"Yes, I was," she conceded. "That was a long time ago."

"And I know that you know that you are still exceedingly good looking and do not in the slightest resemble in appearance your chronological age. Let's start with that. What I want to know is what you have done to achieve this admirable state."

"I've had some surgery," she said matter-of-factly.

"Successfully, I can see."

"Yes. But that's only the start. I have a most marvelous skin man. He gives me all kinds of potions and scrubs that I couldn't do without."

"And Dicky gives you vitamins, I suppose."

"Lordy yes!" she exclaimed. "You wouldn't believe what he forces me to shove down my throat. He calls it my cocktail. Well, let me tell you, mister, I've been around the block a few times, and I know a cocktail when I get one. And those vitamins—they ain't no cocktail, dearie."

"Could folic acid be one of them?"

"Could be. I know there's one he calls thyme. But it isn't."

"That would be thiamine."

"Vile stuff. Smells like rotting fish."

"Good for you, though."

"That's what Dickie says. But sometimes I think he gives me his cocktail just to torture me."

I pointed to the glass in her hand. "At least he lets you have yours."

She snorted. "Oh, he knows better than to take that away. I'd have a new doctor quick as you can say Jack Daniels."

"Even here in the hospital."

"Naturally. You know, at home, I only have two drinks a day, although I suppose you want to count the wine also, which I don't. Wine is good for the heart, you know."

"Yes. A glass of wine…"

"Or two."

"I believe one is enough for the heart."

"Not for me."

"Two then. And if you don't mind my asking, how big are your drinks?"

She frowned. "What do you mean?"

"Well, what I was wondering, just so I can be accurate in my record, is how much alcohol you put in the glass."

She held up two fingers. "Just that much. Never more. One in the morning after breakfast, and that lasts me until lunch time. And one after lunch, and that lasts me until I go to bed."

"Sounds to me that you drink quite responsibly."

"Oh, I do," she said. "I nurse it."

I knew about nursing one's drink. It was a term my parents used when they were drinking their evening sherry.

"And?"

"And I refresh it whenever it is empty."

"Of course. And how often do you have to refresh it?"

She giggled. "As often as it runs out, silly."

It was tedious, and there was a lot of back and forth, but after two hours, I managed to get just about her entire medical history, and when I went back to see Doctor Mansard, I was exhausted, but pleased.

"She's a chronic alcoholic," I said. "She was very careful, but whenever she lifted a glass, her hands shook. And she never got up from her divan. I think she has some alcoholic nerve damage. And some memory loss, although she is awfully good at covering it up."

"In the end, just like the patients you've seen at Boston City, no?"

"Well, yes. Except for one thing."

"She was drinking in the hospital."

"Yes. Served up by the nurse, even."

"That's to control the amount. She still gets two drinks a

day, as she probably told you, but there is no refreshing in the hospital. Doctor Williams brings her in once a year to reduce her consumption from two fifths a day to two fingers. It keeps her out of DTs, and it reduces her tolerance. It will then take her a year to get back up, at which point she comes in again. It isn't what I would recommend, but it seems to have kept her from getting full-blown cirrhosis. And it keeps her happy. Which, as I am sure you discovered, is what you have to do if you want to continue to be her doctor." He sighed, then he said, "And that's what it's like to doctor to the filthy rich."

I learned a lot about the art of medicine from Mrs. Choate. And I learned that when it comes to addictive disorders, that to which one is addicted doesn't matter. What matters is having the money.

I selected Boston City Hospital for my internship.

CHAPTER 12

I could say that Davida took to doctoring as a fish takes to water. Unfortunately, the analogy suffers from two serious defects. In the first place, in the relationship between the fish and the water, the role of the water is a purely passive one. And in the second, there is the etymological complication that the word *doctor*, when used as a verb, carries a very different connotation than the same word as a noun. To doctor something is not necessarily to alter it for the better. So, I will simply say that doctoring and Davida were made for each other and leave it at that.

It wasn't so much that she was a quick learner. That she was. But so were all her fellow students. Medical students are much smarter than we were, and their ability to assimilate the remarkable quantity of data that now forms the knowledge base of our profession never ceases to amaze me. Their empathic skills, however, are less well developed than their quantitative ones. Rare is the individual who both knows the science and understands the person. Davida is one such. She has that remarkable ability, upon meeting someone for the first time, to gain completely that person's trust, and knowing that she has obtained a gift beyond measure, she is certain never to abuse it.

By the end of the first week, Davida had learned all there was to learn from the clerkship, and by the end of the second week, I could almost say she was more of a colleague than a student. Although decorum dictated that this could not be explicitly recognized, we quickly fell into a relationship that was less that of teacher to student than of senior to junior.

As per protocol, she continued to see only two patients each session. Davida could easily have handled a full schedule, however, the chorus of protests from her patients attendant upon each of my attempts to increase her volume—and accordingly decrease the time she spent with each one—precluded any such change.

At the start of each session, we would look at my schedule. Davida already knew them all, "as people," she was fond of saying, and she would pick out of the list the two whom she would choose to see. First on the schedule for the day was Fusswood. As he had already planned to see Davida, he would be one.

Fusswood always arrived early. I was a little surprised, however, to see that he was already in the waiting room when I arrived a little after 7 o'clock. His appointment would not be for another hour.

"Morning, Doc," he said.

"Good morning, Fusswood."

"She here yet?"

"Not yet."

"But she will be?"

"She will."

"Okay, then." Pause. "Good to see you."

"You too, Fusswood."

Davida arrived, and we went over the schedule.

"I'll start with Fusswood."

"Of course."

"We're going to discuss CHIPS today. I read quite a bit about it. The biology is very interesting, but I'm not sure how it will apply to patient care."

"Okay. Whom else do you want to see?"

She looked over the list. Without hesitation, she pointed to a name. "Ray," she said.

In the course of fifty years, I have dealt with many varieties of people. Most are pleasant. A few are not. Some are a treat. Some are a chore. Ray Stottlemyre is an unpleasant chore.

It has nothing to do with his upbringing. As a child, he was not abused. Nor was he neglected. Nowhere in his family history is there alcoholism or violence or poverty, or any of those problems which we use as, if not justification, at least mitigation of a person's antisocial behavior. His mother is milk-of-human-kindness, and his father, although rather a curmudgeon, was a bark-worse-than-his-bite fellow.

Ray's first expression was a frown. His infant cry had a tone of grump. He never had playmates or friends. His mother once told me, "He's my son, and I love him, but lordy, I struggle to like him. Seems he just came out wrong."

I have never seen Ray smile.

Ray was not a bully. Nor was he a whiner. Ray was not violent or mean or cruel. He just radiated an aura of unpleasantness that, like some bad odor, tended to keep people at a distance. He was a terrible student. His classmates expected, and his teachers hoped, that he would quit at age sixteen. But he didn't. It took him three tries at his senior year, but he graduated. Not that he needed a high school diploma. After high school, he went to work in his father's business, Stottlemyre and Sons Tree Surgeons. When his father died from a heart attack at fifty-two, Ray took over the business. The general consensus in town was that he was a perfect fit for his work. "Gets along okay with trees," people said, "and when he don't, he cuts 'em down." Getting along with trees, it seemed, was the extent of his ability to relate to a living thing.

There are patients who don't take their medicines. And there are patients who don't keep their appointments. We call these patients noncompliant. It's not a very nice word. It implies that somehow the patient's condition belongs to us, and that they are shirking their duties by failing to do exactly as we say. There are also patients—far fewer in number—who, although they refuse to take their medicine, come to every single appointment. I don't call them noncompliant. I call them ornery.

Ray was ornery.

Ray had diabetes and high blood pressure and emphysema. He smoked two packs a day and was grossly overweight. His diet consisted solely of foods he was advised not to eat. I regularly gave him prescriptions for his high blood pressure and his high sugar and high cholesterol and his poor breathing. He took the prescriptions without complaint. Sometimes he filled them. Never did he take the medicine. I asked him once why he kept taking the prescriptions if he wasn't going to use them. He shrugged.

"Why you keep writing 'em?"

"Maybe I'm as stubborn as you."

"Not hardly."

I didn't ask Davida why she picked Ray. I didn't have to.

But first we both went in to see Fusswood. Davida said it would be easier to have the discussion together. "Just in case you have anything to add."

Which was unlikely.

"So, Docs, I guess I should say. Whaddya find out?" Fusswood asked.

Davida looked at me. I nodded. "Well, quite a bit. C-H-I-P stands for clonal hematopoiesis of indeterminate potential."

Fusswood frowned. "Can you translate that into English?" he asked.

"Good idea," she said laughing. "*Clonal hematopoiesis* refers to when the bone marrow starts making one single type of blood cell. In this case, it is a cell that speeds up atherosclerosis by facilitating cholesterol deposits in the walls of the arteries. *Indeterminate* is one of those words we use in medicine, like idiopathic—which does not mean caused by idiots. Or essential—which has nothing to do with being necessary. They are words that we use to cover up the fact that we don't have the slightest idea what is going on. They make it appear that it has nothing to do with our own ignorance, but that it is a basic property of the thing itself."

"I like that," said Fusswood. "Next time someone asks me a question I can't answer, I'll just say, 'It's indeterminate.' Sounds much better than 'I don't know.'"

"Three words that doctors never use," said Davida.

"You did."

"I'm not a doctor yet. Anyway, what the researchers discovered is there is a certain kind of blood cell that releases chemicals in the blood that irritate the wall of the blood vessel and make the surface rougher. This makes it easier for cholesterol to stick to the wall and build up plaque."

"Like when you repair a tire puncture," said Fusswood.

"Exactly. You rough up the surface with some sandpaper and then the patch will stick better. Some people are unlucky enough to be born with the gene that makes these cells. And in older people, the CHIP cells get more common in everyone. Which could explain why some people get heart disease early on, even though they have no other risk factors, and why heart disease increases so much as we get older. Of course, one of the problems with any research like this is whether the cells actually cause atherosclerosis or just are associated with it."

"What do you mean?"

"Like snow tires."

"What about 'em?"

"They aren't called snow tires because they bring snow."

"Guilt by association?"

"Yep."

"I get it," said Fusswood. "Like when a doctor gives you antibiotics for a cold, and you get better, but not because of the antibiotics."

"Just like that," she smiled. "So, in order to be sure that the cells actually caused the hardening of the arteries, they injected the gene that made them into a group of mice. And they found that the mice that had the gene developed atherosclerosis much more rapidly than those that didn't."

"Sound like we all should have a CHIP test."

"We don't have a clinical test for the gene yet. What we measure instead is something called CRP. That stands for C reactive protein. It's a very old test. My instructor said CRP is an acute phase reactant, which didn't really help explain anything." She turned to me. "Do you know what it comes from, Beach?"

One of the things about being around for a long time is that you know a lot of stuff that once was quite important but now is old hat. This applies to many of the diagnostic tests we did in my early days. The CRP is one such test. These tests didn't tell us at all what was going on. They just indicated that something was rotten in the state of the body. Most of these tests have been replaced by better, and more expensive, ones. But the CRP has survived.

"Back in the day, there were a couple of researchers at the Rockefeller Institute studying the blood of people with pneumonia in hopes of finding something they could write a paper about, which, in turn, would get them more money to write more papers. They had already found two abnormal proteins in the blood, and they had written papers about them."

"Let me guess," said Davida. "They were called A and B."

"Correct. Well, they had a good thing going with these proteins, so they kept rummaging around. And eventually they found a third."

"Which they called C."

"Which they did."

"But...?"

"What happened to A and B? Well that is one of the great mysteries of modern medicine. At any rate, C is easy to measure, so they started looking for it in all kinds of conditions. And it turned out to be guilty *by association*, not only with pneumonia, but with syphilis and cancer and rheumatism. And now, as you just pointed out, people with heart disease. I am particularly fond of the answer I remember from my training, when I asked the same question of my professor and he said, "Its role remains to be fully elucidated."

"Has a nice ring to it," said Davida.

"It does."

"Better than *indeterminate*."

"Much."

"I heard of CRP," said Fusswood. "Asked Doc once about getting it checked. He said it wasn't necessary." He looked at me pointedly.

"And from what I have learned I would have to say he is right," said Davida quickly. "Turns out the best way to lower CRP is with statins, and you already take one."

"Oh."

"I did find a study that treated people who had an elevated CRP with a drug that was an antibody to the CHIP cells. Turned out the antibody lowered CRP also. The authors said the results of the study were very promising. They wrote that the antibody *significantly* reduced the risk of having a heart attack, even for those already taking statins."

Fusswood was puzzled. "I don't understand," he said. "You just said that there wasn't any reason to get a CRP test, but if it's the way to tell if I need this antibody drug, then I should get the test."

"If only it were that simple," said Davida. "First, you have to remember that when we use the term *significant*, we don't use it in the ordinary sense. All it means for us is that the thing was unlikely to have occurred by chance. Something may be significant in a scientific sense, and yet not at all meaningful."

"Significant, but not meaningful? Now I'm completely confused."

"You're not the only one. I'm not sure all of my classmates understand the distinction."

"Or all of my colleagues," I said.

"I wouldn't say that," said Davida.

"You wouldn't. I would."

"Anyway, once you look at it properly, it makes perfect sense. The key is to understand the difference between *relative* and *absolute* risk reduction. Take, for example, a group of people whose chance of having a heart attack in four years is twenty percent, which is what it was in the study I mentioned. And suppose you cut that risk in half with a medicine. What are their chances then?"

"Ten percent," said Fusswood.

"Right. And compared with twenty percent, ten percent is what?"

"One-half."

"Correct. Which is a fifty percent reduction. And that sounds pretty good. But that's the *relative* reduction. If you have one hundred such people, and you treat all of them, how many people will *not* have a heart attack because they all took the medicine?"

"That's easy," said Fusswood, who had been an accountant. "Fifty percent of twenty is ten. Ten people."

"Correct. Ten people out of one hundred. Ten percent. One out of ten. That is the *absolute* risk reduction. From that we can get what we call the number needed to treat. That is the number of people who need to take the treatment to benefit just one person. How many would that be?"

"That would be ten," said Fusswood quickly. "So, what you're saying is that in order to prevent one heart attack with that medicine, you have to treat ten people, and that the other nine are taking the medicine just to help that one person."

"In a way, yes. And in this particular study, the actual reduction was only fifteen percent, not fifty. Can you figure out what that means?"

"I think so," said Fusswood. "Without the medicine, twenty out of one hundred people would have had a heart attack, right?"

"Right."

"And with the medication, that would be reduced by fifteen percent?"

"Yep."

"Fifteen percent of twenty is three," said Fusswood. "Which means that the *absolute* difference between the two groups was only three percent. And so, if one hundred people took the medicine the whole time, then three of those one hundred people would have been saved from a heart attack, or to look at the number needed to treat, you would have to treat thirty-three people to help one person."

"I think you've got it."

"Thanks, Professor Higgins."

"Glad I can help."

"Which means those *significant* results are not exactly a big deal."

"No. And since the treatment now costs two hundred thousand dollars per person per year, how much would it cost to prevent one heart attack during those four years?"

"That's easy," said Fusswood. "Thirty-three people for four years comes out to a total of one hundred and thirty-two years of treatment. Multiply that times two hundred thousand a year. Wow! That's a cool twenty-six million four hundred thousand to prevent one heart attack. Maybe I'm asking for the wrong signup sheet. Sounds like I should get the stock instead of the medicine."

"Maybe. Maybe not. There is the matter of safety to consider. More people receiving the antibodies died from fatal infections, and of course, we don't know anything yet about long-term side effects."

"Oh well," said Fusswood looking at me. "Guess you were right, Doc. So, I'll stick with the meds I've got."

"Tried and true is still a good idea."

"Yeah. I suppose it is." He turned to Davida. "But you know, I'm not disappointed. Not at all. Even though there is nothing I can do now, just your telling me about it makes me feel good. I know that I'm not going to be missing out on anything, 'cause you are always going to be looking out for me—just like you, Doc."

Davida turned to me. "I hadn't realized how much work it is to figure out what the actual benefit of a new treatment is. We did have some stuff on statistics, but it was one of those classes that nobody pays much attention to. Now I can see that the answer is not in the conclusions; it's in the fine print. I don't know how you can keep up with it all."

"It's not easy," I said. Which it isn't. And there was a time when I relished examining a study as closely as Davida had just done, trying to pick apart the flaws and the caveats. But it was some time ago that I gave that up. I no longer had the energy or the inclination to plow through the long and often tedious discussions of methods, materials, and results, and I had developed what I knew was a bad habit of looking just at the conclusions, which were pretty much always the same. "Treatment X improves condition Y." And "Further studies are needed." To see her enthusiasm for the work, and to see the way she was able to explain it to Fusswood reminded me of the doctor I once was.

And still should be.

Fusswood got up to go. "Thanks," he said to Davida, shaking her hand. "That was great. I was going to say you're gonna be a great doctor, but I won't. Because somehow it seems as if you already are." He turned to me. "Hope you can keep her here, Doc."

"I hope so too."

Davida smiled but said nothing.

At the door, he gave her a salute. "See ya 'round, Doc. Next time it comes around on the gee-tar."

After he left, Davida said, "I have a question, Beach."

"Fire away."

"It's what he said about the guitar. My grandmother says that too."

I nodded. "She would. Ever heard of Arlo Guthrie?"

"The folksinger?"

"That's the one. In the sixties, Arlo wrote an antiwar song called Alice's Restaurant. 'Next time it comes around on the guitar' is from that. It's a good song. Ask your grandmother. I bet she can sing it for you."

"The whole thing?"

"I wouldn't be surprised."

By the time she was finished writing up Fusswood, Ray was ready. She went in to see him.

"That was a strange visit," she said when she came out of the exam room.

"That would be Ray."

"No. I don't mean like that. I knew what to expect. I've seen Ray on the bench all my life, and all the times I passed him on the bench and said hi to the guys, he was the only one who never responded. Looked at me, but never said a word. Never changed his expression. Just a blank stare. As if I wasn't even alive."

"Human relations have never been one of Ray's specialties."

"That's what I thought. And when I first went in, that's just the way he was. He answered my questions all right, but just with a grunt or a shrug, hardly even a yup or a nope."

"He is quite thrifty in his use of words. I wonder sometimes if he thinks he has a limited supply and is afraid he might use them all up prematurely, so that when he really needs them for an emergency sometime in the future, there might not be any left."

"Sure seemed like it. I tried as hard as I could. I even asked him about trees. That was no use either. But then, well, I can't say he opened up, but he actually volunteered some information. And when I asked him if he ever had any chest pain, first he just shook his head. But then he said, 'Don't see how

I could. Ticker doesn't get much of a workout. Lungs give out 'fore I can get up any kinda head of steam.'"

It must have been the longest speech that Ray had ever uttered. Davida is an attractive and engaging person. But I couldn't see that having any effect on Ray. "What happened?"

"It was after I asked him what his dog's name was."

*****

There is a collection of guys who hang out on the bench on the corner of Main and State, next to Busilli's drugstore. They are mostly retired, although one or two work occasionally at odd jobs. In good weather they sit there most of the day, watching the cars and the passersby. Ray occasionally graces them with his presence, always on the end, never too close to the others.

Some time ago, a dog of uncertain lineage showed up. I am very fond of dogs, and I scrupulously try to avoid using a pejorative term when referring to one, but this particular dog tested my vocabulary. Cute I couldn't call him, and ugly I wouldn't. He resembled a pile of old clothes that had been heaped up and somehow come to life. The dog seemed to have a sense of where he stood in the eyes of humans. He didn't wag his tail when a human approached, nor did he perk up his ears. He just shuffled off a bit to the side. "I know you don't like to look at me," he seemed to say. "I wouldn't either. But I can't help it."

The dog approached the bench and ambled slowly past the other men down to Ray's end. He looked up at Ray, paused a few seconds, and then lifted his leg and peed on Ray's shoe. Ray scowled at the dog and gave him a half-hearted kick. The dog backed off a bit and then lay down in front of Ray, just out of reach of his leg.

Ray looked at the dog. The dog looked at Ray. Ray grunted, heaved himself up off the bench, and walked away. The dog got up and shuffled away in the opposite direction. Things went on like this for several days. Ray would arrive and sit down. The dog would arrive and sit down in front of him. The only difference after the first day was that the dog didn't pee on Ray's foot, and Ray didn't kick the dog.

"Looks like you got yourself a dog," said one of Ray's bench mates.

One day, when Ray went home, the dog followed him. Ray lived in an apartment at the back of Stottlemyre and Sons Tree Surgeons, half a mile up Main Street. Ray never let the dog in, but he did leave the door to the shed open, and the dog slept in there when the weather was bad. Otherwise, he slept just outside Ray's door.

*****

"What did he say?"

"He didn't say anything. He just shrugged. So I told him every dog should have a name. He looked at me kinda funny. Then he said, 'Pick one.' And I said, 'No, Ray, he's your dog. You have to pick the name.' And he looked at me again for a long time, and finally he said, 'Dog.' And I said, 'You want to call your dog Dog.' And he nodded. And I said, 'That's an excellent name. I bet he will really like it.' And after that was when he started talking."

"Wonders never cease. Any luck talking to him about his medicines?"

"No. Soon as I started to talk about them, he clammed up again. So I said maybe that was enough for today. But I told him I did have one suggestion—and he actually asked me what it was."

"What was it?"

"To walk Dog."

It was Davida's last day of her rotation. We exchanged the usual compliments. I told her what a great student she had been, and she told me how much she liked the experience.

"It was so interesting," she said. Then she shook her head. "No, that's not the right word. Not at all. It was so fulfilling.

For the first time it made me feel how much I want to be a doctor. And how privileged I am that I can be."

I tried to remember the last time I had thought that.

"Can I ask you a favor?" she said.

"A favor? No."

She smiled. "Weekends would be best."

"You can check the schedule with the switchboard."

"Deal," she said. At the door, she turned back. "See you next time it comes around on the gee-tar."

CHAPTER 13

Not long after Davida finished her clerkship, I got a letter from the medical school.

Dear Doctor Conger,

First, let me say how pleased we all are that you have agreed to be a preceptor in our Primary Care Clerkship. It is the selfless dedication of doctors like yourself who have made this rotation possible. On behalf of all of us here in the department, thank you.

As the new Director of the Primary Care Clerkship, I feel it is important that we at the medical school maintain communication with you in the community. I would like your feedback on what is good about the clerkship and what could use improvement. I would also like to review our current goals and objectives for the rotation, so that we can maximize the value of the experience.

Accordingly, I am scheduling meetings with all our preceptors. I have made an appointment with you for 4:00 next Tuesday the 17th. If this is not convenient, please call my secretary to reschedule.

Looking forward to our chat, I remain,

Yours for medical education,

Robert Roberts, M.D. PhD, MACP

Professor of Medicine

Chair Primary Care Clerkship

It was signed "Rob."

I have been teaching medical students for the past forty years. Periodically I receive a letter like the one above. Although the name and title of the author change each time, the import is always the same, as is the proximate cause of its arrival. A change in leadership in the department.

The visits—chats they were called—were always the same. First came tea and scones. The former served in an elegant Wedgewood tea service that, I would be once again informed, was named Queen's Ware in honor of Queen Charlotte. It had once belonged to Sir John Wentworth, the last in a series of British Wentworth governors of New Hampshire. The service had been crafted by Josiah Wedgewood himself and shipped to America in 1763.

Governor John gave it to the college when he decamped to Nova Scotia after the revolution, presumably not wanting any memorabilia of his time among the heathens. The tea service belongs to the college. It is available, upon request, to members of the faculty of sufficient rank to merit the honor. Its presence connotes a special occasion.

The scones are from Lou's. They are my favorite part of the visit.

The chair always would greet me graciously. As we partook of our tea and crumpets, he would ask me about my career, conveying a sincere and genuine interest in who I am and what I have done. He would compliment me on my teaching. I would say what a pleasure it was. He hoped I could continue, at no cost to the university, to perform this invaluable service. I was happy to do so. Finally, he would say how much he would like to come down to my office, so that he can get a better feel for the community to which he sends his students. I would reply how glad I would be to receive him. And we would never see or hear from each other again.

It is puffery, pure and simple, and we both know it. But as is always true when issued, it is sincere, and when received, it is believed. It makes us both feel we are good fellows. And it puts us both in a good mood.

It is a mood like that which I felt when I was a child after our family had been to church on Sunday morning. Upon leaving the service, I would be full of benevolence to mankind and a do-unto-others spirit. My younger sister would be similarly affected, and we would be exceptionally tolerant of each other as we drove home, eschewing our customary bickering over who got to sit next to the window, a dispute unaffected by the fact that we were a family of four. On a good day it would last the entire one-mile journey from church to home. Most days we got almost to Ashland Avenue.

The letter's mention of goals and objectives unnerved me slightly. There was a bit of being called into the principal's office about it. I knew that I had not been particularly obedient with respect to either goals or objectives, and I had let slip to Davida on more than one occasion that I was not overly fond of them. I was confident she wouldn't say anything, but the proof was in the pudding, and of the pudding I had served precious little.

Doctor Roberts was a handsome, trim man with just enough gray in his temples to make him appear seasoned, but not old. He had a friendly face that made you feel you were going to like him, and he you. Were it not for his eyes, one could mistake him for just another nice, but not particularly interesting chap. Deep-set and dark blue, when directed at you his eyes hinted that behind the benevolent appearance there lay a steely intelligence that one would do well not to underestimate.

Dressed in his uniform of starched white coat, blue shirt, and striped tie, and with a gold-plated stethoscope protruding from one of his pockets, he appeared remarkably similar to his predecessors, and I wondered briefly if he was chosen for the position in part for his ornamental value, much as one would replace an old but beloved sofa with one that fit in with the existing décor.

My premonition that this visit was to be different from the others was confirmed when I noticed that tea and scones were nowhere in sight. Furthermore, Doctor Roberts was not alone. Sitting in the corner was a serious-looking young man who appeared bored.

"So glad you could find the time to get up here to the ivory tower, Beach," Doctor Roberts said, extending his arms in a gesture of welcome that did not require him to get up from behind his desk. "I know it's rather an inconvenience for you, and I would much rather be coming down to see you at your place. It's refreshing to see what life is like in the trenches. But with so many of you to meet and all my other obligations to the department hanging over me, I'm afraid it's just not in the cards. Sort of like trying to see all your patients in their own home, if you know what I mean."

I nodded in agreement.

"I've asked Doctor Bird to sit in with us today. He will be responsible for the day-to-day management of the nuts and bolts of the clerkship, so he'll be your go-to guy whenever there is an issue. Of course, I'll always be available should you feel the need, but Sebastian here..." He smiled and waved vaguely in the direction of Doctor Bird, who nodded ever so slightly but otherwise made no acknowledgment of my presence.

"So," he said, glancing down at a paper on his desk. "You've got quite a CV, Beach. Amherst College, Harvard, Boston City, CDC, UC San Francisco." He looked up from the paper, and, as if noticing me for the first time, looked directly at me. "And then, except for the five years off to manage hospital medicine in North Philly, forty years in Dumster. Interesting choice for someone with your pedigree." He looked at me more acutely, almost as if he were hinting at some hidden skeleton lurking in my professional closet.

"Snow's better here," I said.

"That it is." His lips smiled. His eyes were not amused. "Still, it's a rather long time in a rather small place. Although there is that five-year sentence to Temple." He chuckled at his joke. "I did time myself in Philly, on the other side of the river, so I know the territory."

The other side of the river was the University of Pennsylvania. Although not far in physical distance from Temple, it was a world away, and we both knew it.

"As I said in the letter, I really just wanted to meet you and to thank you for all you have done for the department over the years. It's been a long road you've traveled with us, and you've been a tremendous help. The students have all given highly favorable reviews of their rotation with you, especially Ms. Edwards. She was quite effusive in her praise. It's a real tribute to your teaching and commitment."

"I like doing it," I said with a shrug. "They're so eager for clinical medicine. They're an easy bunch to please." I waited for him to bring up the real purpose of the visit.

I didn't have to wait long.

"Yes," he agreed, turning to Doctor Bird. "And that's what Seb and I were hoping to talk with you about." He paused to let his words sink in.

"As you know, for many years, the clerkship was considered primarily an opportunity for students to see what it would be like to practice in a community. The actual content of their experience was not considered."

"I believe *shadowing* was the word that was used," I said.

"Exactly," he nodded in agreement. "And now, if I could extend the analogy, the time has come to shine a fuller light upon the experience. To eliminate the shadows, if you will." He allowed himself a smile of appreciation at his clever turn of words. "To which end we have been redesigning the clerkship to give students a proper grounding in the bedrock of primary care."

"The medical home."

"The medical home. Which, as you also know, has a rather extensive set of elements."

"One hundred and twenty-one," I believe.

"One hundred and twenty-one," he repeated slowly and turned to Doctor Bird, who nodded. "Exactly." If Doctor Roberts were surprised that I knew the number, he did not show it. It was an ability that was part of the job. "Not that we would expect our students to master all of them in a single rotation, but we do want them at least to have a grasp of the most essential elements."

"Twenty," said Doctor Bird.

"And with an expected rotation of four weeks, at five sessions per week, that allows for one element per session. The details of which element and how it is to be taught are outlined, as you know, in a document that the student brings to each session. It is intended as a guide for both the student *and* the preceptor. You are familiar with the document to which I am referring?"

I was. It went in the trash as soon as I got it. Much to the delight of the students.

"Of course you are," he said. It had not been a question. "So, perhaps we could review the results for Ms. Edwards." He turned to Seb, who was holding a sheet of paper that apparently contained the information in question.

"Seb, did Ms. Edwards have the necessary twenty visits?"

"Twenty-two."

"Two extra?" he raised his eyebrows.

"On her own time."

"Ah," he said. "If I remember correctly, she valued the rotation highly. What was the term she used in her evaluation, Seb?"

Doctor Bird consulted his paper again. "A unique experience."

"Yes," Doctor Roberts said slowly. "Well, we'll come to that in just a minute. But first, how many of the required elements did Ms. Edwards complete in these twenty-two visits?"

Doctor Bird pretended to consult his papers. But he had no need.

"One."

"One," Doctor Roberts repeated. "And that one element was?"

"Blood pressure."

"*Blood...pressure,*" repeated Doctor Roberts slowly. "Well, it is certainly important to acquire skills in the taking of blood pressure. And what is the usual count for our other students in the rotation?"

"Twenty."

"One—and twenty. Quite a difference." He paused. "Ms. Edwards certainly would be correct in classifying her experience as *unique*. And that's the nub of our problem, isn't it then?"

Ignorance was the only strategy I could think of at the time. "I'm afraid I don't understand," I said.

It didn't work. "No, I don't expect you would," Doctor Roberts said. "Let me see if I can explain it to you. There was a time, rather long ago, when we valued innovation and improvisation in medical education. It helped students to sharpen their deductive skills. It was a time when our diagnostic capabilities were more limited than they are today, and deductive reasoning was important. Not that such skills are of no value today. They are, of course. A good keen mind is always valuable, and no more so than right here at the medical school. But reasoning is not for everyone. And for many of today's students, most I would say, the knowledge that there is a well-trod path is preferred over the road less taken, as it were."

Much as I hated to admit it, he had a point. The proliferation of treatment and diagnostic options in the last fifty years has rendered medical decision-making a very complex business. Trying to figure out one's way through it is, at best challenging, but more often frustrating. It is far easier to follow a preordained sequence of steps. Do A; then if A is yes, do B; or if A is no, do C. And so on.

"Out with unique and in with standard," I said.

"Well put," he nodded. "And that brings us to the question of your role as preceptor."

"And the issue of old dogs."

One acknowledged witticism was apparently enough. He ignored my comment.

"Over the years, you have been a valued, and I think I can say without risk of contradiction from my predecessors, an outstanding member of our clinical faculty. We can't thank you enough."

The effort involved in this concession appeared to be too much for Doctor Roberts. He took a deep breath, sat back in his chair, folded his hands, and swiveled away from me to face Doctor Bird. "Seb has come up with a plan that we think will be an ideal match for our needs and your skills." He gestured to Doctor Bird. "Tell Beach what you have come up with, Seb."

"An elective."

"An elective," I repeated. I knew this must be my fond farewell, but I couldn't quite figure out how it was playing out.

"Yes. Students interested in the *historical* aspects of primary care would be offered a two-week rotation with you."

"I see," I said, not seeing at all. "And the expectations for the student would be...?"

"To accompany you on all of your activities, including especially those that take place outside of the office. They would be required to research the evolution of primary care from the early inception of medicine through the present. At the end of the rotation they would submit a report of between one thousand and fifteen hundred words that would summarize their experience and the lessons learned."

"And I would be expected to...?"

"Be yourself. We want it to appear as natural as possible."

Condescension aside, it was an interesting idea. Although I would have fewer students, those who did come would be those who really wanted to. It was a better outcome from the visit than I expected. It almost seemed too good to be true.

"That works for me," I said. "When were you planning to offer this elective?"

Seb made a show of consulting his tablet. "Spring break."

It *was* too good to be true. "Ah," I said.

Doctor Roberts got up from his chair. "Well, Beach," he said, coming over and shaking my hand. "It's been great meeting with you, and I look forward to seeing you again—after we have tried this new plan out. Next time we'll do it down at your place."

It's never very pleasant to be told you are no longer needed, and I tried to make the best of it by reminding myself that what I really valued most in my practice was not my students, but my patients, and that freed from the obligations of teaching, I would be able to concentrate my attentions on them.

It almost worked.

CHAPTER 14

In the days following my meeting with Doctor Roberts I wasn't quite myself. I was not actually depressed, but as P.G. Wodehouse would have said, I was less than fully gruntled. The wind had been taken out of my sails, and I found myself looking about for even the slightest breeze to get me moving again.

It was not a profitable search. The first snag I hit was none other than Fusswood himself. He had returned for a regular visit with me in better spirits than I had seen him in a long time. Then out of the blue, he popped the question. "When are you thinking of retiring, Doc?" Although he was the first person who dared to bring up the subject, I was sure that most, if not all, my patients were harboring the same question. But they understood instinctively it was one of those questions that is fine to ask, as long as it is only to oneself. Fusswood, being one of my oldest and most devoted patients, certainly knew this. I brushed it off with my usual joke that given what I could see about his current state of health, I was confident I could outlast him. We had a good laugh together, and he said how glad he was, but the question still hung in the air. And it stayed with me long after he had gone.

Some people retire early. Many at retirement age. Some retire late. And there are some people who retire *too* late. I have been a doctor a long time. My health is good, and my memory is, if not as good as it used to be, at least good enough. I had never before considered the possibility that I might no longer be up to snuff.

Except when I look at my dashboard. The dashboard is an invention of our new CEO. It is a kind of report card that provides each of us with a monthly set of statistics, metrics they are called, that detail how we are doing in comparison with our colleagues. The metrics determine our pay-for-performance bonus. What that bonus was, I couldn't say. I have never received one.

The metric of greatest importance is productivity. Productivity includes how many patients we see per hour, how much we charge per visit, and how many new patients we have seen. I always did fine with number of patients per hour. I was a little skimpy on the charges per visit. But where my numbers were really outstanding was in the category of new patients. New patients, as we were regularly reminded, were the life-blood of a practice. To grow the practice was the thing, and that could only be done with new bodies.

I had none.

Which is easy to explain. I have a very loyal and regular group of patients, some of whom, like Fusswood, have been with me for forty years. Although there has been the occasional new person in town who liked the idea of an old-style doctor, in the last couple of years they have been few and far between. Whether it was because they were reluctant to invest in someone whose durability was uncertain, or whether it was simply a matter of out with the old and in with the new, I couldn't tell. It had been over six months since I had seen a fresh face. The biological clock on my practice was ticking.

So it was with no little interest that I saw a new name on my schedule one morning: Brittany Menard. Although I was sure I had never seen her before, the name was somehow familiar. However, Menard was a common name in the area, and several Menards had been my patients. She might have been related, I thought.

Under Reason for Visit it said, "new patient."

By birthdate, she was thirty years old. This surprised me. The few patients I had acquired in recent years were of the same vintage as my regular patients. They had come upon recommendation of one of their cohorts and were of such age and health that the last thing they were concerned about was outlasting their doctor. They all wanted the same thing: a doctor who would leave them alone. I couldn't remember the last time I saw someone who was not on Social Security. Which, as it turned out, Brittany was.

I shouldn't have been surprised. Much less shocked. I had Crikett's notes before I went into the room:

Here for meet and greet

VS: BP 65/42, Pulse 110, Wt. 69lbs. Ht. 64 inches. BMI 11.8.
O2 sat 91% on 3 Liters nasal cannula.

Meds:

OxyContin 40mg twice daily- out

Oxycodone 30mg four times PRN breakthrough pain- out

Xanax 1 mg three times daily- out

Ambien 10mg at bedtime- out

Inhalers- not using

Zithromax- not taking

Pancreatic enzymes- not taking

I knew without asking what her problem was. The weight, oxygen, antibiotics, and pancreatic enzymes made it clear.

Brittany had cystic fibrosis.

Cystic fibrosis interferes with the ability of the lungs to manage secretions, causing repeated infections and emphysema. It interferes with the ability of the intestinal tract to absorb food, causing malnutrition. It weakens the bones. It weakens the liver. There is hardly an organ cystic fibrosis does not affect.

Not that long ago, the average survival for a person born with cystic fibrosis was less than twenty years. Now, thanks to intensive therapy and newer medications, a woman so afflicted can expect to live forty years. But that is only if she religiously follows the treatment regimen, and even then, it is a life punctuated by many hospital stays and a perpetual struggle to breathe. It is a miserable disease.

I was puzzled. Why was she coming to see me? Patients with cystic fibrosis are carefully managed from birth by a team of highly trained specialists, although it is required that such patients also have a primary care doctor, the sole purpose of which is to sign the necessary referral papers that allow her to see the doctors who actually treat her. It is a system as inconvenient and unnecessary as insurance companies can make it. So, Brittany needed to have a PCP, but according to her address, she lived in Unity, New Hampshire. Unity was an hour away from Dumster. There were at least four primary care groups closer, in Springfield, Charlestown, Windsor, and Claremont. Travel for her must not have been easy, and I would have expected her to pick someone closer to home. Why she was coming all the way up to Dumster was a mystery. Until I remembered why her name was familiar.

It is customary among the various local hospitals—in a clear violation of the Health Insurance Portability and Accountability Act that is immensely helpful to hospital staff—that when a patient shows up at one emergency room with what is determined to be "drug-seeking behavior," by which they do not mean penicillin, the staff promptly notifies all the adjacent facilities, so that we are on the alert for a similar request. Brittany's name had appeared on our ER list more than once, and from her list of medications, I could imagine why.

*****

When I started my career, the idea of giving opiates for pain was, except for acute conditions or when the patient was ill from cancer, unheard of. The suck-it-up school of pain relief dominated. Then in 1980, Hershel Jick, a professor at Boston University School of Medicine, wrote a now-infamous letter to the editor in the *New England Journal of Medicine*. He stated that his team had reviewed more than 11,000 hospital records of patients treated with opiates for pain and determined that for those not already addicted to opiates, the risk of addiction was less than 1 percent. He concluded that "despite widespread use of narcotic drugs in hospitals, the development of addiction is rare in patients with no history of addiction." Drug safety was Doctor Jick's specialty. Over the course of his career he has written or co-authored almost 400 papers on drug safety. He is considered to be a meticulous researcher and keen intellect.

So, it took him only thirty-seven years to realize that he had completely flubbed the opiate issue. Talking to a public radio host recently, he conceded that "this has recently been a matter of a lot of angst for me."

He then proceeded to excuse himself on the grounds that it was not until some fifteen years after his letter appeared that the epidemic of prescription opiates took off, which is true enough. But it is fair to say that Dr. Jick did his share to help get the ball rolling. His letter was influential in setting off a plethora of studies and editorials commenting on the safety of opiates and the importance of relieving pain. It would also be fair to say that in terms of angst suffered, his would not quite fall in the category of "It hurts me more than it hurts you" for the millions of those who have been affected by the current opiate epidemic.

If the medical profession was slow on the uptake, the pharmaceutical industry was not. As opiates had been a mainstay of medicine for time immemorial, they were available as generic prescriptions and were, therefore, of no value to Big Pharma. Anticipating the marketing value of Doctor Jick's statement, drug companies promptly set to work on developing newer, more potent, and most importantly, patent-protected drugs. And no company was more effective at this task than Purdue Pharma. Taking an old drug, oxycodone, they redesigned it into a new package. They called it OxyContin. Oxy-Contin made its debut on the medical scene in 1996. It was a big improvement over the older opiates. It allowed the user easily to ingest much higher doses of opiates.

Purdue reaped enormous profits from its invention. Liberally quoting medical literature, they embarked upon an aggressive marketing campaign that remains to this day a tribute to both the greed of Big Pharma and the vanity of the medical profession. They peppered us with promotional materials about the safety and effectiveness of their drug. They showered us with gifts. They paid huge sums of money to clinicians who were willing to shill their value to the rest of us. They even had a jingle: "Get in the Swing with OxyContin." If you had thought that highly trained and dedicated professionals were immune to this kind of chicanery, you would have had to think again—and again.

Emphasizing the importance of alleviating pain, Purdue exhorted us not to be reluctant to use OxyContin for chronic pain, even if the patient was not seriously ill. In a modest concession to the potential downside, they did not recommend its use in children under the age of eleven. Early and often became the new mantra. The campaign was a huge success. In its first year, OxyContin generated $40 million in sales. Only six years later the amount had risen to over $1.5 billion. That year, more than 7 million prescriptions for OxyContin were dispensed.

To date, the aggregate sales of OxyContin have generated over $30 billion in revenue. It boggles to think what might have been done with that money were it invested in some more productive activity. Accordingly, no one does.

However much credit Purdue is due for their marketing strategy, they cannot take any for its invention. Some 100 years earlier it had been employed to even greater effect by a company whose reputation, unlike that of Purdue, remains to this day untarnished. In 1898, the Bayer company, in an effort to supplement its sales from its primary pain reliever, aspirin, introduced a new product.

Its name was Heroin (Heroin is capitalized, because it is the trademark name Bayer used for its new product, diacetyl-morphine. The name was selected because the employees who had tried it said it made them feel heroic. I'm sure it did.)

Heroin was initially marketed as a non-sedating medicine for coughs and later as a cure for morphine addiction, which it certainly was. So successful was the marketing that in what must rate as one of the most misguided philanthropic efforts of the century, in 1900, the Saint James Society mailed frees samples of heroin to morphine addicts. By 1910, the potent addictive powers of heroin were apparent even to the most oblivious, and Bayer stopped selling it. But that cow had long been out of the barn.

It is said that those who do not learn from history are condemned to repeat it. And so the medical profession has repeated history. It took twenty years before someone noticed that the Emperor OxyContin had no clothes. After investigations proved that Purdue Pharma knew its claims about the risk of addiction were false, criminal charges were filed against the company. In the end, they and their executives paid some $645 million in fines. Which you might think is a big hunk of cash. At the time it was indeed the largest settlement ever. It represented a little more than 5 percent of their total revenues from OxyContin. In a modest admission of culpability, the company admitted to "misstatements" in its marketing campaign.

We got the message. Younger doctors especially. They became much better at not prescribing opiates, and they were quick to deny a continued legal source to those already addicted, conveniently forgetting that it was their colleagues who had created the addiction. But the effort was more than a day late and a dollar short. Cut off from their supply of the ironically safer drug, opiate addicts turned first to heroin, and then to a more potent and deadlier synthetic opiate, fentanyl. Between

2016 and 2018 overdose deaths from opiates increased 500 percent.

It almost makes one wistful for OxyContin.

*****

In some form or another, this story was running through my mind when I prepared to see Brittany. I pictured yet another person medically addicted to opiates who now had her pipeline shut off by the very profession that created it. I was prepared for an unsatisfying visit, in which the patient would want from me only one thing, and that would be the one thing I would not give her.

It had been over fifty years since I had seen a person with cystic fibrosis. When I was in medical school, I had an evening job at Children's Hospital in Boston, working in the laboratory of Doctor Harry Shwachman. Doctor Shwachman was the head of clinical nutrition at the hospital. He was responsible for the care of patients with cystic fibrosis. My duties involved collecting specimens from the wards where his patients were kept. I can still picture their frail, emaciated bodies struggling to get a breath of air. It was painful to see. I could never imagine what it must have been like to have been in one of those bodies. Whatever else Brittany might be, I knew that my reaction when I saw her would be pity.

The line between staring and inspecting is a fine one, and I would ordinarily be able to keep myself on its professional side.

With Brittany, I could not.

She was in the midst of a coughing spasm when I entered the exam room. Her head was down, and her toothpick-like arms gripped the edge of the chair for support as her chest heaved up and down. There was not an ounce of fat on her body. The outline of her bones protruded from under her paper-thin skin, looking as if they would break through at any minute. It was impossible to feel anything other than compassion for the life she struggled to hold on to.

Until she looked up at me. Then suddenly, my compassion was replaced by an entirely different sensation.

Guilt.

She had fixed me with a stare so scornful that although we had never met, I had the discomfiting sensation I had done something terribly wrong.

"I'm, uh, Doctor Conger," I mumbled.

"I know who you are," she said in a harsh voice. "And you know who I am."

"Brittany Menard."

She made a face. "I don't mean my name, mister. I mean, you know who I *am!*"

"Well, if you mean, do I know your medical history, other than the medication list you provided, I don't. If you released any records to us, they haven't arrived yet. I can see, though, that you have cystic fibrosis."

Another coughing spell temporarily prevented her response. "You can, can you?" she snapped when she had recovered her breath. "A brilliant diagnostician, no less. Oh, lucky me!" She paused to catch her breath. "But are you telling me with that straight face of yours that you have never heard my name mentioned before—not a word about me and my 'drug-seeking behavior'? Or are you not allowed to tell me because it would be a violation of the God almighty HIPAA to tell a patient what you really know about her? Okay, let me make it easy for you. Here's the story of me. I've been kicked out of four practices, banned from three hospitals, and earned persona-non-grata status at the cystic fibrosis clinic. Which is no mean feat, especially considering that I am what you guys love to call an *interesting* case. How did I manage to do it, you wonder? It wasn't that hard actually. I overused my prescriptions. I forged some. When I had to, I sold some of my pills. I told my doctor I was going to strangle him.

"I know," she said, seeing the expression on my face. "Hard to believe, isn't it? And when the security guy came to take me away, I bit him in the hand. Best experience I ever had in a hospital," she said with a grin. "Even though it tasted like shit.

"Why did I come all the way up here from Unity, you're thinking? It's because of what a wonderful doctor I've heard you are, of course. So the fact that this hospital is the only place left I can reach before my portable oxygen runs out has nothing to do with it.

"So, my question for you, before I waste any more of the breath I don't really have to waste is, are you gonna blow me off like the others, or are you gonna give me my meds? 'Cause if you're not, then I'm outta here."

I have treated plenty of difficult patients, including some who were downright nasty. It isn't much fun, but I accepted that it came with the territory. We didn't take the Hippocratic oath only to accept those who were kindly and well behaved—compliant, as we like to say.

But forging and diversion of medicines were problems. Forging was one thing, but the diversion was one wicket that was just too sticky for me to get through. If you were selling your meds, you weren't getting them because you needed them, you were getting them to make money. And you were spreading addiction to others.

As I eventually was to learn, it was a distinction without a difference.

"I'd like to help you," I said. "You've got a bad disease, and I'm sure it has been rough."

"Spare the but, Doc. I've heard that line a hundred times. I know what it means. Sorry, kid. Sayonara."

"The diversion," I said. "That's why. I just can't treat you if you're selling your meds. It's not right. It's against the law. And it could put my license at risk." This last issue, although technically true, was specious, and I knew it. Unless a doctor is knowingly providing drugs to be sold, no prosecutor is ever going to go after her.

Brittany knew it too. "Oh, your precious license," she snorted. "Poor baby!"

"But if you really needed your medicine…"

"Why did I sell them? Simple. I needed the money. You know how much I get on my Social Security? Thanks to this fantastic body," she said, holding out her wasted arms, "I've never been able to get a job. I get SSI—a whopping seven hundred and thirty-five bucks a month. Oh yeah, and food stamps. Ever tried to live on that? I can't. And I don't. So, I do what I got to do with the only asset I have that's worth anything."

"Your medication."

"That was just once. I was in a jam and I needed cash quick."

"I don't understand. What asset are you talking about?

"My body."

"Your body?"

"Yeah. Sounds ridiculous doesn't it. Course I probably couldn't a done it without some assistance from you guys." And she pulled up her shirt to reveal a rather large and obviously acquired set of breasts that looked totally incongruous with the rest of her body. I couldn't help but stare at them.

"See," she grinned. "Even you. Although in your case, I'll grant you a bit of professional curiosity. It's amazing, though. Something about the guy brain. Doesn't matter what else is around. A big set of boobs and zap, everything else in sight disappears."

"You were…a prostitute?"

"Hardly." She laughed grimly. "But I'll bet there are some out there who would have been turned on by banging a skeleton. Nope. Use 'em for gambling."

"You gamble with your breasts?"

"In a way. Twice a month I go down to Foxwood," she said, referring to Foxwoods Resort Casino in Connecticut. "I got a couple of scams I work. Playing the slots is the easiest. First, I check out who's playing. Find me some sad-looking slob of a guy, the older the better, and I set myself up next to him. Play a little bit, give him a friendly smile now and then, just to keep him there, and then, all a sudden I get to crying and gasping and heaving my chest up and down—pathetic little me. Course I make sure he gets a peek at the equipment. So he comes over and asks me what's the matter, and I say the machine cheated me. I'm hardly able to get the words out. He gets all sympathetic and poor-babys me. Sometimes he even puts a hand on my shoulder to comfort me. And then he slips me something. Ten, twenty bucks usually, but if he's on a winning streak, maybe fifty, even a hundred. He may ask me to sit next to him for luck. Depending on how heavy the hand is on my shoulder, I might say yes.

"Playing poker's my favorite though. I check out the tables. Sit myself down next to the same type of guy. After a couple of hands, I pretend like I got a hot hand and get myself all worked up. Get up a good coughing spasm, lose my breath, and get that panicked air hunger look. You know the kind I mean." And she produced such a perfect imitation of acute respiratory distress syndrome that even though I knew she was pretending, I could believe it was real. She stopped abruptly and gave me a big smile. "Pretty good, huh? Should be. Done it enough times for real. Course at Foxwood, my blouse is a little too tight and a little too low, and when the silicones get to flashing, poor guy doesn't stand a chance. Just can't keep his eye off 'em. Swiping a few chips from his pile is easy as pie."

"But doesn't the dealer see you? Or the security cameras?"

"You bet they do!" she laughed. "They think it's a hoot. Even invited me up to their video room once, so I could see myself in action. Usually I make enough to cover the cost of my meds, the cost of the trip, and a little extra."

"And you never got caught? "

"Only once. Had a couple of drinks and got careless. Cost me all my oxys. I didn't get any sleep that night."

"No, I would guess not," I said. "Speaking of OxyContin, this is quite a medication list you've got. These are all your current doses?"

"I wish," she conceded. "But I'm out now. So, if you won't help me, I'll just have to go over to the ER and have me a good old case of respiratory failure. It'll buy me an admission and at least a couple of days of meds. Course, it keeps me on your druggie shit list, but I don't have much choice. A girl's gotta live."

She was certainly right. Going suddenly without her medicines would certainly precipitate respiratory decompensation, possibly even a ventilator and a prolonged stay in the ICU. Her med list was impressive, and although I knew there were doctors who prescribed such doses—for a price—I didn't think there were any around here. "You've been getting these medications by prescription from somebody?" I asked.

"*Somebodies* might be a better word," she admitted. "But don't worry. You don't know them. They're in New York. And it's not cheap. Two hundred dollars cash every two weeks for the visit, plus the medications, plus bus fare. Doesn't leave me much to live on."

"Even with your assets?" I said.

"Yeah, even with them," she smiled ruefully. "Listen, Doc. I'd love to chat. But I'm running out of wind, and I gotta know what you gonna do. You gonna help me or not?"

Out of wind she had been for some time. Our conversation took much longer than is written, as Brittany had to stop at the end of each sentence, and sometimes mid-sentence, to regain her breath. Despite her past behaviors, my heart went out to her.

"I'd like to," I said. "But you're on more medication than I ever prescribe."

"You bet your sweet ass I am," she cried angrily. "And you know who did that for me? Your precious buddies. I was all of fourteen when one of my CF doctors suggested I try some oxys at night to help ease my breathing. He assured me that I didn't have to worry about becoming addicted. Funny thing is, I think he actually believed it."

"He probably did," I admitted. "That would have been back around 2001, wouldn't it?"

"Right. He started low. Didn't want to *'compromise my health,'* he said. That's another hoot," she laughed bitterly. "Course, every six months or so, as my tolerance increased, I needed a boost in my dose. No moral value in pain, he would always say. And he went along with all of it, just as accommodating as you please. Six years ago, he retired, and a new doctor came to the clinic. Arrogant son of a bitch he was. Told me I was an addict. As if I didn't already know that. And that he was going to taper me off my meds and get me into a rehab program. That's when I tried to strangle him."

"And bit the security guard."

"They hauled me into court on assault charges. Judge sent me to a psychiatrist for evaluation." She made a face.

"What?"

"I knew him."

"The psychiatrist?"

"Yeah."

"You were his patient?"

"Nope. Never saw him before, but I knew him all right. Better than he thought."

"How so?"

"My cousin."

"Your cousin was his patient?"

"Nope. My cousin sold him stuff."

"Stuff?"

"Caviar."

"Your cousin is an importer?"

She laughed. "You could say that. But it's not the caviar you're thinking of. At least I hope not. This caviar may have been fishy, but it didn't come from no fish."

"I don't understand."

"My cousin is a dealer. Caviar is a specialty of his. It's a mixture of coke and weed. The shrink was one of his best customers. And you know what's the funniest thing? First off, he wants to know my family history. I told him. My dad's an alkie. My mom is on methadone. My older brother died of an OD, and my younger one is a crackhead. My uncle, my cousin's dad, he used to give us Percs as reward for doing chores for him. After I told him all that, you know what he told me? That addiction ran in my family. I almost said he should know. Course the whole time he was talking to me, he never once looked me in the eye."

"The silicone stare?"

"Yup. Told me I had PTSD and ADD—oh yeah, and bipolar too. Oh, a regular Sigmund Freud, he was."

"You're not talking Freud the analyst."

"I'm talking Sigmund Freud the cokehead. The shrink told me he understood my problems. Which I bet he did. Woulda given me back my stims too, I bet, except he wanted to see me for therapy. I wasn't that hard up."

"And ever since then you've had to go south for your meds."

"Not right off. For a couple of years, I could find a doctor here and a doctor there who would give me some, and as long as I kept switching pharmacies and swiped a few extra prescriptions from his pad, I did okay. But then the damn monitoring system came in, and I had to go to the Big Apple."

"I see. I'm surprised, though. That dose of opiates added to all those benzodiazepines—it's not a very safe combination."

"Might knock me for a loop?" she snorted. "Tell me, Doc, do I look like someone who is about to OD, huh?"

She did not.

"Course if you want to give me my stims back to keep me on the alert, I wouldn't say no. Used to get them as a kid, ya know, but then after I got on the oxys, and they started checking my urine and found THC, they told me that they couldn't give me Adderall if I was smoking pot. Told 'em I never smoked it, but that didn't help. Guess their limit was three poisons. Anyway, it doesn't do much. Can't get high on anything anymore. Marijuana does help me sleep, though."

"How about your CF meds?"

"Sometimes I take 'em. But mostly I don't. Don't see the point. I'm just about at the end of my rope, you know. Life expectancy, as you call it, for someone born in 1985 isn't even thirty. So, I'm living on stolen time."

The thing of it was, I liked her. She was sassy and spunky and smart. And she had a sense of humor. She had a terrible disease, and she was right—she didn't have long to live. But she didn't let it get to her. She deserved whatever break she could get.

"Okay," I said.

"Okay, everything?"

"The Xanax and Ambien…"

"I know," she conceded, "it's a bit much. Tell the truth, Doc. If I get my oxys regular, and I got my vape at night, I can live with that. One thing, though, Doc."

"Yes?"

"You ain't 'zactly a spring chicken."

"How long am I going to last?"

"Not to put too fine a point on it."

"I'll make you a deal."

"Okay."

"I won't retire until after you die."

"Deal."

CHAPTER 15

In the months following Brittany's visit, more new patients appeared in my schedule. At first, it was only one a week, but eventually I could count on at least one or two fresh faces every clinic session. One month I even was the top performer in the new-patient metric. Our rather surprised CEO called me into his office to congratulate me.

"I don't know how you've done it, Beach, but you have really turned yourself around. I was sure you didn't have the lure any more, and that you'd hauled in your last catch. But I have to admit, I was wrong. You're certainly reeling them in now, and I see from your demographics that your haul is from waters outside our usual fishing grounds. I don't know what you're using as bait, but it certainly is working."

He was exceedingly fond of fishing metaphors. "Glad you're still on board," he said, putting his arm around me and shaking my hand. Then he gave me my incentive reward: one free meal in the hospital cafeteria.

I told him thank you but that I didn't really deserve the credit. He said I was being overly modest.

But I wasn't.

The patients had indeed come from far and wide. And, unlike most new patients I had acquired in the recent years, they had no apparent connection with anyone in my current practice. Even the age was different. One was almost sixty, but the rest were much younger, ranging in age from eighteen to mid-forties. They did, however, have one thing in common.

Their diagnosis.

Its location, its cause, and its duration varied, but for every single one, the reason for their visit was the same.

Pain.

Pain that was chronic. Pain that was unrelenting. Pain in the back. Pain in the neck. Pain in the legs. Pain all over. Aching pain. Burning pain. Dull pain. Sharp pain. Pain that kept them up at night. Pain that rendered them unable to work. Pain unrelieved by physical therapy or biofeedback or mindfulness. Pain for which all the medicines the other doctors were now giving them had provided no relief. Pain that, for many, had an obvious cause—an injury, an operation, a skeletal malalignment. Pain of which, for others, the cause was a total mystery. Many had been told they had fibromyalgia.

Some knew exactly which medicine they wanted, and how much it would take to relieve their pain. Some said there was a medicine that some doctor had once given them, but the name of which they couldn't exactly remember, although they might if I gave them some suggestions. A few were putting me on, just giving me a story that they hoped would get them the drugs they wanted. But most were not. Their pain was real. And so was their suffering. For them I felt sympathy. Not only for their pain, but for the way that medicine had offered them a relief for many years only to decide now that we had made a mistake. And all were hoping that I, a doctor about whom they had heard such wonderful things, would be able to figure out what the problem was. And give them a medicine that would work.

Which I did—figure out the problem, that is. I told them I would not be able to provide that which they so desperately wanted. (Except for one Vietnam vet, to whom I just couldn't say no. His leg had been shattered by a landmine in the Tet Offensive, and he had found relief first in what was sold on the

streets of Saigon, and then at the VA, where they had treated
him well, until the no-pain-no-gain philosophy gained ascen-
dance.) I felt bad about this, as I already had my own set of patients with whom I had made the same mistake, and for whom
I had accepted responsibility. I did not quite feel up to taking
on others. I used various excuses. Sometimes I said it was because I no longer practiced pain relief. Sometimes I said it was
because I would be retiring soon and didn't want to get them
started on something they couldn't continue. Sometimes I just
said no.

And so, they trooped in, and they trooped out, and it was
a singularly unsatisfying experience for both of us.

When Brittany came in for her follow-up visit, I mentioned the phenomenon to her.

"Figures," she said.

"Can I ask you something?" I said.

"I didn't send them."

"Okay."

"Didn't have to. Like bees to honey, Doc. It's a small world
here. Soon as people found out I wasn't going to New York for
my stuff, they wanted to know where I was getting it. I told 'em
none of their business. My cousin, though, the one who drives
me up here, he's a blabbermouth. But I'll tell you what, seein'
as how I'm responsible in a way, and seein' as how you've been
so straight with me, I'll see what I can do."

"It would be a big favor."

"I was thinking maybe one more oxy at night."

"Not quite that big."

"Can't blame a girl for trying."

My flurry of new patients stopped as mysteriously as it
started, much to the chagrin of our CEO. He called me in to
find out what had happened. Told him I didn't have the faintest
idea. Must have been some kind of fluke. He agreed it must
have been. And we left it at that.

I called Brittany to thank her. "I don't know what you did, but I'm not getting any more pain patients. I appreciate that."

"My pleasure, Doc," she said. "It was easy. I just let the word out that you were NG. Told 'em you cut me off my meds quick as you started 'em. Said you was under investigation, and the Feds was looking at all your prescriptions, and they might even be calling in some people. But, hey, thanks for keeping Clarence. He's had it rough."

Clarence was the name of my Vietnam vet. "You know Clarence?" I asked. It wasn't really a question.

"He's my uncle."

*****

Nothing is quite so dispiriting as a hope quashed. To wallow in the shallows of a lesser doldrum is not much fun, but after a time, one becomes accustomed to it. But to see a brighter light on the horizon and find upon closer inspection that it is but an illusion is downright depressing. Which is pretty much the mood I found myself in after my recent experience with the pain patients. Each new patient on my schedule brought a frisson of anticipation, and each encounter with the patient left me feeling empty. If I wasn't being used, I was certainly being useless. More than a few times I found myself thinking maybe it was time. Fifty years as a doctor was, as Heather had so pointedly said, a long time. Was it finally *too* long?

There was one bright spot in my professional life still remaining. The emergency room. It provided a respite, however brief, from my ruminations. The pace was brisk, the decisions were quick, and one had to be focused at all times on the job at hand. Furthermore, the patients I saw were a different set from my stable of aging patients, folks to whom I could offer mainly mitigation and commiseration for their complaints. The ER had more than its share of those whose actual needs were less urgent than the perceived ones, but most of them had problems for which something had to be done, and it had to be done then. There were lacerations to be sewed, bones to be set, medicines to give, and every now and then, a life to save.

There, for a brief time, I would be the kind of doctor I used to be, recollecting fondly those days we always call good old, our memories burnished by the rose-tinted glasses of time. It wasn't the best medicine possible anywhere, but I worked hard to make sure it was the best medicine it could be in Dumster on that day.

Medicine has changed a lot since then, and emergency medicine is no exception. But it is still a place where, whatever has to be done, it has to be done by whoever is there. It's not a come-back-after-we've-run-some-tests place. It's demanding. And it's fun.

Today was even better. Davida was with me. Not with any guidelines or goals. Just on her own. Because she wanted to be there.

It was Saturday. The morning had the usual run of parents who couldn't get their child into the office during the week, and now that they weren't at work, had time to worry whether the sniffle or the cough or the earache might be something more serious. And although for pediatricians this would be humdrum, it was not for me. Being around children who, as opposed to my usual crowd, were invariably less sick than they appeared, was, in proper doses, invigorating—like being a grandparent rather than a parent.

"Dumster ambulance to UCRHC," came a voice over the intercom as I was sitting at the nurses' station, finishing my notes. It was a familiar voice. Ray Seewall had been a Dumster firefighter and EMT ever since he was old enough to drive. His father had been a firefighter before him, and his grandfather had been chief. His wife was the dispatcher. His daughter had followed in her father's footsteps, and it was not unusual to have the father-daughter pair teamed up on a run. The Sewall family *was* emergency services in Dumster. Take them away, and you had a gaping hole that would be impossible to fill.

I picked up the microphone. "Emmeline T. to Dumster ambulance," I said, ignoring the official call letters in favor of the name to which we both were more accustomed. "Read you loud and clear."

"Hey, Doc," came in Ray's gravelly voice. "Good to have you back on the ranch."

"Good to hear you still in the saddle," I answered. It was our standard greeting. "What's up?"

"We are in route to the scene. Adult male down. Keep us on hold."

"Will do." There followed that uncertain and anxious period when no one knew exactly what had happened. Was it just a fainting spell? Was it a seizure? Was it cardiac arrest? It always seemed like forever.

In this case it was ten minutes.

"Dumster ambulance to Emmeline T.," came the call again.

"We are in route to your facility with a fifty-two-year-old male who collapsed at the fairgrounds after complaining of chest pain. At the scene he was pulseless and without respirations. CPR was started. The defibrillator indicated, 'shock patient.' We have given him three shocks at two hundred, three hundred, and three sixty joules, with return of pulse and respirations. Patient is now in normal sinus rhythm, with frequent ventricular ectopy and three millimeters of ST elevation. Request permission to administer TPA and call DHART."

"Permission granted." It was a superfluous gesture, and we both knew it. But protocol was protocol, and when the case would be reviewed by the regional emergency medical services, had Ray gone ahead and done the right thing without my formal permission, there would have been hell to pay.

By the time the ambulance had arrived and unloaded the patient, the helicopter was touching down on the helipad outside the ED. I had just enough time to see who it was and say hello. Buddy Crosby, owner of Buddy's Citgo and a new lease on life, gave a weak hi and a brief squeeze of my hand. And then he was whisked off by the air ambulance crew and on his way to Dartmouth, where a cardiac team would be waiting to take him straight to the cath lab and put a stent in his blocked coronary artery. Total time from pain to stent: fifty-five minutes.

It was modern medicine at its best. Davida was impressed.

"Wow," she said after all the dust had settled. "That was amazing."

"It was," I agreed. "And when I think of how we used to treat heart attacks, it is even more so."

"Which would be my cue to ask you how you used to treat heart attacks."

"If you insist."

"I'm all ears."

"First patient I ever treated for a heart attack died. So did the second. The third survived. I treated them all with what we had."

"And now I ask, which was?"

"Two flowers."

"And now, you're kidding."

"Now I'm not. One was the poppy. And the other…"

Davida smiled. "I get it. Foxglove."

"Right you are. Papaver somniferum, the opium poppy, has been the mainstay of medicinal herbs for thousands of years. Cultivated seeds were found in prehistoric archeological sites near lake Zurich. Hippocrates used it as a cure for those palpitating with unrequited lust, and Alexander the Great relied on it extensively to augment his conquering powers. Medieval Chinese used opium to preserve *vital force*, to strengthen sperm, and to regain vigor. Its price was equal to that of gold."

Opium's popularity was considerably enhanced by the fact that one never had to worry about the patient stopping his medicine. It is a sober reminder to those who think that medicine's fondness for opium is but a recent failure in judgment.

"Digitalis purpura, foxglove, by comparison is a relative newcomer to the therapeutic scene," I continued. "In the eighteenth century there lived a physician in Shropshire, England, by the name of William Withering. Doctor Withering made a name for himself as the father of digitalis with a paper on his discovery that patients suffering from dropsy, the term used at the time for congestive heart failure, showed dramatic improvement after being treated with an extract from the foxglove plant. The discovery was not due to any investigative prowess on Doctor Withering's part. Its proximate cause was one of his patients, who, despite his best efforts, continued to suffer from her dropsy. One day the patient returned, miraculously cured of her condition. Upon questioning, Doctor Withering discovered that the patient, having received no benefit from the potions he had prescribed, ventured to obtain a second opinion. The opinion she sought was that of Old Mother Hutton, a local folk herbalist who had a special mixture she employed in such cases. And it was Mother Hutton's herbal mixture that did the trick. Obtaining some for himself, Doctor Withering discovered the active ingredient to be leaves of the foxglove plant. He wasted no time in making a name for himself. Mother Hutton may have been a better investigator, but Doctor Withering was much the better marketer. And so it was he, and not Mother Hutton, who got the credit for the discovery of digitalis."

"You know an awful lot of history, Beach."

"It comes with age."

Later in the day Chet Paquin came in. He had fallen off a ladder and injured his wrist. The x-ray showed a slightly displaced fracture of the distal radius, a Colles fracture as its commonly known. I showed Davida the fracture line and the dorsal angulation that indicated displacement, and I showed her how to inject a local anesthetic into the resulting hematoma. Then, once the area was numb, I asked her to hold on to the arm while I pushed the bone back into place, which made a satisfying crunch. We put a plaster splint on Chet's arm, and I told him to call the orthopedics clinic on Monday to arrange a follow-up.

"That was satisfying," said Davida smiling. "We actually did something. But I didn't know internists could set fractures."

"We can't."

"How did you learn?"

"From Sandi and Loree."

"You mean…?"

"Yep."

"Do I detect another story?"

"You do."

"First week I was in Dumster, Hiram Stedrock came into the ER, because Daisy sat on him."

"Daisy, I'm guessing, being a cow."

"Daisy being a cow. Hiram's wrist being broken. I knew this because after Sandi took the x-ray, she pointed it out to me, adding the useful information that it was nondisplaced. Armed with this information, I asked Loree to contact the orthopedic surgeon on call. 'He won't come,' she said. 'It's a fractured wrist,' I said, 'and he's an orthopedic surgeon.' 'It's a *nondisplaced* fracture,' she countered. 'And it's Saturday.'

"I asked her to call him anyway. She did. And she reported smugly that he was currently in the operating room in Windsor and was unavailable for the rest of the day. When I then suggested she call an ambulance to take him to Windsor, she actually laughed.

"Hiram, hearing all this, asked why I didn't just set it myself. I told him I had never set a broken wrist before. He allowed as how he'd never broke one before neither, and so he guessed we were about even. And then he said that if I would do the best I could, that was okay by him. So, with Loree instructing me, and Sandi looking on for entertainment, I put on a cast that must have weighed at least a pound. Hiram allowed that at least he wouldn't have to worry about getting blowed away in a big wind. Loree's only comment was, 'You'll take it off.'

"And from then on, with the help of Sandi in x-ray and Loree in the emergency room, I gradually increased my competence in orthopedics, until I could handle most of the simple things without any trouble."

"Do you miss those days?" Davida asked when I had finished.

"I do. I was more useful then. But it's a purely selfish nostalgia. When you have to be a Jack of all trades…"

"You did the best you could."

"I did."

"And there was no one else to do it."

"There's that."

The rest of the afternoon was quiet. Then, that evening we had a case the outcome of which was perhaps more significant for me than it was for the patient. Which, in his case, is saying a lot.

"Dumster ambulance to Emmeline T," came the call. "We are on route to your facility with a twenty-five-year-old male, overdose victim, presumed fentanyl. Patient has received two milligrams of Narcan and is now awake and semiconscious. Pupils remain pinpoint, and respirations are eight. We are giving another dose of Narcan now. ETA is three minutes."

Davida let out an involuntary gasp. She was twenty-four. She would certainly know him.

And she did.

Tommy Dufresne—Mister T, as he was known in high school—was a year ahead of Davida at Dumster High. In his day, he was as much of hero on the gridiron as Davida was on the court. The T stood for touchdown. Tommy could thread a pass through a needle, and he could run like a gazelle. Like Davida, he was heavily recruited for college, and not just by the smaller schools that traditionally were the final grazing grounds for Vermont athletes. In the end he accepted a full scholarship to the University of Maryland.

From the start, he struggled. He struggled with the demands of college courses. And he struggled to accept that he was a not very big fish in a very big pond. But Tommy was not a quitter. Accepting that he was not big enough to be a Division One quarterback, he switched to safety, where his speed and agility were more important than his size. And he made the team. He didn't make the traveling squad his first year, but he showed enough promise that the coach told him he would certainly see action as a sophomore.

He never did.

A torn ACL in practice ended Tommy's football career two months after the start of school.

Deprived of his one true love, Tommy lost interest in college. When he came home for Christmas that first year, he didn't go back. His father ran a small-engine-repair business, and Tommy went to work for him.

The people of Dumster are loyal folk, and their heroes remain heroes. Tommy was still Mister T. Wherever he went, he was met with a welcoming smile and a heartfelt greeting. He now had a steady girlfriend, Charlene, and a two-year-old son, Blakeley. To all appearances he seemed to have made a successful transition to adult life.

"Oh, Tommy!" said Davida. "I didn't know."

"Hid it pretty good, didn't I? Even my stay at Maple Tree."

"Charlene said you were on a hunting trip."

"Sounds better than rehab."

"But when…?"

"When? When I was at U Maryland."

"Party life?"

"Nope." He pointed to Davida and then to me. "Doctor's office."

"They sent me home from my ACL repair with sixty Percs. Told me not to be afraid to use them if I needed to. Told me also to be sure to take a couple before PT. Said it would make my rehabilitation go better if I was pain free. Well, I never had much pain, and Advil did a pretty good job with what I did have, but I figured if he gave 'em to me, then I should probably take them, so I did. And then I didn't have any pain at all. So, I kept taking them, before PT, like he said, and then at bedtime, and then first thing in the morning when I was a little stiff. Nothing I couldn't deal with before, but with the Percs, I didn't have to. Pretty soon I found out I liked 'em. They helped me relax before exams. They helped me sleep. They kept me from worrying about flunking out. There's a laugh for you. Well, by the time I had finished that prescription, I was on my way. When I went back to the doctor, I told him I was still having pain. He wrote me a prescription for ninety more. Said it should last a month. Didn't, of course. So I called him and said I had accidentally flushed them down the toilet, and he gave me a refill. Then I told him they were stolen, and I got another refill. This went on maybe three months, and by that time, I was up to more than twelve a day. After a year, Percs just weren't doing it for me. The guy selling to me gave me some heroin to try. Said it would fix me up good. Sure did." Tommy laughed ruefully. "First, I smoked it, and then I shot up. For a bit, I was on top of the world. That didn't last long. Past six years I been using just to keep from getting sick. Getting high's a thing of the past.

"I kept lying to Charlene about being clean, but then one day she came home and found my stuff. Told me I had two choices, her or the needle. She made the call to Maple Tree, and I signed myself in. Was there a month. They detoxed me over about a week and kept me another three weeks for 'intensive inpatient therapy.' Group therapy, individual therapy, psychotherapy. The whole works. They put me on antidepressants. I gotta say, they did a good job. When I left I was feeling better than I had felt since high school. And I didn't have the least desire to shoot up. I knew I had it licked. Seems like ages ago now. Hard to believe it was only last month."

"But…"

"Yeah, but. The guy I used to buy from came by the shop one day to get his mower repaired. Said he didn't have any cash, but he could pay me in dope. Said it was real good. Cut with fentanyl, he bragged. Had it with him, of course. He knew that I could never say no when the stuff was right in front of me. They had told us all about exposure risk at Maple Tree, but I didn't have a clue what it was like until that day. And I didn't have a snowball's chance in hell of turning him down. All he had to do was tell me it was there, and I had a craving like I never had before. I didn't care about my reputation. I didn't care about Charlene. I didn't care about my kid. All I cared about was that needle in my arm. And you can't resist it. You know it's wrong, and you know it won't satisfy, and you know afterwards you are going to feel terribly guilty and ashamed."

"It must be awful," said Davida. "I can't imagine what it's like."

"No," said Tommy. "I don't expect you could. But, okay, everyone has cravings. That's what they always told us in rehab. So there must be something you crave."

"There is," she admitted sheepishly. "Chocolate chip cookies. If I don't see them, I'm okay, but if they're in front of me, even if I've already had my fill, I've got to have one—no, that's not right. I've got to have more than one. Usually, I can resist the urge, but sometimes, I just can't."

Tommy laughed. "Yeah, I know all about *usually*. Anyway, I'd have to say that in the department of cravings, that's pretty wimpy, unless you binge on them, which from looking at you, I'd say you don't. But if that's the best you can do, imagine this: Multiply that craving by ten, by a hundred. Then put that craving in your brain every waking minute of the day, and put that craving into your dreams every night. Make that craving so that you can't think about anything else but satisfying that craving. Then you might be getting close."

*****

If there is ever an argument against the premise of intelligent design, I would simply submit as evidence the existence of cravings and call it point, game, set, and match. They are the monsters inside us. We all have them. They come in different shapes and sizes. Some are more socially acceptable than others. Some are just a minor nuisance. Some can take over your life—like drugs and gambling and cell phones and Facebook.

There are scientists who make a living out of trying to prove the obvious. Like showing that feeling bad is harmful to your sense of well-being, or that breathing on a regular basis is good for your health. A couple of months ago, a psychiatrist determined, by looking at MRI activity, that the brain responds to chocolate chip cookies in the same way that it responds to crystal meth. Which I suppose would be useful information if you could get patients to switch. The brain may not be very smart, but it's not that stupid.

The psychiatrist's finding is, however, a powerful reminder that before you judge an addict, walk a mile in his craving.

*****

By now Tommy was fully awake and ready to go home. Davida asked the obvious question.

"What now, Tommy?"

He looked thoughtful. "Well," he said slowly, "let's see. I've been an addict now for seven years. Before Maple Tree, I was never without it more than a day. Finished a good rehab program. Felt great when I left. Was clean for one month. And first real chance I get, I relapse. I don't think abstinence is in the cards."

"You're thinking of medication assisted therapy?" Davida asked.

Tommy laughed. "I love you guys. Just can't help yourselves, can you? You gotta call a spade a manually operated soil remodeling instrument. But yeah, I'm talking about bupe."

CHAPTER 16

Fueled in part by the addition of a new opiate—fentanyl—we are in the midst of an opiate epidemic. Depending on how one counts, it is the third or fourth such epidemic this country has experienced.

The first epidemic began after the Civil War. Morphine was the driver of that one. Purified from opium earlier in the century, morphine was used extensively to treat wounds sustained in the war. After the war, its use spread to both those who had been treated and their families, the former receiving it by prescription from their doctor for continued pain and the latter by access to the patient's medicine cabinet.

The second epidemic started at the end of the nineteenth century and continued into the early twentieth. It was to some extent an extension of the first. Laudanum, a liquid form of opium, was already a popular weapon in a doctor's pharmaceutical armamentarium. When morphine was added to increase its potency, laudanum became the go-to drug for just about everything. Benefitting from a lack of regulation, manufacturers of patent medicines were quick to jump on the bandwagon. Having relied up to that point primarily on the supplementation of alcohol to a concoction of herbs, chemicals, and anything else they could find lying around, the pharmaceutical industry discovered that the addition of opium not only enhanced their products' popularity, but also ensured the loyalty of the customer.

Because women did most of the purchasing for their family, many of products were designed to treat what was called "women's troubles." But no one was left out. There was an opiate for every age, gender, and affliction. There was Mrs. Winslow's Soothing Syrup for fussy and teething babies. Sears sold a morphine-laced mix for neglected wives to use on their spouses. It was to be slipped surreptitiously into a wayward husband's coffee in order to keep him home at night. There were even opiates that were promoted as the cure for addiction. Habitina was one such, sold as an "infallible cure for drug habits of all kinds." But the most ingenious opiate marketers of them all were, perhaps, a pair of Pennsylvania butchers, the Greens, father and son. Dr. A. Boschee's German Syrup was the name of their product. Using the model by which drug pushers now initiate their customers—offering the first hit for free—they did a mass mailing of product samples to thousands of unsuspecting customers.

The third and arguably deadliest of the epidemics was the heroin epidemic of the 1950s. Its cause was the introduction of the hypodermic syringe, which allowed the intravenous administration of opiates. Because of its more rapid action, heroin became the drug of choice for delivering opiates to the brain. Concentrated in the large inner-city populations, especially New York, which had half of the nation's addicts, the death rate from opiate overdose at its peak was double that of our current epidemic. Its one silver lining was that it also brought about an effective treatment for opiate addiction. Taking Bayer's success to its logical conclusion, the profession recognized that for most addicts, one had to fight fire with fire.

In 1964, two researchers at the Rockefeller Institute, Vincent Dole and Marie Nyswander, began treating a group of heroin addicts with a prescription opiate in the hopes that it would stop their heroin use. It was a synthetic opiate, invented pursuant to the wishes of Hitler, who wanted Germany to have pharmaceutical independence from the rest of the world.

Motivated solely by its patriotic duty, Germany's IG Farben in 1939 created a new opiate. Its name was methadone. Relying on a marketing strategy that Germany's other great pharmaceutical manufacturer, Bayer, had employed so successfully some forty years earlier, IG Farben heavily advertised methadone as an excellent pain reliever with little risk of addiction. Although the addiction claim was a blatant lie, it was nonetheless true that methadone, while still potentially deadly, carried a lower risk of overdose because it was a much slower- and longer-acting opiate. Doctors Nyswander and Dole determined that a single dose a day could suffice, not only to forestall withdrawal symptoms, but also block the anticipated euphoria should the patient happen to inject heroin while under methadone's influence. And discourage further use of heroin.

The results were striking. Opiate overdoses—and criminal behavior—decreased dramatically among those taking methadone. Methadone maintenance quickly became an accepted treatment for those who were addicted and unable to achieve abstinence, and in 1972 the US federal government provided public funding to establish clinics for methadone maintenance.

Addicted persons had to jump through many hoops in order to qualify as methadone patients. Regulations required patients to be directly observed while taking the medicine, and methadone could be dispensed only in federally licensed facilities. In 2002, there was one such facility in the state of Vermont. The feds had created a treatment plan that was both highly effective and largely inaccessible.

Enter buprenorphine, or as Tommy Dufresne and many others called it, "bupe." To explain the difference between buprenorphine and other opiates, I must temporarily immerse the reader into the murky waters of pharmacodynamics. I promise I will make the experience brief, in hopes that you may emerge enlightened from the baptism but will not drown in it.

*****

Many of the functions that the cells in our body perform are dependent upon the action of chemicals that do not reside within the cells. It could be a chemical already existing elsewhere in your body, like insulin or estrogen or adrenalin. Or it could be a chemical that is introduced into your body, like caffeine or Lipitor or aspirin. Before these chemicals can have any effect on a particular cell, they must first gain entry into that cell. They do this by attaching to a kind of a docking station on the outside of the cell. Each chemical has its own personal docking station. It's a dedicated docking station that allows that chemical, *and only that chemical*, to attach to the outside of a cell and then gain entry, so that it can do whatever it is that the chemical intends to do. We call these docking stations receptors. Security at receptors is very high. For example, if you want to dock at an insulin receptor, unless you are insulin or something that is almost identical, you are out of luck. The same is true for all the other receptors. It is very hard to fool a receptor.

The receptor for opiates is called the mu receptor. Mu is a transliteration of the Greek letter μ. Greek letters and words are quite popular in our profession. They lend an air of profundity to things that we do not understand.

Some cells are loaded with mu receptors. Some have none. Certain brain cells are especially rich in mu receptors, particularly those that affect how we feel. Somewhere in the evolutionary past, the need for our brains to respond to pleasurable stimuli so that we could feel good was determined to be important for advancement of the species. For that purpose we got endorphin. Endorphin makes us feel good. It creates what we like to call a natural high. Endorphin is safe. You cannot overdose on endorphin. Of course, for endorphin to work, there have to be endorphin receptors. Otherwise the endorphins would just float around aimlessly in your body, acting about as useful as roadside litter. So we got mu receptors to allow endorphin to work. It's not just humans who have endorphin. Bears have endorphin. When they are hibernating, they have very high endorphin levels. The surest way to arouse a bear from hibernation is to inject that bear with a dose of Narcan. But you better be able to run really quick. Snakes and alligators and toads have endorphin. So do flies and clams. I don't know if anyone has ever studied what increases endorphin in a clam, but I'll bet one thing is high tide. Unfortunately, the human species had no idea that someday the mu receptor for endorphin would allow in a set of imposters that would wreak havoc on us. How could it have?

There are many opiates that attach to mu receptors, but they don't all have the same effect. Imagine that there is an engine in the brain. It's the feelgood engine. The engine has a switch. The settings on the switch include off and full speed and several in between. To turn on the engine, you must insert a key in the switch. The key is an opiate, and the switch is a mu receptor. There are three basic types of keys.

One key turns the switch all the way on, allowing the feelgood engine to run at full speed. This kind of key is called an agonist. Some agonist keys turn the switch to high very fast, others more slowly.

Another key turns off the switch. If the engine is already off when this key is inserted, nothing happens. But if the engine is running, especially if it is running at top speed, the key will shut down the engine immediately, stopping all feelgood activity and precipitating a feelbad—that's withdrawal. This key, the opposite of the agonist, is an antagonist. Narcan is the best-known antagonist. As in Tommy's case, it is used to reverse the effects of an opiate overdose, for which purpose it is very effective.

Then there is the third key. This key is a tricky one. It turns the engine to half speed. If the engine is off, it will turn it on and give you a moderate feelgood. But if the engine is already running at full feelgood speed, it will slow it down, and you will be in feelbad—you will be in withdrawal. We call this kind of key a partial agonist. It can cause a bit of a high, or it can cause some withdrawal, depending on the situation.

We now know that not all brains have the same sized engines. Most engines are of average size, but some are very small, and some are very big and very powerful. There are more brains with these big engines than you might imagine. And when the agonist key is inserted in the switch, the people with these brains feel *very* good. And when it's turned off, they feel *very* bad. Such engines make people much more susceptible to the effect of opiates. It's not their fault. They are just built that way.

Among the agonists, fentanyl is the most rapidly acting. Whether it makes you very high or very dead depends on how much of it you take. Because it is a new drug, many opiate users have to experiment to find the right dose. Which is made difficult by the fact that the person who buys a packet never knows how much drug it contains. There is no truth in packaging in the street opiate business. Unfortunately, that means that often the experiment turns out very bad.

Heroin is almost as quick as fentanyl. Oxycodone and morphine are slower. Methadone is the slowest of them all.

Buprenorphine is a partial agonist. It turns the engine to only half speed. Which makes it a less than attractive choice for someone who wants to get really high. It also stays in the body a long time, several days in fact. During that time, it blocks the action of any full agonist a person might take.

Which brings me to the point of this digression.

Buprenorphine is a kinder, gentler opiate.

Recognizing its greater safety, the Drug Enforcement Administration licensed it for treatment in a doctor's office in 2002. Unable, however, to resist its cravings for creating barriers to medical management of opiate addiction, the DEA required that before doctors could prescribe buprenorphine, they had to take a course to learn about the drug. The administration said this was to ensure that those who prescribed the drug were competent to do so. Which would be a reasonable expectation, were it not for the fact that they allow us to provide full-strength opiates in unlimited doses without any restrictions whatsoever.

*****

"You're talking about going on Suboxone?" Davida asked Tommy.

"Yep. I can't afford to trust myself with sobriety again. At least not now. And I can't take a chance of another relapse like today. Not for Blakeley. Not for Charlene. And not for me. In that order."

Davida turned to me. "Can you prescribe Suboxone, Beach?"

"Excuse me?"

Davida blushed. "Oops! I'm sorry. I mean buprenorphine naloxone sublingual film."

"Much better." Generic is the language preferred these days. At least by students.

"Suboxone is rather easier to say," she said.

"Virtually trips off the tongue."

"Or under it."

"Indeed."

"Well then, by any other name, can you prescribe it?" Davida asked.

"No. I'm not certified as a buprenorphine prescriber."

She looked at me without speaking. But her look said, why not?

The truth was, I didn't really have an answer. It wasn't that getting certified was such a big deal, and it wasn't that I had any real objection to treating opiate addiction with opiates, but some part of me felt that by so doing I was condoning rather than treating.

I wasn't proud of the feeling.

"That's okay, Doc," said Tommy. "Hardly anybody around here does. I only wish you guys had had the same reservations when you gave me the Percs. There is a guy down in Windsor who prescribes Suboxone. Not sure how I can get there, since they took my license away. If I have to, I can buy it on the street. It's a lot more expensive than heroin or fentanyl, but a guy's gotta do what he's gotta do."

Charlene came by to pick him up. She nodded to Davida and after a very few words to Tommy, none of which were particularly sympathetic to a person who had just almost died, took him home.

"Beach…," said Davida.

"I will."

"I'm glad."

That night at supper, as had been our custom for the past forty-four years, Trine and I had our day in review. She would tell me about hers, and I about mine.

I told her about Tommy.

Since we had returned to Vermont from Philadelphia, Trine had been working in Burlington with an organization that she had created. Its purpose was to provide legal representation and social supports to women whose children were under the jurisdiction of Vermont's Department for Children and Families, almost always because of the mother's addiction. It did not enhance her already dim view of my profession.

"I don't know which is worse," she sputtered angrily, "your arrogance or your hypocrisy.

"That's the royal you, of course," she added, after a rather long pause.

"Of course."

"First you pump them full of opiates. And then you cut them off. And then, when they come back in because they have tried to stay away from the drugs that you got them hooked on, and they can't—because you made sure the hook was in good and solid—you turn them away. You're just as bad as the folks in the Department for Children and Families. They say their business is child protection—child confiscation it is, more often than not.

"Last week I was at a termination of parental rights hearing in Burlington with one of my clients. Because the mother was on buprenorphine, the DCF worker refused to let the child return to her mother, even though her doctor and her therapist testified that she had been doing just great for over two years. The DCF worker wouldn't even allow visits, unless they were supervised, and you know how they set up supervised visits."

I did. It is a cruel, although not unusual, punishment. The visits had to be at the DCF office, which was way out on Industrial Avenue in Williston. For most of Trine's clients that meant at least two bus transfers and a half-mile walk on a busy road without sidewalks. And even if they could get there, it could be only when a worker was available to supervise, which would be solely at the convenience of the worker.

"The worker is on the stand testifying about how she just can't be sure the child will be safe, and when I ask her why not, she says, 'Because she's an addict.' And when I ask her about the patient's recovery, she says, 'She's still an addict.' It's the shame-and-blame game. They're so self-righteous—and so young. Most have never been a parent. None has ever been poor. They have not the slightest damn idea what it does to a mother to have her child taken away, and what kind of courage and determination it takes to stay in recovery in order to get them back. And they don't care. My client has been on Suboxone now for almost three years, and you know what she has to do to get it?"

I could guess.

"She lives in Hinesburg. To get to the clinic, she has to take the bus to Burlington and then another one out to San Remo Drive. In order to get there by eight-thirty, which is when she picks up her meds, she has to leave by seven. And that's assuming that the busses are running on time, which in winter is not always true. The first year she had to go in five days a week. She got take-home meds only for the weekend. Now she gets a week's supply at a time. Every time she has to pick up her Suboxone, she misses at least one hour of work. Fortunately, she has a sympathetic boss. Not all of them are. And you know why she has to go through all this? Because of her doctor—the same one, by the way, who had given her the Percocets for what he told her was a bad case of fibromyalgia. Fibro-my-assia! He was just looking for an excuse to give her the drugs so she wouldn't complain about a problem he couldn't figure out. When she asked him for Suboxone, you know what the doctor said? He said he wasn't *comfortable* prescribing it. Gimme a break. What's her doctor's comfort got to do with it, huh!?"

Comfort has been the universal excuse of doctors who are too cowardly to admit the real reason for not doing what they know is right.

They don't want to.

I didn't need to point this out to Trine.

"So," she said, glaring at me, "are you gonna do the right thing—finally?"

"I'm signing up tomorrow."

CHAPTER 17

The certification course was being held in Burlington. It was a two-day course. Since Burlington is only an hour and twenty minutes from Dumster, it was no big deal to go back and forth each day. Which is what I planned to do.

Until I talked to Trine.

"I'll go with you," she said. "We can stay the night and go out to dinner and see a show. And people-watch. Make a weekend of it. Besides, I'd like to listen to what the pontificators have to say."

"Do the Queen City."

"Paint the little berry red."

We had come to Vermont from San Francisco, by way of Boston, London, New York, and Oslo. It would be fair to say that at the time, Burlington felt *very* small. But forty years tends to contract one's view of the world, and now Burlington is plenty big. As Stephen Stills said, "Love the one you're with."

And we do. We love the restaurants. We love the Flynn theater and the Roxy cinema. And we love Church Street. One thing we especially love about a city is watching people. Church Street is the usual place for this activity. In the summer, many of the restaurants have outdoor seating, so one can enjoy a meal, or even just a coffee, and watch the people stroll by. The only problem is that in the matter of diversity, things pretty much peter out after French Canadian. So, we usually prefer to go over to Nunyuns in the Old North End. The best time is 3 o'clock in the afternoon on Fridays.

Back in 1980, Burlington became a refugee-resettlement city. Ever since then, it has been graced by a wave of immigrants from inhospitable lands far away. First from Vietnam and Cambodia and Tibet, then from Bosnia and Nepal, and more recently from Somalia, Sudan, Burundi, and the Congo. In Burlington they have made their home primarily in the Old North End, a one-square-mile neighborhood immediately north of downtown. While 95 percent of Vermonters are people of pallor, the Old North End is different. And when school lets out just around the corner from the restaurant, the stream of kids and their families passing by on their way home or to the local markets can make one feel, if only for a brief time, that one is a part of the world beyond our borders.

Small though Burlington may be, is not without urban problems. There is crime and urban blight in Burlington. There was a murder not long ago over a drug deal, and everybody still remembers it. And there is homelessness too, but the combination of harsh winters and a shortage of shelters make it less than in more hospitable climates. Urban blight is indeed a problem that threatens our idyllic way of life. A developer wants to put a 160-foot-tall building in Burlington, *right in the middle of downtown*. That's more than two stories taller than the tallest building in town, and almost as tall as the steeple on the Ira Allen Chapel at the University of Vermont. Concerned citizens are convinced that this building will destroy life in Burlington as they would like to pretend it is. And these concerned citizens should certainly know what is what, as mostly they come from places where a 160-foot-tall building is just a molehill. So far, we have only a hole in the ground, but if the developer prevails, we will find out if it means apocalypse for Burlington.

The certification course was being held in a downtown waterfront hotel that is 116 feet tall.

The course director was a thin, almost gaunt man with an unruly shock of black hair peppered with gray. He had coal-black eyes; a narrow, pointed nose; and unsmiling lips. His face wore an expression that could have been mistaken for careworn, were it not for a restlessness about him that bespoke more of exasperation. Although he was only about five feet six inches tall, there was an energy about him that made one quickly forget his modest stature. The entire effect was that of a man who was engaged in a furious battle with a greater foe, and who was determined, despite all odds, not to yield. In age he appeared to be about sixty.

"My name is Jonathan Kellman," he said, leaning forward on the lectern and surveying us with a dissatisfied eye—as though he knew we would not measure up to his expectations. "Before I start, I am going to tell you how I wound up being here in front of you.

"I was born in 1972 in Brooklyn, New York. I know," he said, looking at us grimly, "I am not as old as I look. And, in due course, I will tell you why. I grew up on Pulaski Street in Bed-Stuy. Those of you familiar with this neighborhood will know what that means." He paused looking for signs of recognition. Seeing none, he added. "For those who don't, I will explain.

"PS 25 was my elementary school. There was a kid in my class named Harry Johnson. Harry was a sickly kid. He was very pale and completely bald. He missed a lot of school. Harry never played with other kids. We all avoided him, as if just to be near him might contaminate us with whatever it was he had. And we made fun of him. 'Hairless,' we called him. One day an old man came into the classroom. He was small and wrinkled and wore large glasses. At the invitation of the teacher, he sat down at one of the desks in the front of the room and turned around to face us. He had a big smile and an enchanting voice. 'Somebody in this room has a birthday today,' he said. 'Who is it?' We all looked around. Nobody raised a hand. The old man repeated his question. Slowly Harry raised his hand. The old man went over and sat down beside him. 'You Harry?' he asked.

Harry nodded. 'Wrote a song,' he said, 'for your birthday.' And he sang 'I'm Just Wild about Harry.' We knew he hadn't actually written the song for Harry, because we knew the song. It was a song we had heard many times before. Our parents sang it. It was on the radio. But still, we were impressed. Then he turned to the class and said, 'Now everybody, sing it with me,' and he went over the song several times until we got it right.

"The teacher thanked the old man for coming. Then she asked him if he had anything he wanted to say to the children. 'Sure do,' he said. 'Always be kind. Makes you feel a whole lot better than being mean. And don't mess with drugs.' He gestured out the window. 'I grew up in a place like this, so I know what it's like. Stay away from them. They're out there, you know, and they'll be calling for you soon enough—iffen they ain't already. But don't pay 'em no heed. They'll kill you, sure as shootin'. I know. Almost killed me.' They were just simple platitudes, but we all nodded, because we knew we would never touch drugs.

"We were in the fourth grade.

"After he left, the teacher told us his name: Eubie Blake." Kellman stopped talking and looked at us. "Anybody here recognize that name?" A couple of us nodded. "Of course, we kids didn't know that he was one of the great jazz musicians of the twentieth century. After he died, they renamed PS 25 in his honor.

"We were nicer to Harry after that. Harry didn't make it. He died before we got to high school. There were other PS 25 kids who didn't make it either. Some have died from AIDS. Some have died from overdose. Some are in prison. Most of them never went beyond high school, and often, not even to high school.

"I was lucky. I had a good family, and I was a smart kid. I got into Brooklyn Tech, and from there I went to Brooklyn College. I got into two medical schools, Columbia and Downstate. Both are good schools. Downstate was the logical choice. It was only three miles away, so I could still live at home, an idea my parents found exceedingly persuasive. I went to Columbia. Most of my classmates came from top universities and well-off communities. I was the kid from Brooklyn. An urban hick. They liked me well enough, but still could not resist kidding me. Brooklyn became my nickname. It stuck with me.

"My residency was at Bellevue. During the last year of my residency I was working in the ER when a DOA drug overdose came in. It was one of three that day, which was about par for Bellevue. It was common practice then for residents to sharpen our skills at inserting breathing tubes into the lungs by practicing on these unfortunates. That there may have been an ethics issue involved never crossed our minds. We were there to learn, and what better opportunity to do so than on a body to which we could do no harm. 'Hey, Brooklyn,' one of my colleagues hollered at me, 'check out the junk pile in room three.' I dutifully trooped in to take my turn. 'Gang intubation' we called it.

"We saw a lot of death at Bellevue. The deaths we preferred were those in which we played some kind of role, minor as it may have been, in the shuffling off of the mortal coil. They were deaths that came after we had finished fussing with them to our satisfaction and their diseases had run their course. But this kind of death—unexpected, abrupt, arriving as a finished product before we even laid eyes upon them, and arising from someone who in age was not as removed from us as we would like them to be—made us uncomfortable. We were young, and we were guys. We suffered from maturation arrest. So, we resorted to the usual measures of immature guys in uncomfortable situations—crudity and inappropriate humor. It helped us to avoid the there-but-for-the-grace feeling.

"When my turn came, I went in. The fellow before me handed me a bloodied laryngoscopy and endotracheal tube. 'Go for it,' he said. 'Piece of cake. Got in on the first try.'

"But I couldn't. I didn't even try. Lying before me was a body I had seen before. It belonged to who was once Danel Washington. Danel had lived on my street. We used to call him Danny Boy. Not because he was Irish. But because one summer night we were out late playing stickball, when Danel's younger sister came running up. 'Dann-ee! Boy, you better get yourself home right now! Mamma's mad at yo-uu.' From that day on, he was Danny Boy. As we got older, our circles grew further apart, and after I went to college, the only contact we ever had was to say hi on the street.

"I went to the bathroom and threw up. And I remembered the fourth-grade visit from Eubie Blake. That night I told my wife, Maggie, what had happened. We talked it over, and we both agreed—it was time to find somewhere else to raise our family. I wasn't really sure until that night what I wanted to do in medicine. But Danel Washington decided me. We moved to Burlington in 2000, and in 2002, when the state's first methadone clinic opened, I took a job there. Been here ever since.

"I know I look older than I am. Contrary to what you might be thinking, the reason for my premature appearance of age is not the world I came from. The reason I am old before my time is," he said, before pausing and looking around the room, "you.

"By which I do not mean each of you in particular, at least not considering why you have come here today. It would be more accurate to say, if I may quote Pogo, 'We have met the enemy, and he is us.'"

He paused again to let his words sink in, and then signaled for the lights to be dimmed. The first slide on the screen was a picture. It was a drawing in black and white of four men. In the center was a uniformed man in a long, black coat. From his right hand dangled a set of keys. Next to him was another man, who was wearing a white medical smock. He was holding a hose from which he directed a stream of water toward the other two men, who were lying in coffin-like structures. The coffins had a canvas cover so that only the men's heads were showing. Above them were spigots, from which additional water poured onto their heads. From the expressions on their faces, it was apparent that the water was being discharged with considerable force. The men standing had grave looks on their faces. The men in the coffins looked miserable.

"Unless one worked for the CIA, today we would call this torture," said Doctor Kellman. "At the end of the nineteenth century, it was considered a cure for addiction. Water cures, as they were called, were abandoned in the early twentieth century as crude and ineffective. Enlightened scientists of the day realized that it was much better to prevent addiction than to try to treat it. And knowing that those who were addicted had an inherent defective nature, one passed from mother to child, they hit upon an elegant solution. Sterilize the mothers before they could pass on their defective genes to another generation. Eugenics it was called. This simple remedy would, in just a few generations, solve the problem entirely.

"Many of the great minds of medicine sang its praises. Foremost among them was one Professor Henry Farnham Perkins. Doctor Perkins was one of our own. He was the professor of natural sciences here at the University of Vermont. Doctor Perkins devoted his life to helping others. He was a Sunday school teacher, a leader of the YMCA, and one of the first presidents of the Boy Scouts. In 1931, he was elected president of the American Eugenics Society. He died in 1956, living long enough to see the popularity of his teachings extended across the water to like-minded practitioners in Germany.

"Even after the abandonment of these measures, the medical profession continued the strategy of inflicting misery upon those already afflicted with the misery of addiction, the premise being that treatment of the disease was most effective when it was demeaning. Although we now dispense medicine rather than torture to those in need, like our Victorian ancestors, we are unable to pay more than lip service to the notion that addiction is a medical disease. Because in most of our hearts, addiction still represents a defect, not of the neural, but the moral fiber.

"So," Doctor Kellman said, looking us over with an expression of someone who was inspecting a work that had been constructed not at all to his satisfaction. "What, exactly, is my point?"

He showed us another slide. On it were two identical pictures side by side. The pictures were of a bottle of insulin, an alcohol pad, and a syringe with a needle. "Looks familiar," he said, "doesn't it? Nothing special here. But how about this?" He clicked again. The picture on the left was unchanged. On the right, the bottle of insulin and the alcohol pad had been replaced by a packet of white powder, a spoon, and a matchbook. I shuddered. It was an involuntary reaction. "Creeps you out, doesn't it? That is *exactly* the point. If you're serious about treating addicted persons, you are going to need a major attitude adjustment.

"Are you ready for it?"

There was an uncomfortable silence. Nobody knew quite what to do. It had the ring of a call-and-response question, but we weren't a call-and-response crowd. "That's okay," he said in the kind of voice a parent uses when his child isn't quite able to do what he asks, but he doesn't want to discourage the child. "It's a rhetorical question. Let's talk about something easier: diabetes. You all know diabetes. When I say the word, you don't shiver. Quite the opposite. You like *diabetes*. It's familiar, an old friend.

"Diabetes is a chronic disease. Usually it is inherited, but sometimes it arises from events that happen in childhood. Sometimes, even, it is caused by medication, *prescription medication*," he said, emphasizing the last two words. "Multifactorial is the word we use to describe diabetes. It's a pretty neutral word.

We don't blame someone for having diabetes. And we have never proposed sterilizing women with diabetes.

"Diabetes is permanent. There is no cure for diabetes. No one is in *recovery* from diabetes. Diabetes is either controlled, or it is uncontrolled. And there are a host of factors that can contribute to how good the control is.

"Lifestyle is important. Eating the right foods especially. And keeping one's weight where it should be. These are hard things to do, and most of our patients succeed, at best, incompletely. We don't blame them for it. We recognize how difficult it is. Perhaps this is because we are often faced with the same kind of challenge. Avoiding sugar is particularly important, so one of our standard pieces of unhelpful advice is to tell our patients to make sure they are never around sugar, so they won't be tempted to eat it. Don't keep it at home, we tell them. Don't look for it at a party or at work. And when you are offered sugar, just say no. And maybe they succeed.

"But even if they succeed in living the perfect diabetic life, most patients will still need medication. And they will always need it.

"Should a person with diabetes be unable to stick with our recommendations, we wouldn't think of restricting that person's access to their medications. If they do not take their medications exactly as we had prescribed, we wouldn't stop prescribing for them. We would work with them to try to improve things. Because we know they need their medicine.

"Sometimes you might need to modify the treatment due to side effects from a particular medication. But the only reason you would stop treatment altogether is the same reason for terminating any patient—if the patient exhibits inappropriate behavior to you or your staff.

"There are those who say that treating opiate addiction with buprenorphine is just replacing one addiction with another." Doctor Kellman looked around the room slowly and then nodded. "Some of those people are even in this room.

"To you, I say this." He paused.

"So what!

"There are people who just can't stay away from sugar. These people are beset by cravings for sugar, and when they eat something sweet, they feel good. We call that a sugar high. You could say these people are addicted to sugar. We recognize that this is simply something beyond their control. 'That's okay,' we say. 'We understand.' And we offer them an artificial sweetener, a sugar substitute.

"Diabetes and addiction—it's an analogy. The analogy is imperfect, but that is the nature of analogies. They are not a description of things the way they are. They simply provide a different way of looking at something. To allow you to see the thing better.

"There was an expression at the start of a show called *Mission Impossible* that, like the name of the show, is particularly apt at this point. 'Your assignment, should you choose to accept it'—is to treat people with an addiction disorder just the same as you would treat a person with diabetes. Not as addicts."

He stopped abruptly and walked off the stage. We broke for coffee. Trine had come with me to hear his presentation. I asked her what she thought of it.

"He tells it like it should be," she said.

"And?"

"*Det var det.*"

The *Oxford English Dictionary* has almost 500,000 words. The Norwegian language has about 60,000. Norwegians use their words efficiently. *Det var det* means "That's that."

After the break, he went over the pharmacology of buprenorphine. Doctor Kellman reviewed the distinction between full agonist opiates and partial agonists and the properties that both gave buprenorphine a greater margin of safety and made it a less attractive opiate for someone who wanted

to get high—except in the Far East, where it is thought to enhance sexual performance.

He then went over the usual stuff that one needs to know
about any new drug: how it gets into the body, how long it
stays there, and how it is removed—the kind of information I
usually have gotten myself for the hundreds of new drugs that
have appeared in our pharmacopeia since I graduated from
medical school. But Doctor Kellman threw in a few interesting facts regarding alternate ways of introducing the drug into
the body, such as up the nose or in the rectum, both of which,
he pointed out, resulted in substantially improved absorption,
allowing the patient to get the same effect from a lower dose.
This fact, he explained, was well known by those who were unable to get buprenorphine from a doctor and had to buy their
daily dose on the street, where it cost $20 to $25 a day. Being
able to use a lower dose could result in substantial savings. He
reminded us that such people were quite motivated to be in
treatment, as they were paying almost twice as much for the
buprenorphine as they would for heroin, and the buprenorphine didn't produce much of a high. "Less bang for more
bucks," Doctor Kellman said. He finished with a short video
showing us what buprenorphine strips looked like and how
they were inserted under the tongue.

Then it was lunchtime. After lunch we attended a presentation by Martha Padlock on the logistics of medication assisted treatment, MAT for short. MAT is our euphemism for buprenorphine treatment. (Medication assisted treatment is what
most doctors do for most conditions most of the time. We
use the term for these patients because we'd rather not admit
we are treating their condition with more opiates.) Ms. Padlock was the director of the Vermont Department of Health's
Opiate Addiction Treatment Division. She explained the hub-
and-spoke principle that Vermont had adopted. The spoke is a
doctor's office, and the hub is a place for patients who are too
complicated for office management. In the hub, patients may

receive their buprenorphine daily under direct observation—something, she was sure, none of us wanted to get involved with. Once stabilized, hub patients could be transferred to a spoke for ongoing treatment.

She explained that for qualified practitioners, the state would provide the assistance of both buprenorphine-trained nurses and certified drug counselors, who would enable us to provide a *team-oriented* approach. She emphasized that in order to qualify for such support, a doctor needed to comply with the requirements of the program.

We had been told that if we were interested in having a MAT team, Ms. Padlock would be available to meet with us on an individual basis at the end of the day. It was not clear what type of a team it would be—a football-type team on which a quarterback called the plays and the rest of the team carried out the plays in predetermined roles, or a track-team model where each player did his own thing independently. Or did the type of team not matter, the only important concept being a coach who was in charge of everyone? But I liked the idea of working with some people who already had experience with the treatment. I signed up.

*****

Ms. Padlock is a brisk, efficient woman who lets you know right off that she is not one to put up with any nonsense. I introduced myself and told her I was ready to learn about MAT.

"It's a multi-step process," she said. "First, patients will meet with the team counselor for an interview. The counselor will determine if the patient is eligible for office-based treatment. Eligibility is based on the patient's Treatment Needs Questionnaire, a validated assessment tool used to determine the patient's behavioral prognosis. If the patient's score is less than ten, the counselor will then review the requirements for participation."

"What if their score is not less than ten?" I asked

"Then they are not eligible," Ms. Padlock said.

"SOL."

"Pardon?"

"Never mind. Can you tell me about the requirements?"

"It's all spelled out in the contract—the conditions of their treatment, the obligations, and the penalties for violations." She handed me a set of papers. "Here it is."

The contract was eight single-spaced pages long. At the end was a place for the patient to initial and one for me to sign. I skimmed through it. There was the usual collection of *whereases* and *in the event ofs* as well as numerous *consents to* and *complies with.* I couldn't find anything about the doctor's obligations, but I have never been much good at reading legal documents. That's Trine's department. My rule has always been that I'll sign anything, as long as I don't have to read it. I handed it back to her.

"It's quite long," I said.

"We are trying to change behavior," Ms. Padlock said. "That involves many obligations."

"Do you have a cell phone?"

She looked pleased at the question. "Of course. I'll give you my number, and I'll be glad to talk to you at any time. It is a rather involved process, recovery."

"You know that thing you get each time you upgrade your phone?" I asked. "It's about twenty pages long, and at the end there is a button that says 'accept,' and you have to check it if you want to use the phone?"

"Of course."

"Have you ever read it?"

"Heaven's, no!"

"Just accept and get on with it?"

"If I want to use my phone, I have no choice."

"This would seem to be in a similar category."

"Meaning."

"No choice really."

"It's a program requirement."

"Precisely."

"Do you have any *other* questions?"

"Tell me about the penalties part."

"Certainly," Ms. Padlock said. "They are exceedingly important. It's how we both ensure compliance and screen out those patients who aren't really motivated to stay with the program. It includes restriction of take-home privileges, more frequent callbacks, referral back to the hub for daily supervision, and, ultimately, termination from the program."

"I don't understand."

"What is it you don't understand?"

"We consider addiction as a chronic disease."

"It certainly is."

"Like diabetes."

"Your point being?"

"Doctor Kellman told us this morning that we should look at the treatment of addiction the same way we look at the treatment of diabetes."

"Doctor Kellman is an excellent physician. He always has his patients' interests in mind. He is, at heart, a clinician."

"As am I."

"I am quite aware of that."

"He pointed out that if somebody with diabetes doesn't follow the diet or doesn't take the medicine properly or doesn't come in for blood tests, we don't take them off their diabetes medicine."

"Of course not, they need it."

"Exactly."

Ms. Padlock looked hard at me.

"Addiction is different," she said.

"Because it's a chronic disease—except when it isn't?"

"I don't make the rules."

"I'm not sure I can follow them."

She frowned. "Why not?"

"I have to check with my wife."

"You need your wife's permission to treat your patients."

"Yes."

"Quite a relationship you must have," she said, not entirely in admiration. "Do you get your wife's permission for everything?"

"Just for some things."

"I see."

"Probably you don't. But I'll do the best I can. I want to make this work."

"That it will be."

"Pardon?"

"Work."

(There are, as I was to learn, two kinds of people who engage in the treatment of those with addictive illness. The first, and by far the most common, are the eat-your-peas people. The second prefer to splint 'em where they lie. The eat-your-peasers are sufficiently well known to require no further explanation. *Splint 'em where they lie* refers to a well-established principle in the treatment of trauma victims that one should first stabilize and protect the victim sufficiently to guarantee that any subsequent treatment will not inflict further injury. It is a sound principle, and it applies equally well to trauma of all kinds. Martha Padlock is an eat-your-peas person.)

That night Trine and I talked things over. She pointed out that there were a lot of people in desperate need of treatment, and that if the only way I could help them was by accepting a set of rules that I didn't agree with, unusual as it might be for me, it was hardly any different from what everyone else had to do all the time. "Besides," she added, "you can always do what you usually do in a situation like this."

"Refresh my memory."

"Fake it."

The next day, after the conference was over, I met with Martha Padlock.

"You have gotten permission?" she asked.

"I have."

"Then we must address the issue of the team. Do you have any idea how large your buprenorphine practice will be?"

"Well, as of right now, I have one patient."

"One?"

"But I plan to have more—as soon as I can."

"That's good to hear. But I'm afraid one isn't enough for us to assign you a team."

"I see. Okay then, I'll just start out on my own, and when I have a large enough number of patients, I'll let you know, and then we can set up a team."

"I don't think that's a good idea."

"Why not?"

"In my experience, doctors, when left on their own, tend to develop habits that, if not addressed promptly, are not conducive to good teamwork."

"Have a tendency to be rather on the do-our-own-thing side?"

"Some more than others."

"What would you suggest?"

She hesitated, and when she first answered, she sounded a bit surprised that I had asked, but only very briefly. "I'm glad you asked. I have given the matter considerable thought, and I believe I have come up with a solution. The community health center in Burlington has a large number of patients in treatment and a very active MAT team. I have talked with their director, and she is willing to talk to you about allowing you the use of her team for your patients—on a trial basis, naturally."

"Naturally. How exactly would this trial work?"

"That is something you'll have to figure out with her."

"I see."

"Her name is Sara Stensen. She is expecting a call."

"I'm on it."

CHAPTER 18

In 1971 I was in my last year of residency in San Francisco. My boss asked me one day what I was planning to do when I finished. I was thirty-one years old. Never in those thirty-one years had I needed to give a moment's thought as to the question of what I was going to do next. Up to then, all I had to decide every few years was where I would be making the next of the pre-ordained stops on my life's journey—college, medical school, military, residency.

"I don't know," I said.

"How would you like to set up a community health center?" my boss asked.

I liked my boss. I respected him. He was one of those people who always had the best interests at heart for those under him.

I remembered the idea behind community health centers from my time in Mississippi. "Sure," I said.

"It will be located in the South of Market area, on the corner of Eighth and Natoma. Given the neighborhood, the patient population will not be the usual free-clinic group of the young and the restless. The community consists of immigrants, homeless, and those who have been evicted from state hospitals after it was decided that they shouldn't be kept locked up for their entire lives just because they were crazy, and who, no longer having the medication that helped keep them on a somewhat even keel, have had to make do with alcohol and heroin."

The fact that I had no experience in managing anything, or for that matter, ever being responsible for anybody other than myself, was not a consideration for either one of us. Back then, not having the foggiest about what you were doing was never an impediment to doing it.

"Okay," I said.

"Good."

"I do have a question."

"You want to know how to run one."

"A couple of pointers, maybe."

"It's not hard. You hire good people. And you stay out of their way."

It was a satisfying job. The patients, accustomed to being treated at best with disrespect and at worst not at all, were appreciative to come to a place where they were made to feel welcome. The staff was energetic and enthusiastic, motivated by the knowledge that, even in a field that suffered from over-abundance, we were doing work that no one else was doing. We had a sense of purpose beyond the mere treatment of disease. Working there made me feel good about why I had chosen to go into medicine.

The Community Health Center of Burlington was a virtual twin of my old clinic when it opened in 1971, as the People's Free Clinic. It was funded by the same federal money, and it opened at about the same time. It has since grown to comprise eight locations, including the Riverside Health Center, which occupies a recently renovated building in Burlington's Old North End. The Riverside Health Center served, in addition to ordinary residents of the city, people very similar to those I had seen in San Francisco—the homeless, refugees, and those with addiction issues. Entering the building brought back a flood of fond memories. The signs on the wall were in English and Arabic and Croatian and several other languages I did not recognize. The people waiting wore hijabs and embroidered skirts and wrap dresses, as well as ordinary Western clothing. Some wore clothes that had the appearance of having been slept in. Many of the women had bejeweled faces, some traditional Asian, some eclectic Western. Each person who checked in got a smile and a friendly voice. It was a warm and welcoming atmosphere.

I introduced myself to one of the receptionists and told her I was looking for the MAT team.

"Oh, you must be Beach," she said. "They told me to watch out for you. I'll call Jess and Sara."

Jessica Bianconi and Sara Stensen both looked to be in their mid-thirties. One was short; one was tall. One was pale; one was not. But they both had the same expression in their eyes and on their faces—friendly, but inquisitive, and tinged with a hint of skepticism.

"Come on in, Beach," said Jessica.

"We heard you were coming," said Sara.

"So...," said Jessica.

"What brings you?" said Sara.

"I am in need of a MAT team."

"That would be us," said Jessica.

"Always glad to have another player on our roster," said Sara.

"Although we have a feeling that," said Jessica.

"There's more to it," said Sara.

"There is," I said. "You see..."

"You're not planning to join our team."

"You want us to join yours."

"That was my hope," I said.

"Which, as of now, consists of you."

"We plan on expanding."

"The royal *we*."

"As it were," I said.

"Any recruits who might possibly be added to this roster?"

"Not as yet."

"A rather smallish team then."

"As of now, yes."

"And the homecourt for this team would be?"

"Dumster," I said.

"And you were hoping that perhaps, when our team was not playing up here, we could come down and join this team of yours and play for you?"

"That was my thought."

"Make us an offer."

"We'll see if we can refuse."

I didn't know what to say. In truth, I hadn't given any thought as to how it was going to work, and I was hoping that the combination of generosity on their part and irresistible charm on mine would make them jump at the opportunity. I could see now that the whole idea was absurd. I stared blankly.

"Actually," said Sara.

"We did have an inkling that this was what you had in mind," said Jessica.

"As it turns out," said Sara.

"We have talked it over," said Jessica.

"And we have an idea."

"I'm all ears," I said.

"More than that, hopefully."

"We are willing to come down to Dumster to help with your patients."

"In return for which, you will come up here to help us with ours.

"A quid pro quo you might call it."

"One good turn deserving another."

Going to Burlington regularly wasn't something I particularly wanted to do. I did know people in town who traveled that distance to work every day. They did it without complaint. They liked it. "It's peaceful," one of them, who worked at Ben & Jerry's in Waterbury, told me. "Just me and my radio. And if I get tired of the radio, I can shut it off with just a push of the button." But I had become accustomed to a life where the farthest I had to travel was the one mile from our home on Maple Street up to the hospital.

"You're not thrilled with the prospect," said Sara.

"But look at it this way," said Jessica.

"You'd be doing good work."

"And you might learn something."

"It could even be fun."

"There is one other thing to consider."

"You have no choice."

They were right. I could decide that the whole business was too much trouble and go back to Dumster to do the same-old same-old I had been doing for the past forty years. Which made me feel very much a stick-in-the-mud. And not at all sanguine about the reception I would receive at home.

"Fair enough," I said. "But there is one area I wanted to clear up with you before we get started."

"The rules," said Sara.

"Martha Padlock showed me. There are an awful lot of them."

"We know," said Jessica.

"Doctors don't like rules."

"Well, I would rather say that some doctors like them more than others," I said.

"Some doctors like to *make* rules more than others."

"No doctors like to follow them."

"But don't worry about the rules."

"That's good to know," I said.

"Just follow them."

"I beg your pardon."

"You want us on your team?"

"I do."

"Remember Jim Croce?"

"One of the greats," I said.

"Certain things you don't do."

"Like stepping on Superman's cape."

"Or spitting into the wind."

"Bad ideas both."

"And."

"You don't mess around with the team."

"And you will discover that the rules will not be a problem for our patients. They are so accustomed to being ordered around, they expect them. There are many who claim that patients feel better for having rules. Makes them more secure, they say."

"You mean that patients actually like them?" I asked.

"Not a bit. But believing it is so makes the rulers feel better."

"But…" I said.

"You don't have rules like these for patients with other diseases."

"Like diabetes," I said.

"Like diabetes. And Doctor Kellman told you to treat this just like any other disease."

"More along the clinical model and less the criminal one."

"He was pretty definite about that," I said.

"And Martha Padlock told you that it was like diabetes, only different."

"Right. This is the different part."

"For the Marthas, addiction is a *pretend* disease."

"We know it's not fair."

"Which is unfortunate."

"But our patients are used to 'not fair.'"

"So, they accept it."

"If they can."

"You can too."

My proclivities for disobedience aside, the undeniably punitive aspect of MAT treatment just didn't feel right. I told Sara and Jessica.

"We know."

"It isn't right for us either."

"But rules are rules."

"And our patients need treatment."

"Sometimes when you're up against it."

"You just have to compromise."

"Of course."

"There's more than one way to compromise."

"If you think about it."

I thought about it.

"So, if addiction is a pretend disease, I'll *pretend* to follow the rules," I said.

"We can live with that."

"We'll be down next week."

"Thank you."

They smiled and shook my hand, and I left feeling that team play might not be so bad after all.

With the right teammates.

CHAPTER 19

When I got to work, I told Crikett about the course and that, as soon as I got my letter of approval, I would begin treating patients with addiction.

"Was this your idea?" she asked.

"Trine told me to."

"Good. I just wanted to make sure..."

"That it wasn't another of my HBSs?"

"The thought did occur to me. It's been a long time since the last one, and you have been a bit restless recently. You know, it's when you become dissatisfied with just being a good doctor in a small town and feel the need to do something different that harebrained schemes tend to crop up. And sometimes they are a bit, well, *too* different."

"Like the Super Marvel Violet Ray for one."

"And biosurgery for another."

"That didn't turn out so badly. Mister Boyden's toe did heal rather nicely."

"You didn't have to clean up."

Crikett was right. Both the therapeutic adventures she brought up were poorly thought out and poorly executed, and in the end caused more trouble than they were worth, although, fortunately, not to the patients who were subjected to them.

*****

Medicine has always been fascinated with electricity. This is only to be expected. We have a special place in our yearnings for things that have power, especially if we can use that power to augment our own. Doctors as far back as Grecian times employed electricity in their therapeutic armamentarium. The first source of electricity was from nature, in the form of electric fish. The torpedo fish is a skate-like fish capable of administering up to 220 volts of electrical current. Treatment was administered by placing the fish on the body part in need for thirty or forty minutes. It was a popular remedy, particularly for migraine headaches. Scribonius Largus, a first-century physician to Roman emperors, wrote in his treatise on the subject, "To immediately remove and permanently cure a headache, however long-lasting and intolerable, a live black torpedo is put on the place which is in pain, until the pain ceases and the part grows numb." It is neither noteworthy nor surprising that its now-more-popular descendant in the pain relief department derives its name from the Greek word for electric fish, *narka*.

No less a personage than Ben Franklin was known to seek comfort in the embrace of the torpedo when afflicted by his painful headaches. And it is entirely possible that, after he acquired a particularly nasty headache during a family tiff in which his wife told him to "go fly a kite," his literal adherence to her instructions led him to discover a more manageable source for his remedy.

Once electricity had been harnessed, the popularity of using electric current in medical therapeutics—a practice called galvanism—grew rapidly. It spawned a whole host of devices that administered electric current in everything from needles to electric chairs.

I was in Elmer Contremond's general store one day several years ago when he said there was something he wanted to show me out back, in the room where he had once kept excess stock.

After returning from a family outing to the Shelburne Museum, Elmer had cleaned out the room, painted the walls, and sanded and polished the floors. Then he placed a sign over the doorway. "Americana Room," the sign read. The letters were written in large, old-time script. He also placed a sign at the register that read, "Got Stuff? Might Buy It."

Elmer then spent the next several months gathering his Americana. Mostly they were unwanted and useless items that people around town brought in from their barns and attics and basements. There were glass medicine bottles of assorted shapes and colors, horseshoes, iron nails, old license plates, iron cookware, dolls in tattered muslin dresses, and rusted parts of farm implements. The Americana Room, as Elmer expected, was ignored by townspeople, but it proved to be very profitable among tourists, who purchased, at exorbitant markup, anything and everything.

In the early part of the twentieth century, the town's medical needs were administered by Doctor Samuel French. Doctor French, who died in 1920, had three children, the oldest of whom, Betty, died in 1975. Her son, Robert, eventually got around to cleaning out the family home, and in the process, he discovered a collection of his grandfather's medical equipment. In it was a black cardboard box embossed with gold lettering proclaiming that within lay the Super Marvel Violet Ray. It was this box that Elmer wanted to show me.

"Thought you might be interest in this, Doc," said Elmer. "Seeing as how you're his heir, more or less."

"Less, I'd say."

I opened the box. Inside, nesting on a bed of purple velvet, was a long cylindrical handle with an electric cord on one end. Adjacent to the cylinder was an assortment of variously shaped glass tubes.

"Don't know what I'd do with it," I said.

"Don't have to *do* anything with it," Elmer said. "It's a relic."

"That it is." I picked it up. It had a nice feel to it. Despite myself I was curious.

"Still works," said Elmer.

I plugged it in. Nothing happened.

"Gotta turn that dial." Elmer pointed to a small round knob at the base of the handle. "Juices it up."

I turned the knob. A lovely violet light danced up and down the tube. I touched the tube to my arm. It produced a mild and not unpleasant shock.

"Interesting," I said.

"Five bucks. Six if you want the manual."

I bought the device and the manual. Manufactured in 1920, the Violet Ray was the latest and most potent in a line of electrotherapy devices, the special powers of its high-frequency current promoted as the source of its superior performance. It was also the last of its kind. The overly generous claims of electrotherapy proved unable to survive the scrutiny of the profession's newly found determination to define itself as a science. Particularly susceptible to scrutiny were its claims to cure tuberculosis, female troubles, neurasthenia, hair loss, and brain fag. In 1951 the Violet Ray manufacturer pleaded guilty to a claim of misbranding and paid a fine of $2,000. The device was subsequently banned by the Food and Drug Administration. It survives to this day, however, exempted under a grandparental clause in the regulations that allows anything manufactured prior to 1976 to be "generally recognized as safe." It cannot now be purchased from a US manufacturer, but it can be bought online. The scope of cure, however, has been substantially reduced. Its repertoire is now limited to treatment of hair loss and dermatitis.

The Super Marvel is a versatile device. Law enforcement authorities have found it helpful in enhancing the results from interrogating suspects in criminal investigations. As recently as 1981, it was used regularly by one John Burge, an officer of the Chicago Police Department. How effective it was to this end is not reported, but it did result in the conviction of Officer Burge, not for using the Violet Ray, but for lying about it in a deposition, the prosecution having apparently decided that had he just fessed up, everything would have been copasetic.

My Violet Ray was Model 3, a more modest version of the top of the line Model 24, which was equipped not only with the full complement of ten wands, but an ozone generator—the ozone guaranteed to enhance one's immune system and overall well-being.

The three wands of my Model 3 included a multi-purpose wand that terminated in a broad, pancake-shaped tip that could be massaged over any relatively flat body surface; a rake-shaped wand for the hair called a comb; and a throat stimulator, equipped with a pair of horizontal horn-like prongs that, when inserted into the mouth, would cure tonsillitis. The seven additional wands of Model 24 were designed to be inserted into various other body orifices. They were advertised as particularly effective for the treatment of troubles, both of the female and the male.

After a week of painting our garden shed, I had developed a pesky sore elbow. Unable to resist a therapeutic trial, I ran the surface wand over the offending joint back and forth for about ten minutes. It produced a kind of numb tingling, and for the rest of the day, the pain was hardly noticeable. I can't honestly say that the Violet Ray performed any better than ibuprofen or a heating pad, but it did work.

There is ample evidence that electrical stimuli applied to the skin can reduce pain. Nerve fibers are transmission lines. They carry information outward to the muscles, instructing them how to act, and they carry information inward to the brain about what is going on elsewhere in the body. Nerves are not high-capacity lines, and if a competing impulse, say from an acupuncture needle or a transcutaneous electric nerve stimulator, is traveling along the same line, it can cause a traffic jam, slowing, and even stopping altogether, the flow of pain impulses along the nerve. The questions as to what type of electrical stimulus is best as well as to which purposes, other

than the temporary relief of pain, it may be beneficial, are un-
answered. This is in no way a hindrance to its use. For most of
medical history, we have reliably depended upon the unknown
in promoting the benefits of our ministrations, although it is
now rather out of favor. Accordingly, though I was intrigued
by the device, I did not feel sanguine about advocating its ap-
plication to any of my patients.

On the grounds that it was an interesting curiosity, I kept
the Violet Ray prominently displayed on the top of my desk.
To those who expressed interest, I readily explained, offering
the disclaimer that we did not know for sure how, or even if,
it worked. Nonetheless, it was not unusual for patients with a
pain that had proved resistant to all I had offered to show an
interest in trying it out "just to see," our mutual assumption
being that it couldn't hurt. Whether it was the electricity itself,
the mesmerizing violet light it emitted, or merely the desire
for the treatment's success, I cannot say, although I can affirm
it was not unusual that, upon trying it on a sore back, a bum
knee, or a stiff neck, the patient stated it had provided substantial relief. And it was not long before I had a steady stream
of patients returning again and again solely to get a Violet Ray
treatment. What was initially just a bit of curious fun was rapidly turning into a significant business. As these patients were
taking up more and more time in my schedule, I feared I was
risking descent into quackery. Fortunately, I suppose I must
say, there occurred an event with the Violet Ray that brought
an abrupt end to its career.

One night, when I was sitting at my desk after hours, my
eye was drawn to the Violet Ray's comb wand. According to
the manual, the comb could be used to treat conditions of the
scalp, including dandruff, gray hair, and baldness—the last of
which I have.

I pride myself now on not being vain about my appearance, especially with respect to my hair, although there was a
time in my late twenties when I would expend considerable

effort combing the few remaining strands carefully over my scalp in order, so I thought, to diminish its visibility. It was not until I finally gave up on the futile effort that I noticed how absurd the combover looked when I saw it on others.

Almost without realizing what I had done, I found the Violet Ray in my hand. Attached was the comb. We really don't know, I said to myself, whether there might not be some truth to any of the overly expansive claims that had led to its demise. It was patently impossible that it could do everything it claimed, but was it possible that one or two of those claims might have some merit? It was well known, after all, that the skin, when deprived of normal innervation, loses, along with sensation, its ability to grow hair. I had no personal interest in the question, of course, but my shiny smooth scalp did offer, if I may use the words, fertile grounds for experimentation.

"Why not," I said to Self.

"You're a fool," Self replied.

I read the instructions:

Use a weak current at first and increase to a medium strength later on. Refractory cases may require periods at the high setting. Pass the comb back and forth over the entire scalp for four minutes. Do not use the Violet Ray immediately after using hair tonic.

Since this was for experimental purposes only, I resolved to apply the treatment to just one side of the scalp, leaving an equally sized hairless area on the other side un-rayed as a control. I turned on the Violet Ray to the lowest setting. A faint violet light flickered. Applying it to my scalp produced a barely noticeable tingle.

Patience has never been one of my vices. As I have had what I would consider, based on my ability to withstand it when inflicted by me upon my patients, a moderately high tolerance for pain, I turned up the dial. The violet light flashed brightly. Sparks danced inside the tube. The tingling became intense. It felt a bit uncomfortable. I continued, determined to see it through. The handle became very hot. Suddenly there was a loud crackle and a pop, and the Violet Ray went out. A searing pain struck the side of my head. I smelled the pungent odor of burning flesh.

That night I explained to Trine how many of medicine's great discoveries had been made by men who experimented on themselves, offering as evidence the examples of two physicians who had tried to prove the cause of yellow fever by exposing themselves to the purported agent of transmission.

Stubbins Ffirth was the first. In the eighteenth century, yellow fever was thought to be caused by the black vomit of afflicted patients. Ffirth, to disprove that theory, drank the vomit. He bathed in the vomit. He cut his arm and then rubbed the vomit in the open cut. He squirted it into his eyeballs. He did not get yellow fever. Afterward, he wrote a paper describing the experiment.

The second was Jesse Lazear, some 100 years later. In a letter to his wife from his research station in Cuba, he wrote, "I think I am on track of the real germ." He set about to prove his hypothesis by allowing himself to be bitten by a mosquito that had been feeding on a patient known to have yellow fever.

Doctor Lazear got it right. He contracted yellow fever, and in so doing, he proved that the vector responsible for transmitting the disease was not excreta of the afflicted, but the *aedes aegypti* mosquito. Unlike Doctor Ffirth, he was not able to write a paper describing the experiment. His name was, however, attached posthumously to the study, and as a reward for his ultimate sacrifice, a dormitory at Johns Hopkins University was named in his honor.

Trine was not impressed. "Serves you right," she said.

Crikett looked at my bandaged head the next morning. She glanced at the empty spot on my desk where the Violet Ray had been. "Mrs. Paronto is ready to see you," she said.

Fortunately, it was only a superficial burn, and after several weeks it healed without a visible scar to remind me of my stupidity.

But I had learned my lesson, and my next venture into the experimental was on firmer scientific ground. It was a safe and painless treatment, one whose therapeutic effect was first documented over 200 years ago.

As with the Violet Ray, the idea for the treatment came from a Contremond. Stanley Contremond, father of Elmer, was a cantankerous and stubborn old farmer who loved nothing better than a hopeless fight. Which, given that his usual battleground was the soil on which he tilled, and his adversary was Nature, was just about perfect for him. If he could squeeze out a few root vegetables for winter and enough corn to feed his meager herd, he would consider it a draw. If he had enough to sell, he claimed victory. Most of the time he had neither. In the spring of 1992, Nature gained what appeared to be an irreversible advantage. The proximate cause of this setback was a battle wound suffered by Stanley as he was fixing his plow. While working on it, he inadvertently bumped his leg against one of the tines, producing over his ankle what was really just a scratch.

Whether it was the germ warfare the plow's rich culture medium waged against the cut or the diabetes that Stanley never knew he had—because he had paid no attention to the fact that his already slim body had been melting in a stream of heavily sweetened urine—is of no matter. As the cut began to fester, Stanley treated the wound with his two favorite remedies, Bag Balm and denial. Although they had always served him well in the past, this time they were to no avail.

By the time Elmer brought him to the hospital, Stanley was delirious. His temperature was 104, his leg was about twice its normal size, and from a large gaping hole around the ankle oozed a dark green pus that smelled of putrefaction.

I told Stanley I was afraid he was going to lose his leg.

"Thanks for the warning, Doc," he said. "I'll keep a close eye on 'er while I'm here."

By some miracle, the leg survived, but after several weeks of antibiotics, debridements of dead skin, and a fancy new powder that cost $60 an ounce, he still had a large wound that showed no intention of healing in the foreseeable future.

"Might as well go home," Stanley said after I offered another and more expensive poultice. "'Spect I can mulch it 'bout as well as you."

Given the environment Stanley would be going back into, I didn't think it was a good idea, but I couldn't really argue with him. Nothing I had done had amounted to much. So I gave him a supply of antibiotics and plenty of dressing material and advised him to keep it covered at all costs. I told him to come back in two weeks so I could check on how he was doing.

"What for, Doc?" he asked. "You been worry'n' on it ever day now, an' you ain't scared it away yet."

I wrote the discharge orders. Then I suggested I might stop by the farm in a few weeks to see how he was doing. Stanley allowed as how that might be okay.

Three weeks later I went out to Stedsville to see him. Stanley was out in the field on his tractor, determinedly harassing the unruly soil into submission. I waved to him from the road. He got off his tractor and walked over to my car. I asked him how things were going.

"Not so good," he said.

"I'm sorry to hear that," I said. "Maybe going home wasn't such a good idea."

"Mebbe stayin' in, I'd say."

"Maybe. Maybe not. Let me take a look at the leg, if you don't mind."

"The leg?" said Stanley puzzled. "Oh that. Leg's fine, Doc. That's not the problem. What's no good is how late I'm getting my plowing done—thanks to my spell of in-car-ceration." At which Stanley rolled up his pants to show a nice clean scar where the ulcer had been.

I have seen many unexpected results in my day. Often, I have been surprised by them, rarely have I been flat out flabbergasted. If ever I had seen an ulcer that had all intent of staying for the duration, Stanley's was one such. I congratulated him on the outcome.

"Yep. Healed right up—soon as I treated it right."

"That's always important."

"Sure is. First thing I did was get rid of them godawful bandages."

"Oh?"

"Yep. Then I set it out on the porch where the sun could get at it. Figured keeping it locked up hadn't done much good, so I might try some fresh air. Worked real good, I'd say."

"Perhaps," I conceded. "But I suspect it was more the antibiotics that did the trick."

"You can 'spect all you want, Doc, but I'll bet you a day's hay bales them 'biotics had as much to do with it as the bats in the barn. Did the chickens good, though."

"You fed the antibiotics to the *chickens*?"

"Yep. They was kinda puny afore they got 'em—but they's much better now. An' I thank you for that."

"But the leg—what did you do for that?"

"Switched me over to somepin' I knew would work. The ol' Doc Jarvis remedy."

I'd been in Vermont long enough to know the Doctor Jarvis cure. Cider vinegar and clover honey. It was harmless enough, but I couldn't imagine it having any effect on wound healing. Something just didn't add up.

"You're telling me that's all you did?" I asked. "Just drank vinegar and honey, and the ulcer healed?"

"Hell, no," he laughed. "I ain't no fool. I drank the cider vinegar, always done that anyway, one cup ever' day. Put the honey on the sore, though. Cleaned it up slick as a bean. Course I couldn't keep the flies off it—but I dint pay them no never mind. They were jus' looking for a good meal an' a place to raise a family."

*****

During the Napoleonic Wars, Baron Domonique Jean Larrey, Napoleon's surgeon general, noticed that soldiers' wounds that had become infested with maggots never got gangrene. Copying Nature's remedy, he began the practice of applying a larva-laden poultice to deep wounds. Sure enough, they often healed quickly and painlessly, and without the aid of extensive surgical debridement, a painful and time-consuming process. Not infrequently, the treatment even prevented the need for amputation of the afflicted limb. His discovery was eventually adopted as standard wartime wound management. In the American Civil War, for example, doctors would routinely employ blowfly maggots to heal infected wounds. It was still in use up through World War I, but with the advent of antibiotics, the cumbersome and messy treatment has been largely abandoned.

Intrigued by the possibility of resurrecting this ancient remedy, I went to the medical library at Dartmouth to see if there was any current research on the subject. I came across a series of articles written by Ronald Sherman, a doctor at the San Diego Veterans Center. He was using maggots in wound healing, and he described in some detail exactly how to employ them to manage a wound. "Biosurgery," he called it. It had a nice ring to it.

In order to perform biosurgery, I would first have to find an eligible patient. Fortunately, I had not long to wait. William Boyden was a man with diabetes who had been bothered by a persistent ulcer on his right shin. A recurrent bout of cellulitis had necessitated admission to the hospital. After his fever subsided, I approached him with the idea of using biosurgery to promote wound healing. I explained it would involve maggots, and that although I had no personal experience in their use, the value of the treatment was well documented. I mentioned that it was currently being used at a major medical center, and I had researched their procedures. I need not have been concerned. Always an affable fellow, and eager to please his doctor, Mr. Boyden readily agreed to the plan. The nurses were rather less enthusiastic, but after I showed them several before and after pictures from Doctor Sherman's papers, they reluctantly consented to let me try it.

Next, I had to find a source of maggots. This proved to be quite simple. Online I found a bait company in North Carolina that sold maggots for four cents a pound. With shipping and handling, the cost was about $10, a price I considered exceedingly cheap for any treatment. I ordered a pound. The maggots arrived the next day by overnight mail. They were packed in dry ice, in a Styrofoam box. Big and juicy, they looked ready and eager for the task that awaited them. According to Doctor Sherman's protocol, I was to refrigerate the maggots immediately in a bath of alcohol and allow them to soak overnight. This served the dual function of sterilizing them and slowing down their usually frenetic activity, in order to ease the process of application. First thing the next morning, armed with a nylon stocking that would serve as dressing for the wound, I went to Bill's bedside. I pulled the stocking over the leg up to the knee, leaving plenty of extra stocking extending beyond the end of the toes. I taped the upper end of the stocking snugly around the calf. Having sealed the proximal end, I cut a slit in the toe of the stocking. I now had a corral for my maggots and a gate through which they could be herded into it. I then fetched the maggots from the refrigerator. Cold and intoxicated, they were quite sluggish. I poured the sedated maggots into the stocking through the open end and then tied it up in a tight knot. Now they were locked in. Warmed by contact with Bill's leg, they soon began to stir. I was unable to see them actually feeding on the wound, as they quickly formed one large solid mass that filled the stocking, but judging from their activity, I was sure they were doing their job.

It turned out to be less trouble than I expected. Despite what I had read, the maggots were remarkably clean. There was no discharge from the stocking, and the wound was odor free. The next day I opened the stocking and removed the maggots. By now they were barely moving. I presumed they had been sated by their gluttony. To my unpleasant surprise, however, the wound looked exactly the same as the day before. The ulcer was untouched. Something had gone drastically wrong.

Since the best course of action at this point seemed to be to get advice from someone who actually knew what he was doing, I called Doctor Sherman in San Diego. He was quite pleased to hear that I had taken up biosurgery and was eager to help. I told him what had happened with my first trial.

"What kind of maggots did you use?" he asked.

"Blowfly maggots."

"Blowflies are good. How old were they?"

"I have no idea."

"Of course not. How big were they?"

"Plenty big," I said. "An inch to an inch and a half long."

"They're too old."

"Too *old?*"

"The life span of a maggot is about six days, a bit longer if you keep them cold. By the third day they are fully grown and will begin looking for a warm, dark place to make their cocoon. Eating is the last thing on their tiny little minds. The best eaters are the young ones, one to two days old. Where did you get the maggots?"

"From a place in North Carolina."

"A bait shop."

"Yes."

"They're no good. Big maggots are fine for bait, but they're useless for biosurgery. What you need are fresh baby maggots, packed in alcohol and shipped overnight. You put them in the wound as soon as they arrive. And change them each day."

"Where can I get baby maggots?"

"From me."

"How much would I need?"

"That depends. How big is the ulcer?"

"Six centimeters."

"Where is it located?"

"Just above the ankle."

"Given the location, total healing could take anywhere from four to eight weeks. But the maggots should be able to finish their part of the job in two weeks. And with the size of the ulcer, I'd say one ounce for each treatment. If you keep them cold, you can usually get two treatments out of one batch."

"Sounds good. How much do they cost?"

"One hundred dollars an ounce."

The treatment was going to cost well over $1,000. It would be costly, and there was no way I would get it covered by insurance. I couldn't ask Bill to pay for it. Even if it worked, it was prohibitively expensive. Maggots were clearly out of the question.

"I'll take them," I said.

"I'll ship them out today."

"Better send a batch every two days for the next two weeks."

"You got it."

Doctor Sherman was right. The baby maggots were tiny, less than a tenth of an inch long. Hardly seemed up to the work cut out for them. But soon as I put them in the stocking, they went straight to the ulcer, and in just a few hours were excreting a pile of foul-smelling slime. The excreta stayed within the stocking—mostly. The odor did not. When I changed the dressing after the first day, everyone gathered around to look. There was already noticeable improvement. I asked Bill how it felt.

He smiled. "Tickles," he said. "Feels good. Like a foot massage. Keep 'em coming."

I cleaned up the wound and carefully scooped the maggots into a basin. Their performance on the next day was no less impressive. On the third day a new batch arrived, and I repeated the cycle. By the end of the first week, the ulcer was more than half cleaned up. At the end of the second week the ulcer was free of debris. The wound was completely clean, and it was granulating nicely. It was almost healed, all without any more surgical intervention than hundreds of tiny maggot mandibles chewing away day and night. I was quite pleased. Even Doctor Morehouse, our surgeon, was impressed. The housekeepers and nurses were less so. The pervasive odor of dying flesh emanating from Bill's room was readily detectable up and down the corridor. And despite my best efforts, a couple of days after declaring the maggot project a complete success, there appeared a disturbing number of very large flies with pretty blue bodies and iridescent wings. Attracted only to certain patients, they perched on the sills of their rooms and flew in slow graceful circles about the body parts that showed promise as future nesting spots.

"Little vultures," said Ruth Lynch, the head nurse of the nursing home wing of Emmeline Talbot.

"Next time, you clean up," said Rose, the head housekeeper.

"Won't be a next time," said Ruth.

Discouraged but undaunted, I called Doctor Sherman to get his advice.

"Easy," he said. "Treat 'em at home." He explained that the nylon stocking technique was perfectly suited to outpatient treatment, although for those patients who were up and about, he recommended covering the wound in a loose gauze bandage.

Buoyed by his suggestion, I was determined not to abandon the work. The fly in the proverbial ointment, however, was the cost of the maggots. The solution to that issue seemed eminently simple. I would raise my own maggots. I knew from experience with our garbage that maggots were hardy and adaptable creatures. It should be a simple matter to grow them in a more controlled environment, where they could easily be harvested.

"Not in the house," said Trine.

We had a small shed attached to the back of the garage. Reluctantly Trine granted permission for me to build my maggot farm there. I took a couple of old wooden crates, covered the sides in tarpaper, and laid a screen over the top. I put a layer of damp towels on the bottom of the crate and covered it with pieces of raw meat. I then put in a handful of the blowfly cocoons I had saved from the last treatment.

A blowfly's total life cycle spans about fifteen days, and it is a useful maggot for only two of those days. But each mature female fly lays about 250 eggs, so I figured as long as I kept them fed and warm and moist, they would continue to produce abundant crops. And as the baby maggots would be stuck fast to the meat, they should be easy to harvest from the boxes.

Sure enough, the cocoons hatched into flies in about six days, and within twenty-four hours clumps of tiny white eggs appeared on the meat. The next day, the meat was swarming with ravenous baby maggots. As I had no patients upon whom to use them at the time, I left them alone to mature and repeat the cycle, opening the lid at night, when it was cool and the flies were settled down, in order to put in more meat. Pretty soon both boxes were full of a great mass of flies, maggots, and cocoons. Quite pleased with the success of my efforts, I could hardly wait to use the maggots again.

One morning, as soon as I stepped out the front door, I was greeted by a swarm of flies. During the night the boxes had been overturned and dragged onto the yard, strewing their contents everywhere. Claw marks on the boxes told me who the vandals were. Raccoons. It was the opportunity Trine was waiting for. The maggot farm enterprise was shut down. My brief career in biosurgery was over.

In 2004 maggots were formally resurrected by the Food and Drug Administration, which granted them approval as a therapy for necrotic wounds. They can now be ordered online from several commercial sources. Although I am often tempted to try again, the distinct lack of enthusiasm from those upon whom I depend has sufficed to prevent my embarking upon another such undertaking.

CHAPTER 20

My one MAT patient was Tommy Dufresne.

"Tommy is so happy about getting his Suboxone here," said Crikett. "We all are. It's a good thing what you're doing. There's nothing harebrained about it at all—as long as you have Jess and Sara to keep an eye on you."

"Yes, now I have three responsible adults."

"Never can have too many of those."

Tommy was just as pleased. "I can't tell you how great this is, Doc. Turns out the guy in Windsor was full up, so I'm seeing a fellow down in Greenfield, Mass."

"This will be a lot less hassle."

"A lot cheaper too. He didn't take insurance. It was cash only. Two fifty a visit, and I had to drive down every week to pick up my prescription. It was a pain in the you-know-where. Still, I can't complain. It has kept me clean."

There was a knock on the door. It was Jessica and Sara.

"Okay if we sit in?" asked Sara.

"We're Beach's teammates," said Jessica.

I have always considered the exam room to be my territory, my doctor cave. I was unaccustomed, except upon request, to having company. "Uh, no," I stammered. "I mean, certainly. Come on in."

"Actually," said Jessica.

"We were asking Tommy," said Sara.

Tommy grinned. "You bet. Always been a team player."

"Okay then," said Jessica, nodding at me to indicate that there was no need for any contribution on my part to the conversation.

"First things first," said Sara.

"The contract." Jessica handed it to Tommy.

"Where do I sign?"

"You want us to go over it?"

"Hell, no," said Tommy. "Won't remember it. Besides, I got no choice."

"Page eight, at the bottom."

Tommy signed the contract and handed it back.

Tommy had already been on a stable dose of Suboxone, so there would be no induction phase, which made things quite simple. Induction is a more complicated process that involves gradually increasing the dose while monitoring closely for side effects and opiate use. We agreed upon a day of the week for his refills and a pharmacy where he would get them. After that, the only remaining item on the agenda was a urine test. Sara and Jessica had brought down the special cups, which allow for immediate determination of what substances are in the urine and have indicators that show whether the sample has the correct temperature and concentration for urine that has just come from the body. In many places, there is also a special room where the patient can be observed through a one-way mirror while urinating. We had no such bathroom. Neither Sara or Jessica was concerned, but they said that Martha might require one if the state were to provide financial support. It was part of accountability, they explained.

"I can't thank you folks enough," said Tommy as he got up to leave. "You know." He paused. "It's not the travel or the money. That's not it at all. What it is, is that here, I'm not an addict. I'm Tommy Dufresne. I'm a person. That's the difference. And don't you worry. I'm gonna do whatever you want me to in order to make it work. It means so much to me, even more to Charlene. She said that if I stay on treatment, we can get married on the first anniversary. And hey, if there's any machine you got that isn't running right—I'll take care of it, and it's on me.

"Glad I can help," I said. "But seeing as how you're my primary engine provider anyway, we'll just keep it on the same professional basis as here in the office."

"Okay, Doc. Actually, I was thinking more of Sara and Jessica."

"That's a very nice offer," said Sara.

"We thank you," said Jessica.

"There is one more thing," I said. "I've dealt with opiates all my career, but from the other end of the stick. This end is new to me. So, if it's okay with Sara and Jessica, I'd like to add you to my team."

Tommy nodded.

"So, anything I do that doesn't help, or don't do that might, I want you to tell me."

"Sure enough," Tommy agreed. He paused a moment in thought. Then he held out the urine cup. "This business of peeing in a cup."

"Yes, it is a nuisance," I said, "But it's an absolute requirement. Otherwise, I don't get Sara and Jessica to watch over me."

"Which would not be a good idea," said Sara.

"At all," said Jessica.

"I'm with you there," said Tommy. "The thing of it is, when we come in, we want to be treated like an ordinary person. We're coming in because we want to get better. And for just about all of us, our experience with doctors has been, to put not too fine a point on it, less than fulfilling. I know it's different with you and me, because you've known me and been doctoring on me and my family since I was a kid, so I know I can trust you. But others aren't gonna be so lucky. And they won't know you like I do. So, you want to do whatever you can to get their trust. Once you have that, you'll find we are as cooperative and grateful as anyone else who thinks you've saved their life.

"So, here's my first suggestion. Right off the bat you tell them that you understand that their sickness is a medical problem, and that it may never happen, but that at some time in the future, they might find that they're not doing quite as well—better to say it that way than to talk relapse. We're plenty good at punishing ourselves without you needing to pile more wood on the fire. Tell them that no matter what the ups and downs, you'll stick with them, just like you would anyone who'd suffered a setback in any illness. So, there's only one thing you ask, and that is they be honest with you. Otherwise you can't help them when they need it most. And you tell them that it starts with the urine. What I'd do if I were you, I'd say that you can deal with anything that shows up in the urine, as long as you're not surprised. Meaning you ask them before they pee what's gonna be in it, and if it shows opiates or cocaine or amphetamines or benzos, you call it positive, like you would any other test. You never call it *dirty*. Which makes you feel just like the word. You'll do fine, I'm sure." He gestured to Sara and Jessica. "With guidance from your team, of course."

"Of course," said Sara.

"Goes without saying," said Jessica.

"Always worth saying," said Tommy. "And I'll bet you a nickel that what your patients tell you will be a lot more accurate than what the little stripes on this cup show."

"Okay," I said. "We'll start with you."

"Today, Doc, bupe only." He held up the cup in a toasting gesture. "Cheers." And off he went to the lab.

"Good kid," said Jessica after he had left.

"Smart too," said Sara.

"You could learn a lot from him."

"You've known him for a long time?"

"Before his addiction?"

"I sure have," I said. "I wasn't his pediatrician, but I've seen him from time to time over the years. His father and his grandmother and grandfather are my patients, as well as several of the many Dufresnes in town. He or his father has always fixed my equipment. And I served on the school board with his mother for six years."

"Makes a difference," said Sara.

"You're all part of the same community," said Jessica.

"As he said, you know him as a person."

"I do."

"Not likely there will be many like that."

"No," I said, "Dumster is a pretty old-fashioned town."

"Alcohol is the drug of choice?"

"It is," I said.

"As we said before."

"One patient is not very many."

"For us to come all the way down."

"It isn't," I said. "But I know someone who can help me get others."

"People whom you don't already know?"

"Correct."

"So, it won't be like it was with Tommy."

"No."

"They're going to come to you thinking of themselves as addicts."

"I suppose they will."

"You're gonna have to make them people."

"I think I can do that."

"Good."

"I'd say we're off to a good start."

"We agree."

"But it's a long race."

"Been running it a long time," I said.

"Good thing, that."

We shook hands and said goodbye, and we set a day for my clinic in Burlington. As soon as they were gone, I placed a call.

"What's up?" said Brittany. "I'm guessing this ain't a social call."

I told her about my buprenorphine waiver.

"And you're looking for business."

"I prefer to think that I'm looking for people I can help."

"Yeah, that does sound better. And you're wondering if I might know some?"

"It had occurred to me."

"I don't suppose there's any commission?"

"My gratitude and knowing you're helping others was more what I had in mind."

"I'm on it."

"Thank you."

Two days later Alexander Menard came in for a new-patient appointment. Mr. Menard—"Sticks," as he was known—was Brittany's cousin. The reason for his nickname was obvious at first glance. He was tall and thin, with long arms and legs and more angles to him than seemed humanly possible. His herky-jerky action when he moved bore strong resemblance to a collapsing pile of pick-up sticks. His face was deeply lined, and there was a scar that ran down the side of his left cheek that drew the corner of his mouth into a kind of permanent sneer, although when he laughed, which was often, it disappeared into his wide grin. He looked much older than his stated twenty-seven years, but he had the enthusiasm of a kid.

I was to learn over the next year that there were many paths from nirvana. Some of them, like Tommy's, were those of perfectly ordinary people with perfectly ordinary families, until they had a misadventure and were placed on opiates by a doctor—and kept on them by the doctor until they were good and addicted, a process that often took some time. For others the path seemed as natural as the color of their eyes. Often, the family history of such patients was so rife with addiction that it seemed inevitable they would become afflicted, the only question being when. Invariably they told me the same story. With the first hit, they knew—it was something they needed.

Sticks Menard fell squarely in the latter camp.

Although the particulars of how people like Sticks got their addiction vary from family to family, the story is being told not just in New Hampshire and Vermont, but in Delaware and Ohio and West Virginia and Oklahoma, and in virtually every other community where the conditions are favorable to its spread.

The story begins several hundred years ago with a restless young man living somewhere in the Old World. Dissatisfied with the prospects of a life that has been pre-ordained by generations before him, he leaves his native land and comes to the New World to seek his fortune. Here, by dint of hard work and perseverance, and by relying more on his hands than his head, he succeeds. Throughout the nineteenth century and most of the twentieth century, he and his descendants prosper, as he rides the incoming tide of the Industrial Revolution. But then, as inevitably as day turns to night, the tide starts to roll out, and those who relied on it find themselves high and dry. With a clear vision of how much better the life of those before them was than the one they can ever have, his descendants seek a way to obliterate that vision. And in opiates they find just such a way.

The Menard version of this saga begins in the early 1700s, in France, in the province after which Sticks' cousin is named. There in Brittany, in the village of Briec, lived a young man named Jacques Menard. Captivated by the stories of the great explorer Samuel de Champlain and his founding of New France, Jacques made his way to the port of Brest, from which he booked passage on a ship bound for Quebec City. From there he made his way to Trois-Rivières, where he married and settled into a farming life. Over the next hundred years, one branch of the family continued to migrate, following the waterways first west and then south, along the Saint Lawrence, then the Richelieu, and finally down Lake Champlain to Orwell, Vermont. In 1870, Francis Menard, the youngest son of Jean

Paul, restless himself for a new life, left the farm to go work at
the railroad yard in Rutland. Good with his hands and his eyes,
he was quickly promoted from the general labor pool to the
machine shop. The skills he acquired there were ideally suited
to yet another opportunity, the rapidly growing precision tool
industry along the upper Connecticut River. Precision Valley it
was called. He got a job at Jones & Lamson in Windsor, and
when the company relocated to Springfield in 1888, he moved
along with them, settling across the river in the small village
of Unity. He married a Springfield girl by the name of Millie
Parent, with whom he had four children, three girls and a boy.
Like his father, Francis Junior, Frank—the Francois now fully
anglicized—went to work at J & L, as did his son, and the next
succeeding three generations of Menards. The last of them,
Roger Menard, grandfather to Sticks, was working there when
the plant, unable to compete in an international market, closed
its doors. The year was 1984. Roger was unable to find work
either as rewarding or remunerating as the tool-and-die trade.
He took up odd jobs until he finally found steady employment
as a roofer. One day, while working on a new office building in
Springfield, he slipped and fell off the roof. He broke his neck
and died. Young William, his son and Sticks' father, was raised
by his mother, who struggled to make ends meet. She did the
best she could, but she was a quiet and diffident person who
had always relied on her husband for support and guidance.
She was simply not up to the task of being a single mother.
William was pretty much left on his own. At fifteen William
dropped out of school, and at seventeen he met a pretty young
woman from Claremont, Vermont, named Polly Swiderski,
who in short order introduced William first to the wonders
of opiates, and then to the joys of fatherhood. He took to the
former rather better than he took to the latter.

Polly had inherited a family history similar to that of William, the only difference being that the Swiderski elder, Kasi-
mirez, had emigrated from Poland in the 1800s to work in one
of the mills along the Sugar River, and the dissolution of her

family had emanated from the closing of the Joy Manufacturing Company in 1983, a demise hastened by a fire at the already decimated factory.

Polly had two older siblings, Henry and Mary. Henry, the oldest and brightest, recognizing where the future lay, chose to pursue a career in the pharmaceutical industry. Mary, the unfortunate recipient of one of her older brother's defective products, died of an overdose at age twenty-four. At the time of her death, Mary had two children, both girls and both of whom had already been taken into state custody. The older child was adopted by her paternal grandmother, who was a caring woman with a loving home. The younger was not so lucky. She was blessed with a combination of medical and behavioral issues, and the state, with the wisdom it usually employed in the most challenging of its charges, determined that it would be best to share the privilege of her care among as many as possible. Refusing the ardent pleas of her grandmother to keep the family intact, the state placed her in a series of foster homes, where she would last one to two years before, according to their strategy, it was time to move to the next and circle four. This dance went on until she was fifteen, when she ran away from the last of several homes where she had been abused by her foster parents. The state, not so much bowing to the inevitable as writing her off, did not intervene when she moved in with her sister and grandmother. That child was Brittany.

Sticks was raised in an environment of chaos and drugs. He had his first taste of opiates at age twelve, when his maternal uncle gave him an oxy five as payment for cleaning up the garage. It was love at first hit. Soon he was heavily addicted. He graduated to heroin by age sixteen, first snorting and then injecting. "Wasn't no big deal," he said. "Everyone around me was doing it." He went to work for his uncle in the family business, and like all such entrepreneurs, was rather successful until he was caught.

*****

Children are naturally curious. The world is new to them, and they are eager to figure out what it is all about. One of the first words they learn is *why*. Eventually, they get enough of *why* to proceed to *what*, for which purpose curiosity can be a hindrance. There are a few, however, who never make the transition. Some will use this defect to their advantage. They will discover great things and win a Nobel Prize. The vast majority, however, spend their lives ruminating upon questions about which, even if they were to find the answer, no one would give a fig. In the field of addiction, such people devote themselves to solving the Officer Krupke question: Is it just their bringin' upky that gets them out of hand, or is it that deep down inside them they're no good? Is it nurture, or is it nature? Those advocating the former call themselves *social* scientists. They are a more congenial, if less clear-thinking, lot. Their weapon of choice is the statistic, which they wield with considerable versatility. Their opponents, operating under the peculiar delusion that one can best understand the workings of the human brain by examining pictures of it, find proof that people's susceptibility to addiction is intrinsic to their biology.

The possibility that they both might be right is beyond their grasps. But now, thanks to our ability to dissect the human genome, we have determined that Aristotle was right some 2,000 years ago when he proposed the existence of epigenes, genetic material that is formed from experiences early in one's childhood, and which attaches itself to a real gene. These genetic hitchhikers are then passed along on the genes of that person's offspring. This discovery has once again allowed science to take credit for proving the obvious, that both one's nature *and* one's nurture play an important role in who we are, and that for a society to have healthy and happy citizens, all its children must be raised in a nurturing environment, free from want and insecurity. It is rather unfortunate that, at this time, the value of science in informing public policy is less in the ascendant than it has been in the past. One can only

assume that the parents of those currently in authority suffered indescribable childhood horrors of their own, and that
their epigenes are now affecting their need to inflict misery
upon others. When seen in this light, our leaders are more to
be pitied than scorned. I admit it is a rather feeble light. We can
only hope that the next generation will be better.

*****

Sticks Menard is an engaging fellow. Equipped with a
ready smile, quick wit, and a good if somewhat offbeat sense
of humor, he is impossible not to like. Sticks also has a good
head for mathematics and an excellent read of his fellow humans. It is easy to imagine that, had he started from a gate
on a different racecourse, he would have become a successful
businessman, beloved by his employees and respected by his
peers. But the track on which Sticks had been assigned to run
was full of potholes, and it was only a matter of time before
he stumbled and fell.

Opiate sales, legal and otherwise, is a very profitable
business. The annual GDP for illegal opiates is about $30 bil-
lion. The profit, however, is not equally distributed all the way
down the supply chain. While the wholesale distributors do
quite well, retailers like Sticks have a low profit margin, which
is further depleted by the tendency of the sellers to reserve,
for personal use, a substantial share of their product. Sticks
had no permanent domicile. He alternated residence among
business associates, family, and the occasional girlfriend. He
drove a fifteen-year-old Toyota Corolla, and his bank account
had a balance of $57. So, when he was offered an opportunity
to bid on a big shipment at a bargain price, the deal seemed too
good to pass up. Sticks borrowed every dollar he could from a
consortium of like-minded investors, and he made a bid. The
bid was successful. The deal was not. Sticks was arrested in a
sting operation in Nashua, New Hampshire. As it was his first
conviction, he was released after eighteen months in jail, to

drug court, one of the conditions of which was that he enter a
drug treatment program.

Getting to the root of a medical problem can be a lot
of bother. Fortunately, this has never been a real obstacle for
doctors. There are so many things we can *do* without knowing
whether they will do any good, that we are often tempted to
skip the root-getting-to and go straight to the doing. Which is
a much quicker way to satisfy our own irresistible craving to
take the credit.

But when the problem with which we are faced is entirely
new to us, it is particularly important to play the game according to Hoyle. The rules dictate that first we obtain an extensive
history, and then conduct a thorough examination, before we
proceed to our favorite part, the ordering of tests. (So fond are
we of the last step that we honor their results with the title of
objective. This is to distinguish them from what the patient tells
us, which we relegate to the category of *subjective*. Although it
is beyond me why a patient's telling me "The chest pain started
when I was watching *Monday Night Football* and Eli Manning
threw that interception in the end zone on the last play of the
Eagles game" is somehow less objective than an x-ray report
of the lung that indicates an irregularity in the right middle
lobe suggestive of atelectasis, although an infiltrate or mass
cannot be ruled out.)

I have been working with most of the problems I see
for half a century now, and I feel pretty sure of how to proceed when it comes to addressing disorders of a cardiac or
pulmonary or infectious nature. And I am not bad at all when
it comes to matters digestive, dermatologic, and neurologic.
But the treatment of addiction was a new one for me. With
Sticks, I had not the foggiest idea what I needed to know. I
asked him everything I could think of. I asked him about his
family, what they had used and when they had used it and what
had happened to them when they did. I asked him if he was
ever abused. I asked him about how he did in school, including

even his favorite subjects. This last question completely baffled him, as the use of the word *favorite* with respect to school was beyond his comprehension. I asked him where he had lived, and where he had worked. I asked him about partners past and present. I asked him about what he first used, and I asked him what he used next. I asked him when he switched to intravenous. I asked him where he got his needles and if he shared and was he careful about clean needles. Sticks bore it all with good humor, much as a parent would the interrogations of a young child, although he did show some amusement when I asked him about clean needles.

"We're not actually subject to the universal precautions rules of the Joint Commission, you know," he said with a smile, displaying a surprisingly good grasp of hospital regulations. "And usually, when we need a dose, we need it stat. There isn't a lot of time for the sterility stuff, if you know what I mean."

It was only many patients later that I realized something that I should have known from the first. That the *what* of my asking was unimportant. What was important was that I was interested enough in him to ask. Because in the end, I was able to help Sticks—and the many who followed him—not simply because I gave him medicine, but because we established a relationship in which there was a mutual trust that we were both working to the same end: helping him to be as good a Sticks Menard as he could possibly be. After I had asked Sticks all about himself, I asked him if there was anything he wanted to ask me.

"How come you do this stuff, Doc?" Sticks asked.

"My wife told me to."

"Good reason."

Other than being quite thin, Sticks, on examination, was the picture of health. There was the usual collection of scars inside the elbow, but none was recent, and none showed any sign of infection. The large scar on his face came not from any opiate-related misadventure, but when he fell out of a tree at age six and was stabbed by a branch.

With respect to tests, my primary concern was whether, in his communal use of heroin, his colleagues had perhaps also shared with him those shy infections best transmitted by direct injection into the blood stream—HIV, hepatitis B, hepatitis C. Sticks, after directing the phlebotomist to the best vein for the purpose, dutifully supplied a sample that was sent off to the lab for analysis.

The evaluation part accomplished, the next item on the agenda was the business of induction. I knew from my course that, due to the unique opiate properties of buprenorphine, induction was a very tricky business. It had to be undertaken with considerable care. A person who had not used opiates in some time will lose tolerance and be at risk for an over-dose should he suddenly take a dose equivalent to what he consumed when using regularly. One such group of persons are those who have been in prison, or in a rehab facility, where they did not get either buprenorphine or methadone. It is these patients, precisely because they have lost their tolerance, who are at highest risk of overdose.

At the opposite end of the spectrum are those who have been using opiates heavily when they come in for treatment. Because buprenorphine is an incomplete opiate, when a person has a true opiate such as heroin in his body, it will switch roles and play antagonist instead of agonist. In so doing it pushes the active opiate off its perch and takes its place, thereby pre-cipitating an abrupt withdrawal. This is not highly conducive to inducing a positive attitude in the patient toward treatment.

It is essential, therefore, to know just how recently a per-son has been using an opiate, and what that opiate was. Some, like fentanyl, stay in the body for a matter of hours, while oth-ers may last several days. To minimize the risk of miscalcula-tion, the starting recommended dose of buprenorphine is a low one, and the first dose should be taken under supervision, ideally when the patient is already showing signs of opiate withdrawal.

I explained the induction protocol to Sticks and asked him when he had taken his last opiate dose. I then told him I would be giving him a prescription for the smallest dose, which he would bring back to the office so I could monitor him for his response to the drug.

He laughed. "I've been using and selling every kind of opiate there is for close to fifteen years, Doc. I've tried them all, and I've tried them every way you can imagine, and some you might not even. You don't have to tell me how they work, and you sure don't have to tell me about withdrawal. So, just to make things easy for you, I already started a couple of days ago. Bupe is a lot more expensive than heroin, but I figured it was the least I could do, seeing as how you're new to all this. Iffen you need to be sure, just check the urine."

Sure enough, the urine sample he had provided showed buprenorphine only.

"Well," I said, "I don't know. The protocol is…"

"Trust me, Doc. I don't want to get sick."

Somewhat reluctantly, I agreed and wrote a prescription for one day's worth of buprenorphine. It was a low dose.

The next day, he returned looking exactly the same as the day before. He had no signs of intoxication or withdrawal. I was pleased that I had correctly assessed his need. Over the ensuing two weeks I worked him up to what we had agreed would be his maintenance dose. I told Sticks that I thought the induction had gone quite smoothly. He agreed.

"For a first-timer, Doc, you didn't do half bad."

He then explained to me that my opening bid had been rather weak, and he had needed to supplement my prescription with his own, until we arrived at the correct dose.

After that, Sticks followed all the rules. He brought in his medication for a pill count when requested to verify that he had been using the proper amount, a lie that Sticks had already exposed. It is one of the many rules that provide us with the illusion of control over the behavior of our patients, conveniently disregarding the fact that we had no way of knowing whether they were purchasing extra or selling unneeded pills on the open market. And Sticks dutifully provided, under supervision, urine samples that were free of opiates.

One day he came in with a small paper bag.

"Got something for you, Doc. Thought you might like it."

"What is it?"

"It's a Whizzinator."

"A Whizzinator?"

"See for yourself."

I opened the bag. It contained what was from a distance a very realistic-looking plastic penis. At the proximal end was a length of tubing attached to a small plastic bag. The bag was attached to a belt, which contained a small zippered pouch. Sticks explained to me that the bag was for the substitute urine sample, and the pouch was designed to hold a hand warmer, thus ensuring that any urine contained therein was at the proper temperature. One would wear the Whizzinator under his clothing, Sticks said, and with a little practice, it was easy to compress the bag and release urine through the imitation penis. He told me that if one didn't have a reliable source of buprenorphine-only urine, it was easy enough to make one. One could buy powdered urine online, which, when reconstituted, was guaranteed to be drug free. For a higher price, one could purchase buprenorphine urine, but that wasn't necessary. The addition to a sample of a little saliva taken after the daily buprenorphine dose provided a very nice facsimile of the real thing.

"Make a test," Sticks said, "make a way to cheat."

"Yep."

"And today, Doc…"

"Your urine?"

"Could have coke."

"Nobody's perfect."

"Yeah. I slipped up. Went to a party. It was there, and I had to have some. Funny thing, coke was the last thing on my mind, but when I saw it, I had cravings like you wouldn't believe. Seems like the bupe doesn't so much get rid of cravings as switch them. I'm sorry for what I did, and I'm ashamed I let myself go. I guess I just gotta stay away from the opportunity. Out of sight and all that."

"Good idea."

I showed the Whizzinator to Sara and Jessica.

"Cute," said Sara.

"Only time it's easier for a woman," said Jessica.

"Pardon?"

"Concealment."

"As in?"

"Small balloon, sharp fingernail."

"That would work."

"It does."

As it turned out, Sticks' urine that day did not show cocaine. He had used too little too long ago for it to show up. I told him. He smiled.

"There's a lesson there," he said.

"Lesson learned," I said.

Since then Sticks has been a model of recovery. He has a steady job at the Claremont Market, and with the money he has saved on drugs, he managed to make a security deposit and get himself a small, one-room apartment. He even has a girlfriend. She is sober.

I asked him if he thought he would ever want to get off buprenorphine.

He answered without hesitation.

"Nope."

CHAPTER 21

Dumster is not a picturesque town. It does not have a golf course or a ski area or a scenic view. There is no historic landmark in town. Pictures of Dumster have never graced the pages of *Vermont Life*. It does not have a listing on Airbnb.

Excepting friends and family, those visitors whom the town does get are of the drive-through variety, stopping briefly while traveling from the longest covered bridge and Simon Pearce factory in Windsor to one of Vermont's quintessential towns, Woodstock. They might have lunch at Naps or a cup of coffee at Contremond's—where caffeine choices run to cream and sugar, and the muffins are not gluten free. For the rare soul who needs to spend a night, there is the Dumster Motel on Route 5, just south of town. It is clean, and it has cable TV and air conditioning. A room costs $45 a night.

Dumster is a no-frills town.

Its inhabitants are no-frills people. Young people leave, and they are replaced by younger people. Old people die, and they are not replaced. Those looking for a better way of life do not come to Dumster. Those who live there have roots that go back generations.

Dumster folk are averse to change. And even when it happens, they are disinclined to accept it. The fact that something has always been that way is sufficient to keep it that way.

Thus it is that the opiate epidemic has only just begun to touch Dumster. Alcohol remains the drug of choice. Even marijuana has made only a modest appearance. After Tommy and Sticks, who could fairly be considered guests by invitation, there was a dearth of patients seeking buprenorphine treatment with me.

Burlington, on the other hand, is a city of change, a veritable beehive of activity—a hornet's nest, some would say. Hardly a week goes by without a new building sprouting up, or a new store opening downtown. Hardly a week goes by that does not bring a new set of faces to visit those stores. And hardly a week goes by that the ambulance does not bring a new drug overdose into the emergency room. Or the morgue.

I had five patients scheduled to see me my first day at the Riverside Health Center. All of them were already in treatment. For several years they had been on buprenorphine at Burlington's dedicated addiction treatment facility, the Chittenden Clinic, and they were being transferred to my care pursuant to the hub-and-spoke model of opiate treatment. These were people who had done well in the closely monitored environment of the hub and were ready for transfer to a spoke. The Riverside Health Center was one such. These transfers have the dual advantage of giving such patients a substantially greater degree of freedom to live their lives and of making room at the hub to take another new patient. The relationship is reciprocal, so that in the uncommon instance when a spoke patient suffers a setback in treatment, referral back to the hub is a seamless process. The model, identical to the way in which community hospitals refer their more difficult cases to a medical center—from which, once stabilized, they are referred back to their community for ongoing care—has been highly successful, thanks to the willingness of providers like the Riverside Center to serve as spokes, for a wheel without spokes attached to the hub would be a very unstable wheel indeed.

The visits went seamlessly. They were a very grateful group of patients. I felt exceedingly pleased with myself for the care I had provided. I told Sara and Jessica at the end of the clinic how much I had enjoyed the session.

"Good," said Jessica.

"That was the plan," said Sara.

"But just so you know."

"They won't all be like this."

"They were rather an easy lot," I said. "I really didn't have to do anything except continue the treatment they were already on."

"We didn't want to scare you away," said Jessica.

"Which has happened," said Sara.

"More than once."

"But there are a lot more people needing treatment than the hub has room for."

"We need to help them too."

"The difficult ones, you mean," I said.

"*Challenging* is the word we prefer," said Jessica

"Sounds better than difficult," said Sara.

They were right. After the first few weeks of transfers from the hub, I started getting patients who were new to treatment. Some, like Tommy, had been discharged from a rehab program and were concerned they would be unable to stay off heroin without buprenorphine. Others, like Sticks, had already started treatment on their own. Like the transfer group, these patients were highly motivated and happy to have their illness medically managed. They adapted readily to the program and its rules of engagement.

I had accepted about fifteen such patients when Jessica and Sara declared that I was ready.

"For what?"

"To start working."

"Which means?"

"Up to now the patients you have accepted know what they need to do, and they are ready to do it. You can count on them to do the right thing without any help from us. For them, you are not much more than an overpaid pill dispenser."

"I see," I said.

"A very nice one, of course."

"Thanks for the compliment."

"It was nothing."

"True," I said.

"Next week you will get your first real induction. Alison Rondello is an active heroin user, and a pretty heavy one at that. She has lost custody of her three-year-old son, Darren, to her ex-husband's mother because of her addiction. Darren is the most important thing in her life. She has tried repeatedly to get clean on her own but failed. She has been in two separate treatment programs, including one when she was pregnant, but she was unable to keep her appointments. To add to her incentive now, she is in drug court, having been convicted of shoplifting. She has been given one month by the judge to stabilize herself in treatment or she will go back to jail, which means she will lose her child to adoption. She is very motivated to succeed. She is also very impulsive. Delayed gratification is not one of her strong points. Each time she shoots up she swears it will be the last. She will be your next assignment."

"Should you choose to accept it."

"An impossible mission?" I asked.

"As we said."

"We prefer *challenging*."

"Right."

"We have told her she must be free of heroin and in some withdrawal before she can start buprenorphine."

"She promised she would."

"Try."

And she did.

Try.

I entered the room. Sitting in a chair in the exam room was a figure of indeterminate gender dressed in a bulky overcoat several sizes too big. The head was bowed down onto the chest. A large mop of unruly black hair completely covered the face. "Alison?"

The head jerked up. The eyes opened and rolled up to look at me. The spontaneous, unconscious movement reminded me of my sister's Baby Alive when it was picked up. Alison had a smooth, oval-shaped face that might have been pretty had it displayed any expression. Slack-jawed and droopy-eyed, it was, however, blank. The telltale pupils removed any shadow of a doubt as to her state of opiate withdrawal. She looked at me vacantly for several seconds.

"Good morning. I'm Doctor Conger," I said.

Slowly she raised her head. "I tried," she said weakly. Then she perked up a bit.

It is common with those under the influence of opiates for their intoxication to be most pronounced when they are without external stimulus. As a result of my greeting, she awakened from her nod and became alert and coherent. She explained to me that she had gone to bed last night after "only half a ticket," fully prepared for the withdrawal she knew would begin before morning. And despite being shaky and sweaty this morning, she had maintained that resolve. It was only when, frightened by the possibility that she was not in enough withdrawal and the buprenorphine, rather than reducing, would exacerbate her symptoms, that she panicked and took the rest of the bag just before coming in.

There was no way she was going to be able to start buprenorphine this day.

"We thought of just sending her home," said Sara.

"We figured it would be good for you to see what we're up against," said Jessica.

"But there's nothing I can do today," I said.

"Silly goose."

"You're a doctor."

"There's always *something* you can do."

"Show her you care."

"Which, right now, is all that counts."

As always, they were right, of course. I gave Alison

a prescription for clonidine. Clonidine is not an opiate. It is primarily a drug for high blood pressure, and it works by blocking the adrenaline response, which is markedly elevated in withdrawal. It helps, although not very much, to reduce the symptoms. I told her it might help her stay away from heroin when she was in withdrawal. We agreed that she would try again next week.

Alison returned as scheduled. And she had done better. She was alert and cooperative and ready. The only thing she was not was in withdrawal.

"I did wait longer," she said. "Not long enough, I guess."

"Maybe the third time will be a charm."

She did not show up for her next appointment.

Sara and Jessica explained to me that Alison's story was pretty typical. Patients often showed up before they were really ready to quit, and that the requirement for withdrawal was almost as much a way of assessing their motivation as it was a medical necessity.

"She'll be back," said Sara.

"If she doesn't OD," said Jessica.

"Or wind up in jail."

"Sooner rather than later, most likely."

"She's a mother."

"It's Darren that will get her to come in."

The next week, when I arrived in the morning, I saw a familiar overcoat huddled outside the entrance, waiting for the clinic to open. Alison was shaking like a leaf. After I gave her a small starter dose from the clinic supply, she settled down quickly and explained that she was due for a hearing on her reunification petition in court the next day and knew she had to be straight if she was to have any hope of getting her son back.

She did both, and except for two times early in the course of her treatment when she was unable to resist an offer to "share" from an old friend, she has been a model of success. Each time she comes in, she brings Darren. Each time I ask

her how she is doing, and she says "good." Each time I ask
Darren if she really is good. And when he says yes, I give him
a gold sticker to put on the paper he brings in. The paper says,
Mom's Report Card. We are now on the third page of stickers.

It wasn't long before I had a sizeable buprenorphine practice at the health center. Most of the patients were women, and
their stories were depressingly similar to Alison's. Since early
childhood they had all suffered from relentless and systematic
abuse, first at the hands of relatives, then in school, and finally
from the many men in their lives. To add to it all, there was
the additional battle with child protective service that appeared
never to have met an addicted person it could like. Given a
chance for a legal and safe way to manage their addiction, almost to a person, they succeeded.

By three months, I felt I was getting the hang of things,
and I felt I had experienced the full face of addiction.

Then I met Daniel Day Finnegan.

It was a Wednesday morning. I already had a full schedule when Sara told me they had what they called a Blue Light
Special.

"Unadvertised patient?"

"Yep."

"He's sick."

Sick is what many people are when they come to see the
doctor. It can mean almost anything. I looked at Sara and Jessica.

"COWS is thirty-five," they answered in unison.

In Mr. Finnegan's case, sick meant something very particular.

COWS is short for Clinical Opiate Withdrawal Scale. It
is a quantitative score that is determined by assigning point
values to the severity of the signs and symptoms of withdrawal. For example, in order to start someone on Suboxone, it is
recommended that they have a score of at least five, which is
considered mild withdrawal. Alison scored twelve when she
started.

Daniel Day Finnegan was yawning and shaking uncontrollably. His pupils were widely dilated, and his pulse was bounding. Water was pouring off his forehead and out his nose. Every few seconds he was out of his chair, pacing around the room.

In a city in the midst of an opiate epidemic, at a clinic where addicted persons were being treated, this particular sickness was not unusual.

What *was* unusual was the patient.

His face was deeply lined. His hair was thin and gray. His neck barely moved when he turned to look at me. And despite his agitation, there was a weariness in his gaze that told of a life lived hard. He looked like an old man.

I picked up his chart to see how old he actually was.

His date of birth was listed as June 7, 1944.

He *was* an old man.

A sick old man.

I gave him some clonidine. I was surprised to see how much better he rapidly became, so much so that he was easily able sit still and provide me with a detailed account of his addiction.

At the top of the list of what I needed to know was exactly what he had used and when he had last used it. This would help me anticipate the time course of his withdrawal.

"How long ago was your last hit?" I asked him.

"Been a while," he said. "And most folks call me Professor now."

"Professor it is. Easier than Daniel Day."

"Why they used to call me D Day."

I looked again at his birthdate. "Makes sense. Your dad?"

"Omaha Beach."

"Did he make it back?"

"Most of him."

"Sorry to hear that," I said. "Now, *a while* is a pretty flexible unit of time. When did you start getting sick?"

"This morning."

"Did you use anything last night?"

The Professor smiled. "Nope"

"Yesterday morning?"

His smile widened. "Not then either."

Withdrawal occurs rapidly with drugs like heroin and fentanyl, but long-acting opiates like methadone and extended-release formulations can have a delayed withdrawal reaction. As withdrawal can also last longer, it was important to know what he had been using.

"What was it you used?" I asked.

"Woulda been heroin."

"Just heroin?"

"Well, mighta been some fentanyl too, but I doubt it. Wasn't much around back then?"

"Back then?"

"Two thousand thirteen, May fifth, to be exact. In the morning, if I remember right."

"The last time you used was over three years ago?"

"Yep."

"Long time for withdrawal, I'd say."

"Not long enough, I'd say."

"It sure looks like you're in withdrawal," I admitted, "but you can't be. It must be something else."

"Not according to Ivan."

"Ivan?"

"A guy I know."

"I see."

"Not likely. Anyway, I'm guessing you'd like me to give you the full Paul Harvey."

"The rest of the story would be nice."

It was quite a story. Daniel Day Finnegan was born in South Boston, the only boy of six children. Daniel was the youngest by eight years. He was also the smartest. His father worked in the shipyards until the war, and when he came back with one leg less and one set of nerves more, he couldn't go back to work. Instead, he became devoted to drinking himself blind. In very little time his liver gave out. Daniel's father died when Daniel was only three years old. Daniel's mom was a tough woman, and her eldest daughter was cut out of the same cloth. Between the two of them they were able to provide a stable set of parents for the other five children. The girls were no problem, but Daniel was a rapscallion. The two women knew he needed a male role model in order to keep him out of serious trouble. Father O'Connor, the priest at Saint Vincent's, their local parish, was a perfect fit. Born and raised in Southie, he knew how hard it was to get out, and recognizing Daniel's potential, he committed himself to getting him the break he deserved. When Daniel got in trouble, it was Father O'Connor who spoke up for him. When Daniel lost interest in school, it was Father O'Connor who became his tutor. And when Daniel was at Boston Latin, it was Father O'Connor who got him his scholarship to Holy Cross. Daniel graduated summa cum laude and went on to graduate school at MIT, where he got a PhD in combinational optimization, a discipline that I would be glad to explain, if I could.

After two years as a teaching assistant at MIT, Daniel landed a job as an assistant professor in the department of mathematics at the University of Vermont, and over the course of the next seven years he rose to full professor, a tenured position that he held until three years ago, when, due to circumstances that I will explain presently, he was forced to resign abruptly.

*****

The sixties were a time of change. The old ways of doing things were being challenged. Established traditions were being discarded. Alcohol, the mainstay of South Boston ever since the arrival of the Irish during the potato famine, was one of the casualties. Marijuana, LSD, heroin, and cocaine were everywhere, and although the older and wiser of South Boston stuck with their tried and true, the young were less fettered.

Daniel Day was a curious fellow. By which I do not mean he was odd. Daniel was good looking, well-spoken, and sensible, even if he did have a somewhat underdeveloped sense of propriety. But when presented with the opportunity for a new experience, like Alice, he was not inclined to shy away. And if after the experience he became curioser and curioser, he considered it an experience well ventured. His curiosity served him in good stead in academic life. In a young boy, it is less salutary. The drugs were there for the trying, and Daniel Day tried them all. Except heroin. He had seen what the needle had done to too many of his classmates to take a chance. Especially when there were so many other choices. Most of them he didn't care for. Alcohol put him to sleep. Marijuana made him feel like a zombie, likewise the sedative hypnotics. LSD and PCP gave him upsetting visions and awakened a hitherto unknown paranoia. On one particularly unpleasant occasion, having consumed some magic mushrooms, he attempted to rid his sister Mary of a fiendish devil that had invaded her body with a carving knife. He stopped only when Mary screamed in terror, "D Day, you crazy?" at which point, even in his drug-addled state, his instincts prevailed, and having paused to consider the question, he answered, "I think so." And immediately he ended the exorcism.

Cocaine, however, was another matter. For most people it produces little more than a transient euphoria and sense of invincibility. For a select few—including such great minds of civilization as Sigmund Freud, Thomas Edison, and Edgar Allen Poe, to name a few—it was their miracle muse, a stimulant to creativity unmatched by anything else.

Daniel Day was an avid reader. Among his favorite books were the works of Sir Arthur Conan Doyle. He had read them all, over and over again. *A Study in Scarlet*, *The Sign of the Four*, *The Redheaded League*. The night before an examination, he eschewed cramming, preferring instead to immerse himself in one of Sherlock's adventures, convinced that fortifying himself with the detective's deductive powers would be more beneficial to his performance than the mere acquisition of a set of soon-to-be-forgotten facts. When inevitably he tried the drug so favored by his idol, Daniel was hooked. From the first snort, he was amazed by the way it sharpened his concentration and enhanced his powers of reasoning. "This is for us," said Brain to Daniel. To which Daniel answered, "Sure is."

Daniel was smart. And although curious, he was not reckless. He knew the risks. And so, he was careful. Throughout high school, excepting the occasional party, he used it only before final examinations. In college, he used it more liberally, particularly when it came to writing his senior honors thesis, "Metaheuristic Approach to Stochastic Combinational Optimization by Using Simulated Annealing and Boltzmann Machines," which earned him his summa and his admission ticket to MIT.

Daniel may have been smart, but cocaine is smarter. It knows that all it has to do is bide its time, and eventually the brain in question will discover that there is no end to its beneficial uses. Daniel is a strong-willed person, and the fact that he was able to maintain a semblance of control until he finally got tenure is a tribute to that will. But as soon as he passed his final hurdle and became a tenured professor of mathematics, he let his guard down.

Which one can never do with cocaine.

In time, he became increasingly erratic, erupting in outbursts of anger in faculty meetings, berating students in class—calling them imbeciles, slugs, and cretins and persisting in his tirades until he had managed to reduce even the most confident among them to tears. At which point, his aim having been achieved, he would stop abruptly and stalk out of the room, slamming the door behind him. He had a long string of unsuccessful relationships, most of which ended as a result of the same kind of abuse he perpetrated upon students. At the time, such behavior was not condemned in public. It was either ignored or reluctantly tolerated. Eventually, however, things got so bad that his colleagues decided that something had to be done. One Friday afternoon they surrounded him in his office and, refusing to accept any excuses, packed him off to a pre-arranged stay at a rehabilitation facility in Santa Fe, New Mexico.

He spent three months there. When he came back, he was a changed man. Calm and well behaved, he was the model of academic decorum. He spoke only when spoken to, and even then, he often paused before responding. He was courteous to all, and he was solicitous of the well-being of his students, especially the least among them. That he was no longer as insightful as he had been and that at times he seemed inattentive was a small price to pay for the transformation.

No one knew that the Professor's cure had come at a price identical to that paid some eighty years earlier by one of the great surgeons of modern medicine, William Halsted. Doctor Halsted, having fallen victim to the lure of cocaine, was also, at the insistence of his colleagues, admitted to an asylum for many months. There he succeeded in curing his cocaine addiction by means of the treatment deemed safest and most effective at that time.

The treatment was morphine.

One of the best places to get drugs is in the vicinity of a drug rehabilitation center. Early in the course of the Professor's stay, a fellow patient, sympathetic to the pains that the Professor was experiencing during his withdrawal, offered him the modern version of the Halsted remedy. One hit was all it took.

It was easier to hide his opiate addiction, especially as the Professor kept his promise never to use the needle. Nasal remained his only route of administration. The bigger problem, however, was financial. Relative to the salary of a professor, heroin was quite costly. The professor found it necessary to take on an additional job to make ends meet.

The Professor tried hard to generate income by socially acceptable means. He offered himself as a tutor. He tried his hand at consulting. He even signed up as a substitute teacher at the local high school. But the market was skimpy for tutoring in combinational optimization, and the demand for consulting in such was nonexistent. Substitute-teaching opportunities there were plenty, but he quickly discovered that a high school math class had nothing to do with math and everything to do with crowd control. And so, he turned to the business he already knew well—as a consumer.

Doctors had just turned off the prescription opiate pump. Heroin was an emerging market in Burlington. It was a small-business enterprise managed by sole proprietors who handled commodity acquisition, product manufacture, and distribution with the help of at most one or two friends or family members. The Professor didn't have to read *Freakonomics* to know that there was no real money to be made in retail. Combining a good head for numbers and his Irish affability with a business acumen he never realized he had, he soon developed a highly successful wholesale heroin business. He recognized that product quality in an industry that had no consumer protection would be a big draw. The Professor personally oversaw every step of his manufacturing and supervised closely his distributors, ensuring that what they sold was not adulterated. So highly was his heroin valued that a bag of Professor, as it became known, was the standard against which all others were judged. It sold at a premium price. He knew he was in a risky business, and he was very careful. He never overextended his supply lines, he never sought more profit than what was necessary for his own needs, and he never sold directly to the consumer. As a consequence, he was able to avoid arrest for over ten years.

Sentenced to ten to twenty years, he was released from federal prison in Upstate New York after three for good behavior. The bus ride home was uneventful. But when he disembarked at the station on Cherry Street in downtown Burlington, everything went to hell in a handbasket. As in most cities, the bus station in Burlington is one of the prime locations for those whose pharmaceutical needs are of a nature not accommodated by CVS or Walgreens.

******

"It's actually quite interesting, when you think about it," the Professor said, his voice professorial now. "This business of cravings. Whole time I was in prison, I never had a single one, not even when I went in. I had withdrawal big time, of course, but after it was over, I never thought a bit about heroin. Well, that's not strictly true. I did have dreams sometimes where white powder made a guest appearance, but other than that, nada. And all the way home on the bus I was thinking how good it felt to be clean *and* free. And then, soon as I stepped off that bus and I saw the old dealing grounds, it hit me like a ton of bricks. Shakes, sweats, yawns, and trots, the whole shooting match. Just like old Ivan would have predicted.

"Ah," I said, at least seeing the reference to Ivan Pavlov. "That Ivan. The one with the dogs."

"And the buzzer."

"We call it a trigger now."

"Call it what you want, Doc. Sets the brain to craving either way. This old noggin may not be smart in a lot of things," he said, tapping his skull twice, "but it sure knows how to get what it wants. Does an impressive job at virtual reality. I don't think there was a single symptom that it didn't call up. Didn't help that I knew it was fake, 'cause I also knew that there wasn't anything going to stop it until I got a fix. So, unless you get me started on bupe right now, I'm going to be back out on the street looking for stuff—which I would rather not do."

It was indeed just another variation of the story of the dogs, the buzzer, and the salivation. As Pavlov had shown over a century ago, conditioned behavior is very easy to induce, and very hard to change. The Professor had long since lost his tolerance and was not in literal physical withdrawal, so I gave him a low starter dose and said I would come back up tomorrow to see how he had managed.

The next day he was fine. We talked over what to do next and agreed on two things. First, that he shouldn't need much of a dose to keep his cravings at bay. And second, that we hadn't a clue whether our assumption was correct. He agreed to call me promptly should he feel he was losing control, and I promised I'd give him however much buprenorphine it took to prevent that.

It took twenty-four milligrams, the maximum I prescribe. It wasn't right off, but every week or so, we would increase the dose by a couple of milligrams until finally the powers above were satisfied.

I asked him, after he had been stable for a couple of months, if he thought he would ever want to try to get back down off the medication.

He may have been a professor, but his answer was no different from those of any of the others I had treated. "Not on your tintype," he said. Just to make sure I got the picture, he added, "No way. Never. Not a snowball's chance in hell—which is where I'd be if I did."

CHAPTER 22

One evening I was sitting at my desk, finishing up my charts, when Crikett came in.

"The ER called. Brittany's here."

In the past several months, Brittany had been a frequent visitor, and the interval between her visits was declining. Although she had not yet required admission, each time it took longer to break her episodes of respiratory distress, and she usually left, not because she was better, but because she'd had "about as much of it as I can take for now." Her oxygen flow had been steadily increased and stood now at six liters a minute, which was the limit of effective delivery by a nasal cannula. In order to get an adequate supply, she would have had to wear a mask, which she adamantly refused.

"No way I'm going to Foxwood with a mask," she had declared resolutely. "They'd never let me in."

On her previous visit, she was accompanied by a quiet, nice-looking young person. More a boy than a man, he didn't look even twenty. He was slightly built, with closely cut light brown hair and a pair of pale blue eyes that stared at me with a deer-in-the-headlights expression.

"This is Tim," said Brittany. "Tim is my friend."

"Ah. A *friend*."

Britany grinned. "With… *limited* privileges."

I put out my hand. "Well, Tim, I'm pleased to meet you."

Tim looked at his shoes. Then he looked at Brittany.

Brittany nodded. Then, looking back at his shoes, as if to make sure he hadn't overlooked anything of importance upon first inspection, he shyly put out his hand.

Tim was in the waiting room when I arrived. He was ashen and trembling. Until I went into the examining room, I thought he was going to be worse off than Brittany.

Because I saw her regularly, I hadn't noticed how much weight she had lost. But when they put her on the bed scale, it was a lot. Ordinarily ten pounds wouldn't amount to much, but when one starts at only sixty-nine pounds, it is substantial. Whatever muscle and fat she once had was completely gone. Her paper-thin skin was stretched so tightly over her bones it seemed as if any sudden movement would tear it to shreds. As she sat bolt upright on the stretcher and heaved her chest up and down, gasping for air, I could believe that her skin might actually tear.

Her temperature was 103, her oxygen level, even with 100 percent oxygen through a nonrebreathing mask, was only 85 percent. Things did not look good.

A portable chest x-ray showed pneumonia in her right lower lobe. There was a large collection of fluid at the bottom of the lung.

"That's good news," I told her, "in a way."

Unable to speak, she just shook her head.

"It means there's something I can do that will make you better. Intravenous antibiotics will treat the infection, and I can take off the fluid to help the lung expand. You should get some relief right away. But you're going to need to be admitted."

Brittany shrugged.

After giving her morphine to settle her down and putting her on a BiPAP machine to assist her breathing, I drained about a quart of fluid from the right lung. The fluid was clear and pale yellow in color. This was reassuring. It meant there was no abscess, and the tube wouldn't have to stay in. Within minutes her oxygen level had climbed to 90 percent, her breathing had slowed, and she was able to come off the BiPAP.

She managed a half smile.

"Feel better?" I asked.

She raised her arm and extended her fingers, placing her thumb and forefinger about half an inch apart.

"Call the ICU, please," I said to Dennis McInerny, the nurse on duty, "and ask them please to get a bed ready."

With a strength I couldn't believe she had, Brittany grabbed my arm and shook her head violently.

"I can't send you home like this."

She took off her oxygen mask. "The Morgue," she wheezed.

"The ICU would be better."

She shrugged.

"Okay, then."

On her second visit to see me, Brittany had asked that I show her around the hospital. She was particularly interested in one of the rooms we had fixed up for patients with terminal illness—hospice patients. It was a lovely room. Instead of the standard hospital drab, it looked like an actual bedroom. There were two upholstered armchairs, a wood-frame bed with large fluffy pillows, and a soft floral-patterned down comforter that matched the wallpaper. It had a huge television screen and a DVD player. A small single bed for anyone who might want to spend the night was in the corner. The bathroom had a walk-in shower and large tub with a Jacuzzi. Fresh flowers were everywhere. A set of French doors opened out onto a terraced courtyard, in which were a set of patio furniture and a gas grill. The courtyard was bordered with high shrubs that concealed it from the rest of the hospital grounds. It could have served equally well for a couple beginning a new life as it did for a person ending an old one. It is an unfortunate fact of medical care that a person has to be dying before a hospital provides reasonable accommodations.

The staff called it the Flower Room. Brittany had renamed it the Morgue.

By midnight her breathing had settled down, and her oxygen level was holding steady at 95 percent. I went home.

The first call came at 4 a.m. It was from Ellen Pritchett. Ellen is seventy-five years old. She has been a nurse at the hospital for fifty-six years, going back to the time even before Emmeline Talbot, when it was Dumster Hospital in the large Victorian building on Main Street that now serves as assisted living for seniors. That she was the only one who still wore a white nurse's cap, with dress and stockings to match, didn't bother her one bit. She was as old-style as they come.

"Mrs. Menard is refusing her vital signs," she said, making no effort to conceal her irritation. "I told her how important it was in monitoring her progress. She told me to stuff my progress."

"Sounds like she's better," I said.

"It is not a subject for amusement, Doctor Conger."

"She didn't really tell you to stuff progress, did she?"

"No. But I'm not going to repeat what she *actually* said."

"Thank you for letting me know."

"I'm going to have to write her up."

"That would be the proper thing to do."

"Yes. Unlike some, *I* know what is proper."

The next call was at 6 a.m. It was Mrs. Pritchett again.

"Mrs. Menard has refused her antibiotics."

"You told her how important it was in her treatment, I expect."

"I did. She told me to stuff my treatment. Said if it was so important then she could get it at a civilized hour."

"I see."

The last call came thirty minutes later.

"Mrs. Menard is demanding her morphine. It is not due until seven. When I reminded her of this, she said nobody told her pain that it had to wait."

"And she told you to stuff the wait?"

"No."

"Hmmm."

"She told me to go stuff myself."

"She didn't bite you, did she?"

"No. But she threatened me. Said if I didn't get out of her sight, she was going to whip me good."

"That wasn't very nice. Most likely she isn't quite herself right now."

"You know what I think, Doctor Conger? I think she is *exactly* herself, and I'll tell you what she is, whether you excuse my language or not. She's nothing but a stuffing bitch. And I for one am not going to have anything to do with her. And if anyone tries to make me, I'll quit."

"I don't think anyone will try that, Ellen."

She rang off.

Sarah Trotter, our head nurse, took me aside as soon as I arrived on the floor.

"She's been here less than twelve hours, Beach, and she's already a disaster. I had to send Ellen Pritchett home practically in tears, and now all the other nurses are saying they're not going to go in the room either. They know about what happened at Dartmouth. Word like that gets around. I went in myself to give her the morphine and the antibiotics, but I'm not here all the time. I understand the poor thing is deathly ill, but I've got a rebellion on my hands. Can you talk any sense into her?"

"I don't know."

"Well try. It's not just her whose care is being compromised. It's everybody else on the ward."

There was an inescapable irony in the fact that the only thing that had kept her alive so long was that Mrs. Pritchett's diagnosis was correct, although I might prefer for purposes of this work to use the less misogynistic choice of ornery.

"Morning, Beach," Brittany said, greeting me with a broad smile. "How'd you sleep?"

"Often."

"Me too."

"Quite a coincidence, that."

"You want to know how I am, I s'pose."

"I do, but first…"

"You want to know if I'm going to behave myself."

"I do."

"Maybe."

"I don't know if *maybe* will quite work."

"You gonna throw me under the bus if it doesn't? Wouldn't look too good if I up and died after a *premature discharge*, would it? Feds never too happy 'bout that."

"I'm not going to discharge you. But unless we work out some kind of solution, it could get out of my hands. The administration could declare that you require services beyond our capability and arrange a transfer to a more suitable facility."

"Might take a while to find one."

"And in the meantime, you'd be spending all your energy fighting the nurses and none getting better."

She shrugged. "Worse things to do with my time. Kinda entertaining sometimes."

"So, tell me, how can we get past *maybe*?"

Brittany gave me a sly grin. "Thought you'd never ask. You know, Beach, it's not that I enjoy giving them such a hard time. Well, I do enjoy it, course, but that's not the main thing. It's about power and control. They got it, and I need it. I ain't got much of it left, but it is my life, after all. And I got a right to live it out best I can."

She was absolutely right. But the idea that she could do what she wanted to, when she wanted to, was completely at odds with the business of converting a person into a patient, something that all hospitals rely upon to proceed expeditiously. I didn't see how things could be resolved.

"Any chance for a compromise?"

"A little."

"A little probably won't be enough."

"You're a smart guy, Beach. Make it enough."

It turned out not to be that hard. First, I added post-traumatic stress disorder—PTSD for short—to her list of diagnoses. This, I thought, was fair. There had been more than enough trauma in Brittany's life. This helped quite a bit. Nurses, themselves subject to more than their share of abusive behavior in an ordinary workday, are an intrinsically compassionate lot. Having some reason to justify unreasonable behavior made it a lot easier for them to tolerate it. Then I switched her pain medicine to a PCA pump. PCA stands for patient-controlled analgesia. The pump allowed Brittany, just by pressing a button, to deliver as much morphine as she needed, as often as she needed it. There was a theoretical risk of overdose, but Brittany was smart enough to know when she had received too much, and assuming she didn't want too much, which at least for now, she didn't, the pump should work just fine. I simplified her vital signs. I cancelled weights and blood pressures, writing that I would document these, which I did by asking Brittany what she would like them to be. I restricted the others to meal time, when she was sure to be awake and at least in some mood for receiving. I did request that she do me the favor of putting up with this on the grounds that it was now a relatively minor indignity, and the inconvenience to her life would be more than made up for by the convenience to mine.

"Sure," she said. "I'm not trying to be unreasonable, ya know."

"Perish the thought."

There was a rustling in the corner and a shuffling sound, the kind a dog makes when preparing a place for himself on a rug. I looked over.

I had forgotten about Tim.

He was sitting up on the single bed, scuffing his feet back and forth on the floor. He was staring at Brittany with a terrified expression.

"Tim," I said. He turned to me with a pleading look.

"It's okay," I said. "She's going to be fine."

There was a single harsh cough from Brittany—more like a snort. It was a lie, and we all knew it. But it worked. Like declaring victory in a lost war, the declaration itself had the effect of making us almost believe it, at least for a time.

For the rest of that day, she *was* better. She was still unable to get out of bed on her own, and she still required the mask for oxygen, but her temperature had come down, and the repeat x-ray showed no fluid had accumulated again in her lung. I told Brittany the good news when I stopped by in the afternoon.

"Looks like maybe I'm gonna be here a bit. Best make myself comfortable."

"I think things are all set on my end," I said. "I can't say we have an actual truce with the nurses. It's rather more like detente."

"Mutually assured destruction, I believe is the expression," said Brittany. She winked. "Don't worry, Beach. Things will be fine. Just you wait and see. Soon enough, they'll be eating out of my hand, as it were."

"Really?"

"Trust me."

"I'll try."

She turned to Tim. "Bring in my Mac and a USB cable. We're gonna have us some fun."

And she did.

By the end of the day, nurses were vying to be assigned to Brittany, and by the end of the next day, even those not assigned to her care could be seen making frequent trips into her room, "just to make sure everything was okay." From time to time exclamations of joy and disappointment could be heard emanating from behind the closed door of her room.

The cause of Brittany's remarkable rise in popularity was ingenious. Using her contacts, she had managed to obtain an online connection to the gambling site for Foxwoods, thereby enabling her computer to recreate a virtual casino where one could play any of the games of chance one desired—video poker, blackjack, roulette, or for those who just wanted to throw away their money without the pretense of skill, slot machines. Nurses would pay Brittany an amount of money of their own choosing. This served as their stake. They were then allowed to play their games of choice until they had lost the amount of their stake. Although it would have been only reasonable for her to charge a commission for the service, Brittany steadfastly refused to take any payment. She did let it be known, however, that chocolates of any kind would be graciously accepted in appreciation of services rendered, adding that because of her cystic fibrosis, she needed more than the average person.

"What could they give me that I could possibly use that I don't already have?" she said. "The only real pleasure I have these days is gambling, and now I've got a whole new game to play, even if there's no money in it."

"Which protocol dictates I should ask you about."

"Well," she said with a grin, "if you insist." She reached over to her night table, opened the drawer, and pulled out a sheet of paper.

The paper was ruled in tabular form with rows and columns. The headings across the top read, "Name, CC, Roulette, Blackjack, Poker, Slots." In the rows of the first column were the names of most of the current staff on the floor. In each of the remaining columns were numbers from 0 to 10.

"CC?" I asked

"Candy Crush."

Brittany loved everything sugary. "You could say my tooth is the only sweet thing about me," she often joked.

"I can understand the games and what looks like some kind of scoring system, but why the candy?"

Brittany rolled her eyes. "Not a candy, silly." She picked up her phone, clicked a couple of times, and handed it to me. On the screen were a set of variously colored objects of differing shapes arranged in rows and columns. I looked at it uncomprehending.

She took the phone and held it so that we both could see the screen. "These things," she said, pointing at the objects, "are the candies. The idea is that you move them about to get them in groups of at least three, being sure, of course, to get rid of the jelly and to remove any bombs that might be lurking."

"Of course."

Her fingers flew over the phone. Explosion-like bursts cascaded across the screen. A scoreboard at the bottom lit up each time. The number on the scoreboard increased by leaps and bounds with each explosion. She handed the phone back to me. "Here," she said, "you try." Painstakingly she showed me how to make a move. Sliding a green blob to the right and a blue square to the left, I produced a line of three green blobs in a row and was rewarded with a small fireworks display. I handed the phone back to her.

"So, what do you think of it?"

"Looks like loads of fun."

She handed the phone to me again.

"Want to try some more?" she asked slyly.

"I think not. Don't want to ruin my perfect record."

"Ever been to a casino?"

"Once—in Reno."

"Play the slots?"

"I tried. It didn't work out so well."

"Because."

"I had twenty-five dollars' worth of quarters. I planned to play until they were gone. On my third try I hit some kind of jackpot, and quarters came pouring out of the machine. I realized it would take forever to get rid of them, so I gave up and went home."

"Figures," Brittany said. She picked up her paper. Under the last entry in the name column, she wrote, "Beach." Under CC, she put a 0. The others she left blank except slots, where she entered another 0.

She put the paper down. "I got a theory."

"Always interested in theories."

"My theory is that this game, Candy Crush, is an excellent predictor of addictive potential. So, before I let anyone do online gambling, I give them Candy Crush to see how they react. Their score depends on how addicted they become to the game. Zero at one end, and ten at the other. You know what zero is. Ten is when a person can't put it down, even when talking or eating. A few—women—told me they even keep it next to the bed during sex. Then I look to see how well it correlates with their attraction to the different casino games. The best correlation, of course, is with the slots, but you can see the others are pretty close too."

They were. There was a remarkable similarity between the Candy Crush scores and those for the games of chance.

"Very interesting,"

"Not really. But you know what would be?"

"I think I can guess."

"I bet you can.

"Which maybe you discovered before all this."

"Which I did."

"I'm guessing you found that people addicted to drugs have a high propensity for addiction to Candy Crush."

"They do."

"So, what you're suggesting is that maybe if we tested kids with their response to Candy Crush, we would have a good predictor of their risk later in life of developing an addiction to drugs."

"It's possible. the thing of it is…"

"Be a really good idea, if we knew what to do about it."

"You said it."

"You know, Brittany," I said, "you missed your calling."

"I missed a lot of callings, Beach."

"You did."

She shrugged. "I'm not complaining," she said. "What's the point?"

"Doesn't stop most people."

"I'm not exactly most people."

"No, you're not."

It could have been the chocolate, it could have been the attention, but most likely is was just one of those things that happens when life gets the urge to defy expectations. Regardless, Brittany got better. She put on weight. She used less oxygen. And for the first time in weeks, she was not only able to transfer out of the wheelchair to a sitting position, she was able to walk almost the length of the corridor. She made plans to go home.

The night before her discharge she slipped in the bathroom and fell against the sink, breaking three ribs and sustaining a 50 percent pneumothorax that collapsed her left lung. I told her that without a chest tube, she would almost certainly die within the next couple of days. Reluctantly she agreed to the tube.

The chest tube cleared the pneumothorax, and in three days it was out. Unfortunately, a significant part of her left lung did not re-expand, and the collapsed portion became infected. The infection, caused by one of those multi-resistant bacteria that hospitals love to give to their patients, spread to her blood stream. I gave her potent antibiotics. The bacterial infection resolved. It was replaced by another hospital favorite, an opportunistic fungus that lies in wait for a body's protective bacteria to be killed off before taking over. Anti-fungal antibiotics destroyed the fungus, but in the process, they damaged the kidneys. Throughout it all, Brittany was unperturbed. "Could be worse," was her response whenever I asked her how she felt. Then she would add, "And probably will be." Three weeks into her stay, she hadn't actually turned the corner, but she had stopped her backward slide.

Then she started to bleed. Not a lot. Some bruising under the skin from her IV, a small nosebleed that stopped with packing. Then, each time she had blood drawn, a pressure dressing had to be applied to keep it from oozing. I didn't need any test results to know what had happened. Her bone marrow, not the strongest at best, attacked first by the infections and then by the medicines used to treat them, was worn out. And her antibodies, roused to combat the foreign invaders and now lacking any to repel, turned their fire against her own clotting factors, delivering a one-two punch to her coagulation system that left her bereft of means to control bleeding. Although not absolutely a point of no return, it was one requiring a treatment that we could not provide. She would have to be transferred to the medical center, which, as she had burned her bridges at Dartmouth, would have to be at the University of Vermont Medical Center in Burlington. I told Brittany.

"Que sera, and all that," she said. "But if you don't mind, I think I'll pass on the offer."

"There is a treatment that might well work," I pleaded, knowing full well that of the many things to which Brittany was immune, persuasion was at the top of the list. "Besides, what have you got to lose?"

She looked at me hard. "My dignity."

"Not likely."

"Maybe not. Anyway, it's way more fun here."

"That it is."

She looked at me. "You know that Kenny Rogers song?"

"'The Gambler?'"

"That's the one."

"It's time for this gambler…"

"To fold 'em?"

"*The best I can hope for.*"

So, Tim moved back into the room. And with him the morphine pump. While she could, Brittany did the dosing. And then, when she couldn't, she left strict instructions with Tim as to exactly how much, how often, and when to increase. For two days she slept peacefully. Tim did not sleep a wink. He never took his hand off the button on the pump. Any attempt to relieve him was rebuffed with a quiet but determined response. "Thanks anyway, but I got my orders."

She got the best she could hope for.

Hospitals are very fond of naming things after people. This is not so much out of any desire to personalize what is essentially a sterile and impersonal place as it is to reap the appreciation, expressed financially, by the recipients of the honor. The room in which Brittany was staying had one such honorific plaque declaring that it was donated "In Memory of Harriet Jenkins" by her devoted husband in appreciation for the care she had received there.

The hospital staff asked the administrator how much they would have to raise to get a plaque added in Brittany's name. The question of whether a single object could be named in honor of two separate people had never been raised before. The CEO suggested that a tree in the courtyard or a chair in the lounge would be more suitable. Both offers were politely but firmly rejected. The CEO said it was highly irregular, and he didn't really see how it could be done. The staff said perhaps it would help if they refused to work in that room until their request was accommodated. The CEO referred the question to the board of trustees. The trustees, in deference to the grateful and very wealthy Mr. Jenkins, thought it prudent to ask his feelings on the matter. Mr. Jenkins talked to the nurses, and after a rather extensive conversation, agreed to the plaque on the condition that he be allowed to make the necessary contribution, and that he could be present at the ceremony when it was put up.

On the plaque there was no name.

There was a picture.

It was the picture of a playing card.

The card was the queen of hearts.

CHAPTER 23

It was a morning in mid-January. It was dark as I walked to work, and it would be dark when I walked home. Ordinarily, my spirits this time of year would be a bit on the dampish side. This day, however, they were tip-top.

The storm had started in mid-afternoon and continued all through the night. By morning there was two feet of fresh snow on the ground. It was lovely. Having covered the indignities that man has wrought, Nature looks her best in fresh snow.

There were no people out. There were no cars on the roads. All was quiet and peaceful and clean. The twenty-minute trip took me over an hour. Every step was a pleasure.

Very few employees lived as close to the hospital as I did, and not everyone was committed to coming to work regardless of the weather. All the nurses made it in, and a few of the doctors did. No one in administration came to work that day. They viewed a snowstorm not so much as a challenge for getting to work than as an opportunity to avoid trying. The patients showed up right on schedule. We did the best we could, but by mid-morning, when the CEO called from his home in New Hampshire and said the clinic was officially closing down, no one objected.

I was getting ready to leave when Crikett came into my office.

"Bill Johnstone is on the phone."

"Marie?"

"Marie."

Bill Johnstone is the one-person road crew for Stedsville. In summer he spreads gravel. In mud season he fills ruts. And in winter he plows. On a day like today he had already been working for eight hours when he called.

Fast Brook Road is the highest of Stedsville's roads. It crests out at the town line on Steds Hill before heading down a long, circuitous route into East Pomfret. At the top of the hill, in a small house set back from the road, lived Marie Stahler. Marie was eighty-eight years old. Her husband, Otto, had died ten years ago. There were three of them in the house now: Marie, Franz, and Helmut. Marie the human, Franz the cat, and Helmut the goose.

Marie had a car, a battered, old, red VW Beetle. Once a week, weather permitting, she drove into town to do her shopping. The driver's side door was sticky, so she would wait in the parking lot until someone came to open it for her. She never had to wait long. She left the door open while she shopped. How she got out of the car at home was not clear, but it was generally agreed that Helmut was a very smart goose.

She had two sons, both of whom lived in New Jersey. Every weekend one of them drove up to make sure everything was okay. Each time they came, she told them she didn't need any help, but if they wanted to do something, they could split and stack some wood.

When he plowed Fast Brook Road, Bill Johnstone turned around in Marie's driveway. He would always stop in for a cup of Bavarian cocoa and, if he was lucky, her apple strudel. If Bill wanted to tell me something about Marie, it couldn't be good.

I picked up the phone. "What's up, Bill?"

"That's just it, Doc. I don't know. You know how heavy the snow is out her way. Drifts up there this morning were up to my waist. When I got up to her drive, I could hear Helmut carrying on something awful. I tried to get to the house, but the snow was too much for me. I couldn't call, because the lines are down, and besides, as you know, she never answers. Claims it's because she's hard of hearing, but I don't think that has anything to do with it."

I did know. Marie did not like the phone. It was installed at the insistence of her children, but she never answered it. She said that if she needed something from someone, she would use it, but if someone needed something from her, they could come to the house. She had all the noise she needed from Helmut.

"That knee of mine," Bill said. "I couldn't go more 'n a couple of steps before it started hollerin' at me. Besides, I know how you like to get out on those skinny skis, so I figured maybe you might want to take a little expedition. I'm guessing things are pretty quiet right now for you."

He was right on both counts. Bill had a knee that was ready for replacement about five years ago. I had told him he ought to put it off as long as he could, and then put it off a little longer. He did that for four years. For the last year it had been a lot longer. The thought of a winter excursion under cover of house call was appealing. And there was nothing else I could do in the office.

"I'd love to," I said.

*****

Marie and Otto had emigrated from Germany in 1960, when Otto, a chemical engineer, was offered a job at a pharmaceutical company in New Jersey. They bought the Stedsville place in the 1970s. It reminded them of the small town in the Black Forest of Bavaria where they had lived. They came up every chance they got. When Otto retired in 1995, they sold their home in New Jersey and moved up here. Steds Hill is a lovely area, and their house, sitting on the highest point of land, was in a perfect location. On three sides is a forest of birch, aspen, and sugar maples, with a few small stands of spruce. To the east, the property opens onto a long grassy field that looks out to Mount Abenaki and over to New Hampshire. On a clear day, you can see the top of Mount Washington. The area is one of our favorite places for outdoor activity. In summer we bike on the roads, and in winter the horse and snowmobile trails that crisscross the region are perfect for cross-country skiing.

When I arrived in Dumster, one of the things Doctor Franklin gave me was his house-call list. He explained that I didn't have to make house calls. He understood that doctors of my era did not generally do them, dismissing them as little more than a social call, and an inefficient one at that. "But if you want to stay here," he said, "you'd best learn the value of socializing."

Which I did. And I still value socializing. A few of the calls are to people who can't get out, and who, except for the devoted care of family, would be in a nursing home. And I can pretend that in so doing I gain some special insight into that person's real problems. But that would be a lie. Most of the house calls are to people who are simply good company.

Marie and Otto were such a couple.

Sometimes I would put my stethoscope in my pack and stop by the house when I was on an excursion in Stedsville. I would take a listen to their chests and opine that they appeared to be still alive. They would thank me and, as payment, give me the same they gave Bill—a cup of hot chocolate and a slice of apple strudel.

Ten years earlier, I had gotten a call from Bill Johnstone.

"Just saw Marie. She's wondering if you could stop by on your way home."

"*On the way* is a relative concept."

"I told her you'd come."

"Do you know what it's about?"

"Says it's Otto."

"Tell her I'll be there after work."

"Can't. I'm way over on the other side of town now. But she said any time that worked for you was okay for her. Didn't have to be today even."

Otto was in the bedroom lying quietly in bed. The right side of his face drooped. His right arm hung limp outside the covers. He had the blank expression of someone who had suffered a large stroke. "Hello, Otto," I said. "Good to see you."

Otto smiled.

"He seems to recognize me," I said. "That's a good sign."

"It's not just you," she said. To prove her point, she banged her walking stick against the iron bedpost.

Otto smiled.

"He's had a stroke,"

"I know."

"Can he talk?"

"No."

"He may get better. Time will tell."

"It always does."

"At least he's content."

"Now he is. It wasn't like that at first. Twitching about and looking wild-eyed and making this horrible kind of groan. It like to broke my heart."

"That's not unusual in the early stages. Fortunately, things usually settle down."

"I suppose so. I couldn't wait for that to happen. So I helped him."

"I'm sure you did. Having you around must be a great comfort to him."

Marie looked at Otto. "We comfort each other."

Otto smiled.

"When did he have the stroke?"

"Tuesday."

Today was Monday.

"He had the stroke *last* Tuesday?"

"Would be Tuesday before last."

"Two weeks ago."

"Yes."

"But you didn't call me until just now?"

"I wanted to make sure he was safe."

"Safe from what?"

"Safe from you. You're pretty good, Doctor Conger. But I couldn't take a chance. I wanted to make sure you wouldn't be fussing about, putting him in the hospital or any of those other doctoring holes that, once you start digging, you can't get out of. Also, wanted to make sure I got his medicine right. So that…"

"I wouldn't try to get you to use some of mine."

"I'm old school, Doctor Conger."

"Not completely."

There was an unmistakable aroma in the room. It was not disinfectant.

"You noticed?"

"Hard not to."

"It's not very common around here."

"No, it isn't. But when you're from Berkeley…"

"You too?"

"Me too."

Marie was raised in a time and place when the question of whether a person would be made better or worse by the medications her doctor dispensed was an open question. She remembered all too well that any time she complained to her parents of an ache, whether in the stomach or not, the invariable remedy was castor oil. The premise back then was that bad humors needed to be flushed out. The result was such that it made her permanently suspicious of the profession's potions. She was reinforced in this belief by a friendship she developed with her nearest neighbor, a young woman who had emigrated from Berkeley to live on twenty acres of forest land she had inherited from her grandfather. The neighbor lived in a yurt and had an assortment of farm animals with whom she shared the property. Her name was Sunrise Holbode. Sunrise was a firm advocate of the natural school of treatment. She also considered herself an herbalist.

In order to allow Marie to indulge in her favorite activity, Otto had built a greenhouse, which he attached to the back of the house. Facing south and east, it soaked up every bit of sun that the day had to provide. In addition, to augment the less robust offerings of winter, he had installed a set of grow lights across the ceiling.

Sunrise, a firm believer in the sanctity of all life, trees included, had very little sunlight around her yurt. It was not an environment conducive to horticulture. Despite their age and cultural differences, Marie and Sunrise shared a common world view. They bonded over the greenhouse. Marie gave Sunrise the vegetables she could grow in winter and spring. And she reserved a spot for Sunrise to grow her medicinal herbs, which Sunrise offered to Marie, along with advice for whichever ailments each was indicated. There was the usual set—comfrey, chamomile, lavender, aloe vera. There was also one plant about whose powers Sunrise was particularly enthusiastic. It had long, dark green, serrated leaves. The female plant produced clusters of grape-sized gray-green buds. The buds could be brewed into a tea or baked into almost anything. They could also be smoked, but as Sunrise explained, smoking was bad for your health, so she preferred to eat them or inhale them through a vaporizing device.

"How do you give it to him?"

"I put it in his food."

"He can swallow, then?"

"Not very well."

"What are you feeding him?"

"Jello."

"Anything else?"

"No, just jello. Lemon-lime mostly, but sometimes I give him cherry. I don't think he can tell the difference, but it gives me the illusion of variety."

"There's not much nutrition in jello."

"We know."

"But at least he does get some calories."

"We thought about that. It's sugar-free."

"You and Otto have already talked about this."

"We have."

"And you decided this was the best approach for whichever of you needed it."

"We did."

"I don't know how long he can live on sugar-free jello. But I expect you talked about that also."

"We did. And we decided it doesn't really matter. As long as it wasn't *too* long."

"Sugar-free jello and cannabis. It's an interesting treatment plan."

"It's worked well, Doctor Conger. You might want it sometime—for any patients that might be in a similar situation, that is."

"I think it takes a very special patient and a very special caretaker for it to work."

"We thank you. We will do it anyway, but it does feel better knowing you approve."

"I think it's rather I who should thank you—for making me feel useful."

"What is it you say here? One good turn deserves another?"

"That is what we say."

Otto lived for three weeks. I stopped by every day, to talk with Marie. I always said hello to Otto. He always smiled.

I told Marie it was longer than I expected.

She said it was just right.

Marie was a tough and stoic woman. But Otto had been her love and her best friend for over fifty years. Her grief was palpable. Nights were the worst, she said. Which they always are. A bad night not only destroys sleep, it ruins the day after. I offered Marie a mild sleeping pill, emphasizing that I knew she did not like medicines, but that for a short period at least, it might make things easier. Firmly but politely she refused.

"I had to offer," I said.

"Thank you," she said.

The next time I stopped by, although she was still sad, her spunk had returned. She sounded more like the Marie of before. I asked her if she was sleeping better. She said she was.

"Otto and I always had a small glass of schnapps before we go to bed," she said. "Since he isn't drinking anymore, I decided to take his glass too. It was a way to share. And I thought it might help me sleep. It did, but I would get a terrible headache in the morning, so I gave it up. We have a saying from back home: What's sauce for the goose is sauce for the gander."

"We have it too. You figured maybe the reverse was true."

"It was. So I have a small bowl of jello before I go to bed. Otto thinks it's a good idea."

It was several months before Marie stopped speaking of Otto in the present tense.

And stopped having jello every night.

*****

From what Bill had told me, I figured snowshoes would be a better choice than skis. I went home, changed clothes and put the snowshoes in the car. With our four-wheel drive I was able to make it just about to her driveway. The house is set back a hundred yards from the road. A stand of spruce in front obscures it from view. Snow-laden branches lay on the ground everywhere, and those that hadn't broken were severely bent. The scene made me think of a group of bearded, white-haired old men, their backs bent by years of toil, standing about, waiting for a little sun to lighten their load. Were it not for Helmut's raucous honking it would have been a peaceful scene.

As in most Vermont houses, the entrance one used was not the front door. For the Stahler home, it was a rear door that opened onto a covered breezeway connecting the main house to a small shed.

To the right of the rear door was a small window about waist high. The pane was broken. Marie's body was sprawled over the sill. Her head and shoulders were inside the house. Her legs hung down on the outside. Under them was a stack of firewood. In her left hand was her walking stick.

It was obvious what had happened. Marie had gone out to the shed to get some firewood and upon returning was unable to open the door to get back in. She had tried to climb in through the window by breaking the glass and using the firewood as a stool, but the window was too high. Most likely, she had died of a heart attack as a result of the frustrated effort. It may not have been pleasant, but from the look of things, it was at least quick.

I tried the door. It opened easily. Once inside I pulled her body the rest of the way into the house. In the process I made two unexpected discoveries. On the sill, lying underneath her, was a dead mouse. And the expression I saw on her face when I turned her over was not pain or anger. It was what one would see on the face of an athlete who has just broken the tape while crossing the finish line. It was the look of exultation for a victory hard fought.

I realized I had misinterpreted the sequence of events. The latch that secured the back door was a bar that slid across to fasten it shut. It must have accidentally slid over when she went outside. By breaking the window and leaning in, she had been able to use her walking stick to push it back. It was an awkward reach from the window, and she must have struggled hard to accomplish the task. But she had persisted. It had cost Marie her life, but the effort was successful.

I barely had time to recover from my surprise when Helmut was upon me.

I don't know if you have ever been attacked by an angry goose. I would strongly urge doing everything you can to avoid it. He pecked ferociously at my legs and my arms and would have pecked at my face had I not shielded it. Helmut was highly protective of his mistress. However, I knew from my prior visits that Marie had an infallible way of quieting him down for company. As quickly as I could, I made my way to the refrigerator. Fortunately, it had what I needed. I set it on the floor, and Helmut abandoned his attack. His rage was apparently directed not at Marie's death, but at her failure to supply him with his daily portion of jello.

Something rubbed against my leg. It was Franz, the donor of the dead mouse. Whether intended for sustenance or merely to add to the graveyard, he did not say. What Franz was saying, in no uncertain terms, was that I had not finished my chores. Taking the hint, I opened the refrigerator again and fetched some milk. I set it down in a saucer beside Helmut. Mission accomplished, Franz devoted his attention to the saucer.

I called Ralph Johnstone on my cell phone. Ralph is Bill's brother. He is the town constable and the animal control officer. He would be responsible for the care of Helmut and Franz.

"I'm out here at Marie's," I told him. "Looks like she died trying to get back into her house."

"Bill said you might call," he said. "Sorry to hear that, Doc. She had a good life, though."

"That she did. It's a natural death, so I'll call King's to come get her. And I'll let the boys know. It was a sudden thing. I'm sure she didn't suffer."

"Thanks for that. Guess I should come out and pick up the animals."

"Helmut's on his jello."

"Good," said Ralph. He was familiar with the wrath of the goose. "Nothing else you need from me then?"

"Not about her. But there isn't just one body here. There are two. And the other one, by the looks of it, could be a homicide."

There was a long pause at the other end. Homicide was way beyond the jurisdiction of the town constable.

"You want me to call Jeff?"

"Not unless you think you need to. I gave the perp a saucer of milk, so everything's under control."

I heard a sigh of relief. "That would be Franz."

"It would."

"You gotta be careful with your jokes, Doc. You know what kind of shape my ticker is in."

"Sorry. I was just trying to lighten the mood a little."

"Maybe I will give Jeff a call—just to jerk his chain a little."

Jeff Kapise was our local state police officer. He was very conscientious. And he was *very* serious.

I had the number for Marie's sons back at the office, so I went there and called them. They were good sons. They were sad to hear of her death but not shocked. They asked me how she had died. I told them.

"They say the best you can hope for is to die in your sleep," said her older son.

"They do."

"From what you told us, it seems our mom did even better."

"She did."

CHAPTER 24

It was April, an ambivalent time of year in Vermont. Sometimes it is the end of a winter that refuses to take a hint. Other times April can be the start of a glorious spring. Mostly it is neither fish nor fowl. This was a year for glorious. There had been little rain in March, and a spell of warm, sunny days had terminated mud season almost before it had a chance to get its foot in the ground.

It was early afternoon. I was sitting at my desk, having just finished my work for the day. Ordinarily, I would be contemplating what I was going to do next—take a walk in the woods, ride my bike, dig in the garden. I would be in a very good mood.

Instead, I was thinking. Thinking is not one of my favorite activities. By which I am not referring to the business of figuring things out. Figuring things out is just the kind of activity a brain should be doing on a regular basis. It keeps one's cerebral functions running smoothly and in peak form. It has a start, a middle, and an end. And if you reach the end and still haven't quite completed the figuring, you are sure to have made progress, so that by the next time, or maybe two, you are certain to succeed. But even if, try as you might, you never should quite get it, the old noggin will not leave you in a tizzy, for noggins are particularly adept at abandoning unproductive figurings on a moment's notice and moving on with nary a backward glance.

But thinking has the rather unhelpful tendency to get stuck in the mire of some particularly unsatisfying muddle, one over which you have no control whatsoever. And then it wallows around in it, until you start to ruminate, and from there, things turn too quickly to festering.

Recognizing, as soon as I sat down, where things were headed, I had attempted to protect myself with my standard preventive, a cup of Earl Grey tea and a muffin, eschewing in this case the less potent cinnamon blueberry in favor of a fresh sample of the cafeteria's *specialité du maison*, Marie Furman's jalapeno cheddar bacon.

As I had feared, these remedies were ineffective against the thoughts that were now insinuating themselves into my consciousness. They were the where-am-I-now, and where-am-I-going thoughts. And the particular going upon which they were now thinking was that of my career, a journey for most of which I had been a general internist who tended to older and sicker people with too many medical problems. The kinds of people for whom someone with my training and skills was ideally suited, ensuring, as best as possible, that the treatment of one medical problem would not exacerbate the others. I was the kind of doctor who once was highly valued, but has all but disappeared. I was ruminating on the fact that I had just saved my career from obsolescence by taking up the treatment of opiate addiction, which, although important and rewarding and, I must say, more fun than I had imagined, did not really require any of the medical skills I had acquired over the course of my professional lifetime. I was recognizing the inescapable fact that management of addiction had been granted exclusively to the MD solely because of the paternalistic nature of medical care, and not because of anything the degree conferred on one's ability to treat it. For truth be known, were Sara and Jessica to be allowed a license to prescribe buprenorphine, the patients would fare just as well with them in charge—better even. So here I was, the titular head of an activity over which I had no right to preside, and fully aware of it.

In short, I was feeling sorry for myself.

I was staring disconsolately at the remains of my sustenance when I was interrupted by Crikett, who announced that Davida was here to see me.

It was impossible not to be cheered by this news. Davida is one of those people around whom none but the most persistent of miserators can maintain a funk. I went out to say hi.

I asked her how school was going, and she said it was going well. And I asked where she was going to do her residency, and she said she was staying at Dartmouth.

This didn't surprise me. Residency programs at any given hospital know their own students quite well, and they make a special effort to recruit the best among them. Not only do they know their abilities, but having already been inculcated into the whys and wherefores of the hospital, including, not least importantly, the medical record, their own students require none of the tedious orientation needed by those who arrive from elsewhere. The latter students are well versed in the medicine but ignorant of the institution.

When I asked her which residency she had chosen, I was surprised by her answer.

"Internal medicine," she said with a smile.

For someone with her commitment to primary care, family practice would have been the more common path to follow. I asked her the reason for her choice.

"I like doing my bit to preserve an endangered species," she answered. "Besides, it seemed to work okay for you."

I offered her congratulations, and I told her that I would be sure, when referring any of my patients up to the big house, to let her know. Then I turned to go.

"Actually," she said, "I'm going to be here for the next month. For my fourth-year primary care rotation."

"That's great," I said, not fully hiding my disappointment and wondering with which of my fortunate colleagues she would be working. "Who's your preceptor for the rotation?"

"You are."

"That would be nice," I said with a shrug. "But I'm no longer a preceptor for the medicine clerkship. There must be some mistake."

Davida smiled. "There was," she said. "I fixed it."

"You would."

"I went to Doctor Roberts. I told him I wanted to do my fourth-year rotation here. He thought that was an excellent choice and gave me the list of preceptors. You weren't on that list."

"I've been removed for conduct unbecoming a preceptor."

"So I gathered. Disobeying a superior officer, it sounded like."

"And dereliction of duty."

"I explained to him that if it was all right with him, I'd just as soon have you as my preceptor. He said that it just wasn't possible."

"And?"

"I asked him to make it possible."

"And?"

"He did."

"Just like that."

"More like several thats. And a few thisses as well."

"A hard nut to crack, was he?"

"Depends."

"Okay, so, I'll ask. What did you do?"

"I stood there."

"That's it? No carefully reasoned argument or impassioned plea? You just stood there?"

"Yep."

"And that was enough?"

"You know how he likes to sit behind that big desk of his and lean back in his throne and fold his fingertips together and look at you with an expression that says he is listening to you very carefully and will take what you say under advisement, but you should not for a minute believe that it will have any effect whatsoever on what he will do?"

"I am familiar with that demeanor."

"Well, when I came into the room, instead of sitting in that hard, wooden chair that pushes you forward, so it makes you look like you are a supplicant begging for something, I went over and stood in front of the desk. He hemmed and hawed and said there really weren't any provisions for my request. I didn't say anything. I just stood. Then he explained about the difficulties that the department had experienced with your noncompliance with the course objectives, which, he emphasized, existed only to ensure that I would get the best possible value out of the rotation. I didn't say anything, just stood there. He hemmed and hawed some more. Finally, he said that he supposed maybe he could make an exception, but he was concerned, *very* concerned, he emphasized, about the objectives. So, I told him that I wanted just as much as he to get the most value out of the rotation, and that if he would just give me a copy of the objectives, I would make sure that we followed each and every one to the letter. And he did."

"And?"

"And I have them right here."

She handed me a sheet of paper. On it was a list of twenty-four objectives, with a space for documenting the way in which each one had been met. It was an impressive list, all the more so because it had already been completed—names, dates, and all.

I smiled. "A person after my own heart."

She pointed to a line on the bottom of the last page. "Sign here."

I signed the form "I'm impressed," I said admiringly. "He's not an easy one to persuade."

"Not for you, maybe."

"Oh?"

"You're a guy."

"That I am."

"So is he."

"Peas in a pod."

"Well, there are guys—and there are guys. And whenever a not-guy wants to get something from a guy, it is important that she knows which kind of guy she is dealing with. Doctor Roberts is the kind of guy who will give me exactly what I want."

"And that kind would be?"

"The kind who can't deal with tall women."

"Good to know."

"If you're a tall woman."

"All right, tall woman, tell me what you want to do. I'm putty in your hands."

"If it's okay, I'd like to set up my own schedule, and when I have questions, which I certainly will have lots of, I'll check with you."

"Just like a real doctor."

"Which I will be in a month."

"Which you already are."

"Well, since you bring it up, there is one more thing."

"You want my office."

She laughed. "No silly. I'm not trying to replace you."

"Not yet."

"But…?

"But?"

"I would like to have my own panel of patients. The residency includes a continuing-care component, where the resident is supposed to have her own panel of patient that she follows over the course of her residency."

"Until, in two years, she turns into a pumpkin."

"We'll see about that."

"If I remember correctly, that component takes place in the resident's clinic up at the medical center."

"Usually it does."

"But in your case?"

"The residency director is willing to make an exception."

"He's that kind of guy?"

"Nope. She's my kind of woman."

*****

As she promised, Davida was careful to let me know what she was doing with each patient, and when occasionally she asked my opinion, it was because she wanted it. She started by calling back all the patients she had seen during her third year, and all of them readily accepted. Fusswood, of course, came in, which was only to be expected. And so did Ray. I couldn't say he was exactly transformed, but he certainly qualified as improved. Over the past year he had grudgingly accepted two of his medications, but more importantly, he had lost thirty pounds that seemed to have every intention of staying lost. And no longer was he spending his day on the Main Street bench. When I saw him in town, he was often in the company of a woman with two dogs, both of whom looked of similar pedigree to Dog. I asked Davida if she knew who the woman was.

"Maria Weston," she said. "She owns the consignment shop. She also runs an exercise class in the evenings. It's for people who hate to exercise. The Lesser of Two Evils Class, she calls it."

"Sounds like an interesting person."

"She is. She also has a soft spot for stray dogs."

"And their owners?"

Davida smiled. "I was in the shop one day, and I told her about Ray, emphasizing his life as a new dog owner and going light on his curmudgeonly tendencies. I mentioned that Dog was a very social animal and seemed rather lonely, and seeing as how she was downtown anyway, if she introduced her dogs to his, that might be a good thing."

"Seems to be."

"It's a work in progress."

Toward the end of Davida's rotation, John Bowers came into the office. Mr. Bowers had taught fifth grade at Dumster Elementary for the past thirty years. He had known Davida as a bright student and as a great athlete, but not as an adult. As with all of the patients Davida saw, Crikett asked him if it were okay for her to examine him. And as with all of the patients, he agreed readily. Everybody knew Davida. Everybody trusted her. Nevertheless, it was remarkable to see how easily the two of them accepted their new roles with respect to each other. After she had finished listening to John's story and examining him, she came to me and asked if I would see him also.

"His neck has been bothering him for a couple of weeks. Now the pain is getting worse and traveling down his right arm. Occasionally he gets electric shocks that make his fingers numb. He was painting his garage when he first noticed it, and he thinks that's the culprit. He told me he has had some pain for a long time, which always goes away after he has seen the chiropractor. But that is on the opposite side. There is an x-ray in his file from three years ago that shows he does have arthritis of his cervical spine, with some narrowing of the disc spaces. He went to the chiropractor last week, but it didn't help and maybe even made it worse. Last couple of days, his shoulder has been hurting, and it's getting hard to write on the blackboard at school. He's been taking ibuprofen pretty much around the clock. It helps the pain, but now he can't really do much of anything. He looks miserable."

"Miserable as in unhappy?" I asked. "Or miserable as in sick?"

"Both."

"He is quite muscular on exam," Davida said, "but he can't raise his right arm above his head. He's got good passive range of motion in his shoulder, but when I get to full abduction, his neck pain increases. He's got brisk reflexes on both arms, and his sensation seems intact, but the grip in his right hand is a little weak. It could well be just because of the pain, but I'm concerned he may have a disc problem with radiculopathy rather than just sore muscles. I'm wondering if he might benefit from a short course of steroids, but I'm not sure. He's restless. Something about him isn't right."

We went to see him. John was pacing about the room, obviously uncomfortable.

I asked him how he felt.

"Awful," he said. "I think maybe I got too much Advil in me. I been eating it like candy."

I examined him. As I expected, Davida's observations were spot on. The shoulder itself was fine, but his neck was not. When I tapped on the spine, he flinched, and when I turned his neck to the right and pressed down quickly on the top of his head, an electric shock ran down his right arm. His grip was indeed weaker on the right, but for someone with his development, I thought, the left was below par also. I asked John, and he agreed that both hands were not quite what they should be.

"You're right," I said to Davida. "It certainly looks like a neurologic problem in the neck. And you're correct that something's not quite right. Three somethings, in fact. First, it appears that both hands are involved. It's just that the right is worse. Second, his spine itself is quite tender, which you don't usually get with a simple disc problem. Third, he's restless. People with back and neck pain from a disc usually sit quite still. They don't want to exacerbate the symptoms by movement. When someone with pain is restless, it can be a sign of an inflammatory business. We should check his temperature."

It was 99.2.

"With ibuprofen." I turned to John. "You haven't by any chance had any kind of infection in the past month, have you?"

"No," he said slowly. Then he corrected himself. "Wait. Four weeks or so ago I had a boil on my calf, just a big pimple really. It was pretty red and sore, but it's fine now." He raised his pant leg and showed me a small, innocent-looking scab on his right thigh.

"Did you see anyone about it?"

"Well," he admitted, "I didn't. I'd had one before and knew what needed to be done, so when I couldn't squeeze it out, I got my X-Acto knife and opened it up. After I sterilized it, of course."

"Of course. Still, it may be important. What bothers me especially is the combination of pain in the spine itself and a low-grade fever. A simple slipped disc doesn't cause a fever. The boil could have been a staph infection. Staph, as you know, is notorious for spreading to other parts of the body days, even weeks, later. Osteomyelitis of the vertebra, discitis, and even an epidural abscess may not be the most likely diagnoses, but they are the most important ones not to miss. They are the kinds of problems that once you suspect them, you have to be sure."

"You're saying we should get an MRI," Davida said.

"I am. It's not a diagnosis that should be delayed. I'll call radiology and see if they can do an MRI of the cervical spine today."

The MRI unit was available, so over he went. The MRI showed a fluid collection along the right side of the cervical spine, with a small extension into the spinal cord itself. It was an epidural abscess. We packed him off in an ambulance and shipped him up to Dartmouth, where Doctor Santelli from neurosurgery took him straight to the operating room and drained it.

At the end of the day we talked about him.

"That's two for the rulebook," Davida said, taking a small notebook out of her pocket.

"Rulebook?" I asked. "Your guidelines and algorithms?"

"Yep."

"Gotta keep the powers that be happy."

"Gotta keep *me* happy. Also, Mr. Bowers goes on the List."

"Ah," I said. "*The List.* Yours is probably shorter than mine."

"He's number two."

"A *lot* shorter."

"It's early."

"Mind if I look?"

"Not at all." She handed me the book. I opened it. The first page was titled "Rules." Each rule was numbered and dated, the last three of which were dated today. All the others were in the previous year. There were eleven in all:

Medicine is a service industry.

Patient is just a role played by people.

The disease you are treating does not belong to you.

It's first do no harm, not first do.

A heroic measure is one that puts you at risk, not the patient.

Before ordering a test, know what you are going to do with the results.

When a treatment doesn't work, consider another diagnosis before another treatment.

In your differential diagnoses, start with the diseases most important not to miss.

If something doesn't seem right, it probably isn't.

Always be on the alert for when you are completely wrong.

The second page was titled "The List." On it were two names. John Bowers was the second. At the bottom of the page there was an inscription: "This is a list of my mistakes. Read it regularly. Don't make the same ones twice."

"John Bowers is not exactly a mistake."

"That's okay."

"The Rules were from your course?"

"In a way."

"It's better than I would have expected of them."

"I got them from you."

"Oh?"

"Not in so many words, maybe."

"It's missing number one."

"You mean the one that is the most important?"

"And that for some of us takes the longest time to learn."

"Turn the list over."

There it was, all by itself on the other side, in boldface letters:

1. Do the Right Thing.

AFTERWARD

After Davida finished her residency, to no one's surprise and to everyone's delight, she joined the practice in Dumster. That she was an excellent doctor and a great colleague should go without saying, but it won't. Her reputation was well known, and patients came to see her, not just from Dumster, but from more distant towns as well. Most of my patients stayed with me out of loyalty, but I noticed that more and more of them arranged to have some urgent problem that required attention on my day off. By the third time I had made a recommendation to Fusswood and he asked if it would be all right if he went over it with Davida, I could read the handwriting that had been on the wall for some time.

When we moved to Vermont, we had planned to live in Burlington, but fate having decreed otherwise, we wound up in Dumster. After many pointed hints from Trine, we decided it was time to finish the journey that was interrupted some 100 miles short of its destination. We bought a small house in Burlington, we sold our Dumster home, and I had a grand retirement party where everyone told me how sad they were to see me go. No one mentioned how relieved they were as well.

But I was not quite ready to hand over my stethoscope. Fortunately, the community health center, accustomed to serving the homeless and the refugees, was willing to take me in. The people I work with are smart and dedicated and younger, by and large, than my youngest daughter—a few are even younger than my oldest granddaughter. They are exceedingly deferential without making me feel old. And no one ever asks me when I am going to retire.

A few of my old patients come up from Dumster to see me, but it is more for old times' sake than for my skills. Nostalgia is a drink that tastes better when shared. The rest of my practice now consists almost entirely of patients who are in treatment for addiction to opiates. I have treated more than 200 such patients. I am both pleased and impressed that 180 are still coming to the health center for treatment, and that the vast majority have not used any opiates.

It is not necessarily the best treatment for everyone. And it is not necessarily the best treatment forever. But I do know it is the best treatment for these people right now. They are happier, and they are healthier and more productive. Their lives are better.

I am continually humbled to see that, despite the terrible traumas these people have gone through, they maintain a resilience and determination to better themselves. They are excessively grateful to me for their care, and I am embarrassed that they give me so much credit, when all I do is treat them exactly as I would any other person who came to me with a chronic illness.

But, of course, that is what makes all the difference.

As to the question of how much longer I will be working, I cannot give an answer. I am pleased that I can still be of some use and am averse to gazing into my crystal ball. At this stage of my journey, it is more comfortable just to put one foot in front of the other and keep my head down, watching out for potholes into which I might stumble and keeping my gaze fixedly *off* the horizon. I do know this much. However long it may be that I continue, under the watchful eye of Trine and all those who work with me, of one thing I am certain.

It won't be *too* long.

If in this work I have given the reader the impression that I think medicine has gone badly astray, I have misled you. Because it is so much easier to speak in critical terms than in laudatory terms, the former has a way of dominating conversation. But any disparaging words you may have heard from me are nothing more than wind rattling harmlessly against the windows of the House of Medicine. Inside all is just as it should be, a warm and comforting place where I am constantly rewarded by the joy of doing good for others. And to be able to dwell in it for the past fifty-two years has been a privilege for which I am immensely grateful.

ACKNOWLEDGMENTS

First to Colleen Mohyde, my editor, agent, and friend. She has stayed with me on my thirty-three-year foray into the forest of literature, keeping me, if not quite on the straight and narrow, at least from getting completely lost. Without her support and guidance, I would never have managed to keep at it.

No less important are all those responsible adults who have worked tirelessly to keep me out of trouble, and through whose wisdom and diligent supervision I have been a much better doctor. Especially to Helen George and Betty French, and Crikett French, who took me under their wing when first I arrived in Vermont. Patiently and without complaint, they taught me how to be a good doctor.

At the Riverside Health Center, where I now require more than one person to keep me in line, those who watch over me have been a cheerful and encouraging group. Their forbearance of my aging decrepitude has been a source of pleasure and wonderment. I have had more fun working there than anyone deserves to have in what is considered work. Everyone has pitched in to share the burden, and I can't possibly thank you all, but some have worked on me especially diligently—Leo Kline and Janice Emmanuelson, Stephanie Yahn and Carrie Steele and Jessica White and Emily Nicholson and Katie Lee, Sarah Steenbeek and Hata Pasic. And especially Caroline Donohue, who has been not only a valued colleague, but also a vital source of support for our patients. To all of you I am more grateful than all the chocolate at Lake Champlain Chocolates can express.

And to all those folks who have allowed me the privilege of being their doctor, thanks for your patience.

And to Trine, who has always been my editor-in-chief.